D1598493

Palgrave Studies in Leadership and Followership

Series editor
Payal Kumar
New Delhi, India

Foreword by William L. Gardner

Leadership has traditionally been defined as a process whereby an individual exerts influence over a group of individuals to achieve a common goal. While earlier theories placed the leader at the center of the model, only recently has the other actor in the picture, the 'follower,' become a focus for significant research and exploration. Within this context, however, the follower is still largely seen as a recipient of the leader's influence and power, who is subservient and passive, rather than as an organizational agent in his own right.

Palgrave Studies in Leadership and Followership aims to bring the follower-centric leadership approach to the fore. It is based on the premise that followers are largely proactive sense-makers who react in different ways to leadership and to change management. Adding value to leadership theory as well as organizational behavior literature, this series situates leadership in the eye of the beholder, exploring how followers make sense of leaders and leadership, and what impact this has on their own identity, work relationships, the leader and the firm.

Series Editorial Board:
Stacy Blake-Beard (Simmons School of Management, USA).
Juana Bordas (Mestiza Leadership International, USA).
Jerry Biberman (University of Scranton, USA).
Michelle Bligh (Claremont Graduate University, USA).
William (Bill) Gardner (Texas Tech University, USA).
Richard Harris (California State University, USA).
Marc Hurwitz (University of Waterloo, Canada).
Shaista E. Khilji (ITBA, Argentina).
Dušan Lesjak (International School for Social and Business Studies, Slovenia).
Oswald A. J. Mascarenhas (XLRI – Xavier School of Management, India).
Jeff Miller (Greenleaf Center for Servant Leadership, USA).
Eddy Ng (Dalhousie University, Canada).
Peter Pruzan (Copenhagen Business School, Denmark).
Birgit Schyns (Durham University, UK).

More information about this series at
http://www.palgrave.com/gp/series/15637

Dorianne Cotter-Lockard
Editor

Authentic Leadership and Followership

International Perspectives

To Dad & Corienne,
With love and
gratitude for your
consistent support and
encouragement.
Love,

Dorianne

palgrave
macmillan

Editor
Dorianne Cotter-Lockard
Fielding Graduate University
Santa Barbara, California, USA

Palgrave Studies in Leadership and Followership
ISBN 978-3-319-65306-8 ISBN 978-3-319-65307-5 (eBook)
https://doi.org/10.1007/978-3-319-65307-5

Library of Congress Control Number: 2017950825

© The Editor(s) (if applicable) and The Author(s) 2018
This work is subject to copyright. All rights are solely and exclusively licensed by the Publisher, whether the whole or part of the material is concerned, specifically the rights of translation, reprinting, reuse of illustrations, recitation, broadcasting, reproduction on microfilms or in any other physical way, and transmission or information storage and retrieval, electronic adaptation, computer software, or by similar or dissimilar methodology now known or hereafter developed.
The use of general descriptive names, registered names, trademarks, service marks, etc. in this publication does not imply, even in the absence of a specific statement, that such names are exempt from the relevant protective laws and regulations and therefore free for general use.
The publisher, the authors and the editors are safe to assume that the advice and information in this book are believed to be true and accurate at the date of publication. Neither the publisher nor the authors or the editors give a warranty, express or implied, with respect to the material contained herein or for any errors or omissions that may have been made. The publisher remains neutral with regard to jurisdictional claims in published maps and institutional affiliations.

Cover illustration: Jerome Murray - CC / Alamy Stock Photo

Printed on acid-free paper

This Palgrave Macmillan imprint is published by Springer Nature
The registered company is Springer International Publishing AG
The registered company address is: Gewerbestrasse 11, 6330 Cham, Switzerland

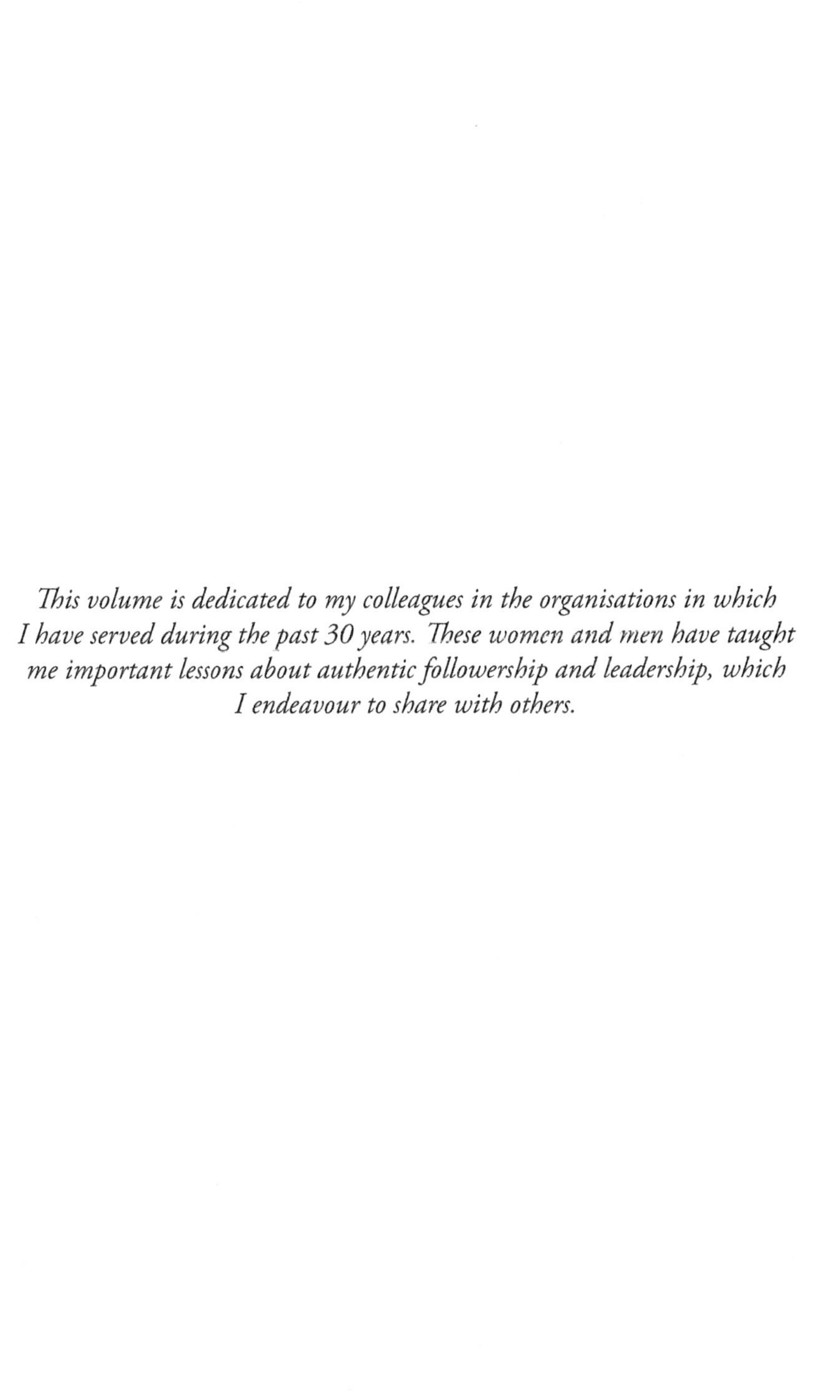

This volume is dedicated to my colleagues in the organisations in which I have served during the past 30 years. These women and men have taught me important lessons about authentic followership and leadership, which I endeavour to share with others.

Foreword

What is authenticity? And what is authentic leadership? The former is a question that humankind has been seeking to answer throughout the ages – from the ancient Greeks to today's existentialist philosophers. The latter question has only recently gained attention, but has become a prominent theme within the scholarly and practitioner leadership communities during the past decade and a half. Although these questions are difficult to answer, they hold promise for the spread of more humanistic and values-based leadership practices within our organizations.

For the past 15 years, I have had the pleasure to work with many talented and inspired colleagues in pursuit of answers to these questions. Along the way, others have joined our quest to bring more diverse perspectives to bear on these questions, including the authors who contributed to this volume. Together, the ideas advanced in the pages that follow add to our collective insights by raising new questions about authentic leadership, authentic followership, and how both are manifest across a broad array of cultural and organizational contexts. And many of the authors have gone beyond asking these questions to pursue answers through quantitative and qualitative research.

Reading these chapters has stoked my excitement about the potential for authentic leadership and followership to promote high moral standards, enhance employee well-being, elevate levels of organizational performance, and foster corporate social responsibility. At the same time,

I have become more conscious of potential contextual constraints, as well as the shortcomings of extant authentic leadership theory in recognizing these contextual influences. And, at a more personal level, it has caused me to reflect on my own journey of exploring authentic leadership, while identifying new avenues to pursue. To clarify the lens through which I view the work included this volume, I chose to briefly share those reflections below.

In the Fall of 2003, I joined the faculty of the University of Nebraska-Lincoln (UNL) as a member of the newly formed Gallup Leadership Institute (GLI). This was a unique opportunity, as GLI worked in partnership with the Gallup Organization, with a vision "to provide a global laboratory for the discovery of authentic leadership models, methods and best practices that contribute to enhancing the full potential and performance of all individuals, groups, organizations, communities and services." We had the good fortune of working with talented faculty and doctoral students, and Gallup executives, researchers, consultants, and trainers with the goal of expanding knowledge about leadership. Bruce Avolio, the founding GLI Director, and I had previously worked together studying charismatic leadership. We benefited from the wisdom, experience, expertise, and enthusiasm of Fred Luthans, the elder statesman of UNL faculty. Fred is my academic grandfather – my dissertation chair's (Mark Martinko), dissertation chair. These connections contributed to my excitement about my new job.

Inspired by the emerging field of positive psychology with its focus on enhancing individual well-being, Fred advocated for the study of positive organizational behaviour, soon to be renamed psychological capital or PsyCap. Importantly, Fred's focus aligned with the strengths-based approach to management, which provided the foundation for Gallup's corporate training and development. Together, the forces provided the impetus for Fred and Bruce to publish an influential chapter on authentic leadership in the edited volume titled, *Positive Organizational Scholarship.* The excitement that pervaded GLI, which included conversations with Bruce, Fred, ethicist Doug May, and the cohort of dedicated doctoral students, inspired me.

When Bruce talked about his interest in authentic leadership, he explained that shortly after his move to Nebraska he observed the genuine and humble, yet powerful, influence displayed by leaders in the area. No one exemplified such leadership better than Warren Buffet, the oracle of Omaha. For years, he has demonstrated extreme transparency through his day-long annual shareholder meetings, where he openly shared information with investors. Buffet's commitment to long-term investments also inspired our thinking. He emphasized that a strong moral compass could lead to sustainable gains in organizational performance. And, given the many corporate scandals of the time, we found Buffet's leadership to be especially refreshing.

To enlist others in our quest, we decided to host the 2004 GLI Summit at Gallup University. We issued a call for papers soliciting contributions from scholars and practitioners with the goal of generating new insights into authentic leadership development. A subset of the papers presented at the 2004 GLI Summit were published in a 2005 Special Issue of *The Leadership Quarterly,* while others appeared in the Volume 3 of the *Monographs in Leadership and Management* series.

From the outset, we sought to elicit diverse perspectives. While our own model of authentic leadership was grounded in in social psychology, other views were derived from fields such as philosophy, political science, and history. Hence, the 2004 GLI Summit achieved our goal of generating insights from a broad spectrum of disciplinary and practitioner perspectives. Independent of our efforts, Bill George, the former CEO of Medtronic and then Harvard Professor, authored two popular books – *Authentic Leadership* and *True North: Discovering Your Authentic Self* – that strongly resonated with practitioners.

To recap, these are the factors that fostered our quest to study authentic leadership at GLI. We had a powerful corporate partner in Gallup. We had a bright and dedicated cohort of doctoral students committed to the endeavour. Bill George's writings fuelled interest in the topic. And, our call for papers produced diverse perspectives. All we lacked was a theory.

My GLI colleagues and I set out to fill this void. In doing so, we found Michael Kernis' writings on authenticity and Deci and Ryan's self-determination theory to be essential. Indeed, their work provided the foundations for the self-based model of authentic leadership, authentic followership, and their development that we eventually advanced. In our introduction to *The Leadership Quarterly* 2005 Special Issue on Authentic

Leadership, Bruce Avolio and I sought to articulate the key tenets of this model. We specified the core components of authentic leadership, distinguishing them from those of charismatic, transformational, servant and spiritual leadership. We argued that authentic leadership serves as the "root" for positive forms of leadership, in that transformational, charismatic, servant, and spiritual leaders will be more impactful if they are also authentic. We also argued that authentic leadership includes an inherent ethical component. We emphasized the importance of the *development* of authentic leadership and followership as a core objective. And, we stressed the role of the follower, through an explicit discussion of authentic followership. Finally, we discussed the importance of contextual factors such as the ethical climate and cultural influences.

I hope this discussion of my personal quest to study authentic leadership will clarify the lens through which I view the work presented in this volume. Using this lens, I examine each chapter and suggest directions for future research.

In Chap. 1, Wernsing examines the relationships between the self-awareness dimension of authentic leadership and follower psychological empowerment across ten national cultures. Her findings raise several research questions. First, given the more sophisticated conceptualization of the leader self-awareness she advances, is the 4-item scale included in the ALQ adequate to capture the full content of this construct? Or, is a more extensive multi-item measure needed to operationalize the introspection, self-reflection, and feedback-seeking components she identified? Second, given the lack of support she obtained for the scalar invariance of the ALQ's self-awareness scale across cultures, what can be done to create a measure that achieves scalar invariance? Finally, what factors explain the cross-cultural differences in the relationship between leader self-awareness and follower psychological empowerment that she identified? Cross-cultural research that uses cultural dimensions and clusters derived from the GLOBE study may help to answer these questions.

In Chap. 2, Karacay, Ertenu, and Kabasakal explore differences in the conceptions of authentic leadership among male and female followers within a Middle Eastern context. In addition to documenting cultural influences on such gender-based differences, this study raises several intriguing questions. First, to what extent do the gender-based expectations of followers within Middle Eastern cultures become manifest in the actual behaviours of authentic leaders? Second, are there differences in the behaviours of male and female leaders within this context, and if so, how do such differences impact perceptions of leader authenticity and effectiveness? Third, what explains the absence of leader self-awareness as a perceived quality of authentic leadership in this sample? Did followers have a hard time deciphering the extent to which leaders are self-aware? If so, this suggests a limitation of asking followers what it means to be an authentic leader, rather than talking directly to leaders. Fourth, in contrast to prior research, followers identified a strong vision as a requisite attribute of authentic leaders. This raises the question as to whether they differentiated between charismatic, transformational, authentic, and other positive forms of leadership, or if they simply described the qualities that they associate with 'good' leaders. Hence, research is needed to ascertain if these findings reflect culture specific manifestations of authentic leadership behaviour, rather than more generic implicit leadership theories (ILTs).

In Chap. 3, Bravo explores within the context of Latin America the extent to which leaders use empathy as a means to achieve authentic leadership, whether such empathy impacts their followership and followership commitment, and how national culture shapes the role of empathy within leader-follower relationships. She concluded that the vast majority of the leaders she interviewed reported that they regularly employ empathy as part of their leadership and that the majority of followers reported that a leader's use of empathy induced them want to follow the leader. However, the small sample size and retrospective reporting by respondents raise questions that suggest opportunities for future research.

First, to what extent is empathy a component of, as opposed to a correlate with, authentic leadership? Put another way, must a leader possess empathy to be authentic, or do the self-awareness, relational transparency, balanced processing, and internalized moral perspective dimensions elicit empathy, or at least follower perceptions of leader empathy? Second, to what extent do perceptions about the importance of empathy to authentic leadership reflect empirical relationships, as opposed to ILTs? While respondents may think that empathy is a requirement for authentic leadership, especially when primed by interview questions, it is an open question as to whether it is, and the extent to which it produces the gains in trust, open communication, and follower commitment and motivation, that the participants reported. Finally, given that the idiographic findings are derived from retrospective interviews and the researchers' subjective impressions, nomothetic research using representative samples is needed to assess their generalizability.

In Chap. 4, du Plessis and Boshoff explore the interrelationships between authentic leadership, followership, and psychological capital (PsyCap) within a South African context. The results revealed significant positive relationships between authentic leadership and PsyCap, as posited. However, the expected relationships between authentic leadership and followership failed to emerge. Finally, an exploration of demographic differences revealed that male versus female respondents rated their leaders as exhibiting higher levels of balanced processing, and that male managers were seen as exhibiting higher levels than female managers of behaviours related to balanced processing, relational transparency, and self-awareness.

As du Plessis and Boshoff acknowledge, a key limitation of their study stems from the cross-sectional, single-source survey design, which makes it vulnerable to potential common method biases and prohibits causal inferences. Hence, a question arises as to whether authentic leadership cultivates the development of PsyCap among followers, as opposed to PsyCap eliciting follower perceptions of leader authenticity. Future research using multi-source, longitudinal surveys, as well as experimental designs, is warranted to answer these questions. In addition, given the psychometric shortcomings of the adopted followership measure, the authors' recommendation to develop and validate a measure of authentic followership has merit. Finally, cross-cultural research that compares the South African context with other cultures which reflect less power distance and male dominance is needed.

In Chap. 5, Monzani describes how 70 years of dysfunctional Argentinean leadership has emerged from a 'toxic triangle' composed of destructive leaders, a conducive environment, and susceptible followers. Using two former Argentinean presidents, Carlos Saul Menem and Cristina (Fernandez de) Kirchner as examples, he considers how the conduciveness of the Argentine business ecosystem to 'Corporate Machiavellianism' and the tendency of the population to romanticize charismatic leaders, have contributed to a vicious cycle of economic collapse and recovery. As an alternative, he presents a model of positive leadership, which is composed of three *spheres of virtue*: authentic leadership, eudemonic organizations, and self-determined followers. Future research could explore the extent to which the lessons Monzani derives transfer to other cultural settings. Additionally, because the proposed model reflects spheres of virtue, without specifying the causal relationships among the constructs they encompass, future iterations of this model should go further in fleshing out these relationships.

In Chap. 6, Pembleton, Friend, and He use a case study approach to describe the leadership of Lee Kuan Yew, the first Prime Minister of Singapore. This case offers a powerful example of the manner and conditions under which transformational leadership promotes authenticity within the leader-follower relationship. That is, Lee Kuan Yew's leadership illustrates how cultural forces impact leader–follower relationships, because his 'Asian Values' vision, while well-received in Singapore, did not resonate with a larger East Asian audience. Subsequent research could apply more extensive cross-cultural comparisons to further explicate how cultural dimensions and leader visions shape follower perceptions of leader authenticity.

In Chap. 7, Bradley-Cole describes an interpretive study of how followers assess the authenticity of their leaders. Experienced leaders were interviewed about their relationships with early career leaders (ECLs). The results revealed five master themes associated with authentic leaders: (1) inclusive, (2) integrity, (3) collaborative, (4) transparent, and (5) courage. In contrast, inauthentic leaders were described as: (1) self-centred; (2) emotionless; (3) autocratic; (4) critical and (5) manipulative. Further, the findings revealed that positive and enduring benefits accrued for followers who had the opportunity to work with an authentic leader at an early career stage, as they came to better understand and develop their own leadership identities and behavioural preferences. By tapping into followers' experiences with ECLs, Bradley-Cole sheds light on how they formed their personal conceptions of authentic leadership. Future research with leaders from more diverse cultural and professional settings is needed to assess the generalizability of such perceptions. Additionally, research is needed to ascertain the extent to which these conceptions translate into actual leader behaviour, and the degree to which such behaviour is associated with felt and perceived authenticity by leaders and followers, respectively. Finally, research is required to determine whether these attributes are required elements as opposed to correlates of authentic leadership.

In Chap. 8, Brown describes how leaders and followers can develop greater awareness of their 'true self' by observing and displaying somatic cues to connect with a bodily based sense of felt authenticity. She applies Douglas McGregor's classic writings on Theory X and Theory Y, embodied leadership, authentic leadership, and followership theories to contrast two case studies from the United States and Israel. For the former, she selected Steve Jobs as a well-known leader who had complex relationships with followers characterized by autocratic leadership and Theory X assumptions. She concludes that Jobs lacked self-awareness due to a disconnect between his inner and outer worlds. For the latter, she selected Hanan Lipskin, the CEO of Keepers Child Safety, who exemplifies Theory Y assumptions and authentic embodied leadership. She concludes that the strong emphasis placed on teamwork and voice within Israel serves to foster a higher level of relational transparency relative to the United States, where followers are expected to be more passive and obedient.

Future research could extend Brown's work by developing psychometric measures of embodied leadership and followership, thereby making it possible to quantitatively assess their relationships with felt and perceived leader and follower authenticity. Additionally, given that only one organization and leader from the United States and Israel were used in her case studies, nomothetic research is needed to assess the generalizability of her tentative insights. Finally, more extensive cross-cultural comparisons are required to assess the extent to which specific cultural dimensions and configurations are conducive to the alignment of leaders' and followers' inner and outer worlds.

In Chap. 9, Braun and Hornuf invoke self-concept maintenance theory to explore the extent to which authentic leadership influences the cheating behaviour of followers. They posited that the presence of an authentic leader would lower the perceptual threshold under which followers can cheat while preserving a self-concept of integrity. Results from their laboratory experiment revealed that most participants cheated, but not to the full extent possible – presumably because doing so would have been inconsistent with their self-concept of integrity. However, the predicted main and interactive effects failed to emerge. That is, participants were no less likely to cheat under the high authentic leadership condition relative to the baseline and low authentic leadership treatments.

Despite the null findings, the video-based approach used to operationalize authentic leadership in this study shows much promise for future research. While survey measures such as the ALQ and the ALI are useful, particularly in field settings, they have notable shortcomings. Indeed, other-reported measures are only capable of capturing *perceptions* of authentic leadership and may be impacted by followers' ILTs or the extent to which they like the leader, while self-reported measures may be impacted by social desirability. Given these shortcomings, experimental studies that adopt alternative operationalisations of authentic leadership and permit causal examinations of the focal relationships are particularly attractive.

In Chap. 10, Fortin, Baron, and Renucci explore the psychological and existentialist conceptions of authentic leadership as they relate to individual authenticity. To do so, they adopted Wood and colleagues' model of authenticity which proposes three elements of experience: self-alienation, authentic living, and acceptance of external influence. Wood and colleagues' self-report operationalization of these elements was used to measure authenticity. Berkovich's model of authentic leadership development was used to represent the existentialist perspective. This model identifies eight interactive components – self-exposure, open-mindedness, respect, critical thinking, empathy, care, contact, and mutuality – that promote authentic leadership.

The results of this research revealed that authentic living and acceptance of external influence were significantly related to ALQ scores, but self-alienation was not. With regard to Berkovich's model, the empathy and critical thinking scales were positively related to authenticity, but not the self-expression measure. The authors conclude that both the psychological and the existentialist models of authentic leadership received generally positive, but incomplete, support.

Fortin and associates' chapter suggests that concerns among existentialists may be warranted that the psychological approach underestimates the challenges leaders and followers face in achieving authenticity in organizational contexts. Thus, it behoves proponents of the psychological view to pay greater attention to relational and organizational constraints on the development of authentic leadership and followership. However, while positive correlations between empathy and critical thinking with authenticity provide some support for the existentialist model, this conclusion must likewise be tempered by the lack of evidence of a positive relationship with self-expression.

Future research could extend Fortin and colleagues' work through the adoption of probability sampling, longitudinal designs, control groups, and multivariate analyses, while examining all eight components of Berkovich's model. Additionally, the inclusion of control variables, such as measures of socially desirability, personality traits, and contextual factors, would reduce concerns about endogeneity. Finally, I endorse the authors' recommendation that future research explore the utility of mindfulness training as a means of increasing the congruence between authentic leadership, authentic followership, and authenticity.

In the final chapter, Crawford, Dawkins, Martin, and Lewis consider in depth the role of authentic followers within leader–follower relationships. They propose that an authentic leader will exhibit five behavioural dimensions: (1) awareness, (2) sincerity, (3) balanced processing, (4) positive moral perspective, and (5) informal influence. Next, they introduce a conceptualization of authentic followers that reflects two underlying dimensions: (1) the psychological capacity for authenticity and (2) positive organizational engagement. The latter dimension makes a distinction between passive versus active followers. Combining these axes identifies four types of followers: (1) inauthentic passive, (2) inauthentic active, (3) authentic passive, and (4) authentic active. The authors also assert that as the amount of informal influence increases, the individual eventually shifts from a follower to a leader role. Hence, two types of leaders, inauthentic and authentic, are identified.

Crawford and colleagues' chapter provides a fitting conclusion to this volume as it presents thought-provoking ideas about what it means to be an authentic follower. Here, I offer some considerations for scholars seeking to build on Crawford and colleagues' promising model by sounding some cautionary notes while identifying opportunities for further advancements. First, the rationale for the authors' decision to limit the focus of the proposed model to authentic followers and authentic leaders, as opposed to the processes of authentic followership and authentic leadership, requires further justification. Clearly, it is difficult to separate the roles of authentic follower and authentic leader from the processes whereby individuals who occupy these roles. Additionally, referring to authentic followers and authentic leaders gives the impression that some are purely authentic, whereas others are inauthentic. In reality, authenticity is not an "either/or" condition, as no individual is completely inauthentic or authentic. As such, it is more appropriate to refer to followers and leaders as being more versus less authentic, while recognizing that the degree of authenticity they achieve will vary from one situation to the next.

Second, scholars should evaluate the merits of including informal influence as a behavioural dimension of authentic leadership and authentic followership. While the authors offer a compelling rationale that doing so helps to differentiate between passive and active followers while clarifying when and how actors move from the follower to the leader role, the implication that informal leadership is required to achieve authentic leadership and authentic followership is suspect. Indeed, there is nothing to preclude leaders and followers who exert high levels of informal influence from being authentic, and one can readily think of instances where this is the case. Hence, further justification is needed for including informal influence as a dimension of authentic leadership and followership. Nonetheless, I strongly encourage scholars to build on Crawford and colleagues' work by exploring the interaction of follower authenticity with the level of positive organizational engagement.

My personal quest to understand authentic leadership and authentic followership and how they contribute to individual well-being, a positive ethical climate, and sustainable organizational performance has produced many rewarding moments. Reading the chapters included in this volume and the novel insights they provide is among the most rewarding. The many thought-provoking and impactful ideas contained within the pages of this book suggest multiple pathways for studying, and being, authentic leaders and followers across diverse cultural and organizational contexts. As you read these chapters, think about your own quest to understand what it means to be authentic, and how you can best achieve authenticity as a leader and follower. Like me, I suspect you will gain new and valuable insights that may inspire your research, or better yet, help you to lead and follow in ways that reflect your true self.

Texas Tech University
Lubbock, Texas, USA

William L Gardner

Preface

During the years that I served as a consultant to Fortune 500 companies, and later as an executive in a major financial services firm, I observed numerous instances of leadership in which the followers felt unempowered, disrespected, and essentially 'a part of a machine' rather than as valued contributors to a meaningful enterprise. As a leader, I believed I had an obligation to develop my capabilities so I could lead with a high level of integrity, and to help others in my organization to develop their capabilities. Thus, within my organization, we began a several-year journey of personal and organizational learning, during which we incorporated Covey's *7 Habits of Highly Effective People* (1989), Kouzes & Posner's *Leadership Challenge* (2002), and Goleman's *Emotional Intelligence* (2005), among other programs to develop colleagues at all levels of the organization. We implemented cross-organizational communication structures and practices to ensure all voices were heard throughout, and we embedded our core values into every aspect of our work to ensure that we "walked our talk." In more recent years as a practitioner-scholar, I came to realize that we developed an organization which fostered authenticity for all participants.

The concept of authenticity has been in vogue since the Greek philosophers. According to the etymology dictionary, the Greek word *authentikos* means, "original, genuine, principal," and is derived from *authentes*, "one acting on one's own authority." Bhindi and Duignan (1997) introduced one of the earliest definitions of authentic leadership as comprised of authenticity, intentionality, spirituality, and sensibility. In Bill George's 2003 bestseller, *Authentic Leadership*, he said, "Authentic leaders use their natural abilities, but they also recognize their shortcomings, and work hard to overcome them. They lead with purpose, meaning, and values. They build enduring relationships with people. … They are consistent and self-disciplined."

AL scholars began to explore the theoretical constructs of follower attitudes and behaviours in the mid-2000s, including a special issue in 2005 on this topic in *The Leadership Quarterly.* During this period, Avolio, Gardner, Walumbwa, Luthans, and May (2004) drew upon multiple theories of emotion, trust, positive organizational behaviour, and identity to devise a theoretical construct for follower's attitudes and behaviours. Fields (2007) later explored theories related to followers' judgements of authentic leaders based on followers' observations of leaders' actions.

The Authentic Leadership Questionnaire was initially tested and validated in multiple cultures, including China, Kenya, and the United States (Walumbwa, Avolio, Gardner, Wernsing, & Peterson, 2008). Walumbwa and his colleagues emphasized the importance of conducting leadership research in non-western cultures, observing that most of leadership theory originated from the United States. During the past 25 years, the Global Leadership and Organizational Behavioural Effectiveness (GLOBE) project investigated differences in leadership styles and the impacts on organizations in different cultures. GLOBE scholars inferred that the definition and characteristics of authentic leadership (AL) and followership will differ depending on the cultural context.

The topic of authenticity in organizations, along with AL and its impact on followers is primary to my current scholarly and professional work. In addition, I have always fostered an interest in the perspectives of different world cultures. It is my belief, founded in my research, that in order to collaborate effectively within teams and organizations, we must learn to see the world from a variety of perspectives. Therefore, I am curious about whether the meaning of 'authenticity' related to leadership and followership differs depending on the culture context. This book was born from these two intersecting areas of study. Working on this project has given me the opportunity to take a deep look at the current concepts and research on this topic, and to consider how it might be incorporated into practice.

This volume contains research, theoretical, and practitioner contributions which represent different cultural perspectives of authentic leadership from a follower ontology. The contributions to this volume represent perspectives from Latin America, Europe, Middle East, Asia, Africa, Australia, and North America. The book is organised into two sections. Part 1 is focused on international perspectives of authentic leadership and followership and Part 2 shines a light on conceptual perspectives. William L. Gardner, a foremost expert on the topic of AL, has beautifully written the foreword for this book, which includes the history of the study of AL, along with recommendations for future research in response to his reading of each chapter.

In Part 1, the first chapter is written by one of the original scholars of AL, Tara Wernsing. She studied leader self-awareness, which is one of the key characteristics of AL. Tara Wernsing examines leader self-awareness across ten national cultures and its relationship with follower psychological empowerment. In Chap. 2, Gaye Karacay, Behice Ertenu, and Hayat Kabasakal explore how perceptions of male and female followers in the Middle East differ regarding different attributes of AL. Chap. 3 is written by Patricia Bravo from a practitioner perspective; she explores the expression of empathy in Latin American leaders as a vehicle toward AL.

The research reported in Chap. 4 is set in the context of South Africa; Marieta du Plessis and Adré B. Boshoff examine psychological capital in relation to authentic leadership and followership behaviours. Although these researchers found the followership instrument had serious psychometric shortcomings, AL and follower psychological capital were found to be related, indicating that leaders had an impact on the development of their followers' hope, optimism, resilience, and self-efficacy. In Chap. 5, Lucas Monzani looks at the dark side of leadership and followership and its impact in Argentina, offering a proposed model for positive, authentic leadership adapted to the Argentinean context. In Chap. 6, Deborah Pembleton, John Friend, and Zhiyuan He offer a case study of Singaporean leader Lee Kuan Yew and his 'Asian Values' vision, concluding that Lee's leadership style ultimately failed because his vision was incongruent with the ontologies and values of other societies in Asia, resulting in a message that appeared inauthentic.

In Part 2, Kim Bradley-Cole investigates in Chap. 7, how followers who are early career managers, determine the authenticity of their leaders in the context of their formative work relationships. In Chap. 8, Sharon Davis Brown uses a nonverbal body–mind model, Laban Movement Analysis, to examine authentic leadership, embodied leadership, and followership in relation to leadership theories and embodiment concepts by examining case studies from the United States and Israel. Susanne Braun and Lars Hornuf present in Chap. 9 the results of a lab experiment designed to assess whether followers' perceptions of authentic leadership attenuate cheating. The authors interpret the results using self-concept maintenance theory. In Chap. 10, Cloé Fortin, Louis Baron, and Cécile Renucci assess similarities between the traits of authenticity and authentic leadership, using two different perspectives related to authenticity: an existential perspective and a psychological perspective. They explore these perspectives further with a study of French Canadian students. Finally, in Chap. 11, Joseph Crawford, Sarah Dawkins, Angela Martin, and Gemma Lewis consider the role of authentic followers in the leader–follower relationship in greater depth, providing an updated conceptualization of the construct characterized by psychological capacity for authenticity and positive organizational engagement. As a fitting end to this book, the authors consider how authentic followers interact with leaders, can be leaders, and interact in teams.

In summary, this book explores a breadth of perspectives related to authentic leadership and followership, using multiple approaches to examine the topic more deeply. The fact that the research contained in this volume raises more questions than it answers is a good thing, indicating that the exploration of this topic has not been exhausted by any means. It is my sincere hope that readers will contemplate how this research can be applied to create thriving organizations which foster authentic relationships, and then find ways to realise positive results.

References

Avolio, B. J., Gardner, W. L., Walumbwa, F. O., Luthans, F., & May, D. R. (2004). Unlocking the mask: A look at the process by which authentic leaders impact follower attitudes and behaviours. *The Leadership Quarterly*, *15*(6), 801–823.

Bhindi, N., & Duignan, P. A. (1997). Leadership for a new century: Authenticity, intentionality, spirituality, and sensibility. *Educational Management and Administration, 25*(2), 117–132.

Covey, S. R. (1989). *The seven habits of highly effective people: Restoring the character ethic.* New York, NY: Free Press, a division of Simon & Schuster.

Fields, D. L. (2007). Determinants of follower perceptions of a leader's authenticity and integrity. *European Management Journal, 25*(3), 195–206.

George, W. (2003). *Authentic leadership: Rediscovering the secrets to creating lasting value.* San Francisco, CA: Jossey-Bass.

Goleman, D. (2005). *Emotional intelligence* (10th anniversary trade pbk. ed.). New York, NY: Bantam Books.

Kouzes, J. M., & Posner, B. Z. (2002). *The leadership challenge* (3rd ed.). San Francisco, CA: Jossey-Bass.

Walumbwa, F. O., Avolio, B. J., Gardner, W. L., Wernsing, T. S., & Peterson, S. J. (2008). Authentic Leadership: Development and Validation of a Theory-Based Measure. *Journal of Management, 34*(1), 89–126.

Acknowledgements

I am grateful to our series editor, Payal Kumar, for inviting me to contribute a volume to this wonderful series, Palgrave Studies in Leadership and Followership. Many thanks to Payal and to Lucy Kidwell at Palgrave Macmillan for answering my numerous questions during the editing and publication process. I am grateful to my colleague and friend, Crystal Davis, who has taken this journey with me, one step ahead throughout, as she put together her volume for this same series. Thanks goes to Edward Breslin, who generously performed the early APA edit reviews of chapters, as well as to the esteemed blind peer-reviewers who provided thoughtful, detailed feedback to the authors. I am grateful to the contributors to this book, who have made significant contributions to the knowledge related to authentic leadership and followership, and who responded quickly and diligently to my requests for revisions. Finally, I am grateful to my husband Jim Lockard, who patiently gave me space, time, and support to work on this project.

Series Note

Leadership has been defined as a process that involves exerting influence on followers (Yukl, 2012). It is also said to consist of power dynamics in which leaders are bestowed authority and legitimate power by the organization, largely because of their technical, human, and conceptual skills (Katz, 1955).

Earlier theories of leadership such as trait theory, or charismatic theory, placed the leader at the centre of the model. Followers were seen as recipients of a leader's influence and power, rather than as organizational agents in their own right, akin to devotees revering the leader as a God-like figure (Gabriel, 1997). From the role-based perspective of a follower in a hierarchical setting, even the word 'follower' implies that the agent is subservient and passive (Katz & Kahn, 1978).

More recently the 'other' actor in the picture, namely the follower, has become the focus of significant scholarly work (Baker, 2007; Bligh, 2011), including the follower's perception of the leader (Antonakis, House & Simonton, 2017; Gottfredson & Aguinis, 2016). 'It is now widely accepted that leadership cannot be fully understood without considering the role of followers in the leadership process' (Uhl-Bien, Riggio, Lowe & Carsten, 2014, p. 88).

Based on the assumption that the identities of both leaders and followers are socially constructed, interlinked, and can transform each other (Meindl, 1995), this series intends to bring to the fore the follower as a largely proactive sensemaker who reacts to and shapes both leadership and organizational change. This merits deeper study, because the multi-faceted and ever-changing follower identity is possibly more complex than was once thought (Collinson, 2006).

Gaining deeper insight into followers' identity, sensemaking, and co-construction of leadership is essential for the advancement of leadership knowledge (Brown, 2012) for several reasons:

- Followership determines how leaders are perceived (Carsten, Uhl-Bien, West, Patera & McGregor, 2010).
- Followership identity predicts how a follower will follow, which affects both individual and organizational outcomes (Dasborough, Ashkanasy, Tee & Herman, 2009).
- Followership predicts how a follower will lead (Koonce, 2013).

This book series follows seven different perspectives of key components in the follower–leader dynamic. Each volume consists of empirical and conceptual chapters on leadership and followership, interspersed with a few chapters by practitioners in the first-person narrative style.

Each volume editor has chosen a specific aspect to explore in order to expand the full range of understanding of how followers shape leadership dynamics, largely from two levels of analysis:

1. Follower identity and behaviour at a micro level
2. Follower relationship with the leader at the dyadic level

What distinguishes this series from books in this domain is the distinct international appeal: The volume editors themselves span five countries (America, France, Australia, Canada, and India), and the research contributions are from scholars from all over the world. In fact, many of the volumes—such on Authentic Leadership and Followership; The Dynamics of Role Modelling in the Workplace; and Inclusive Leadership: Negotiating Gendered Spaces—explore this topic specifically from international and diversity perspectives. This series also has a strong interdisciplinary appeal, with the volumes drawing on perspectives spanning gender studies, philosophy, and neuroscience.

I have had the privilege of working with some fine scholars, who have worked diligently over the last few years to produce volumes, some of which are described below:

1. ***Servant Leadership and Followership: Examining the Impact on Workplace Behaviour*** 978-3-319-59365-4
   Editor: Crystal Davis
   Providing a deeper understanding of servant leadership and followership theory, this volume contributes to the literature on servant leadership and selfless service through the lens of the servant as follower. The collection brings together both empirical and conceptual research from around the globe that showcases servant leadership from the viewpoint of the follower.
2. ***Distributed Leadership: The Dynamics of Balancing Leadership with Followership*** 978-3-319-59580-1
   Editor: Neha Chatwani
   Challenging the current definitions of leadership by exploring more inclusive and holistic paradigms, this volume contributes towards the current discourse on distributed leadership by examining this as an inclusive form of leader–follower engagement. Qualitative and quantitative studies showcase the dynamics of followership in distributive leadership, covering several themes such as collective decision-making, leadership identity, roles and demographic composition of groups in a variety of settings, and human development processes.
3. ***Inclusive Leadership: Negotiating Gendered Spaces*** 978-3-319-60665-1
   Editors: Sujana Adapa and Alison Sheridan
   Questioning traditional perceptions of a leader as white and male, this volume presents leadership from a gender equity lens and includes topics such as feminine leadership, leadership legitimacy, and co-creating creativity between leaders and followers. With contributions from scholars in Australia, India, and the UK, this volume also touches on diversity within these countries, for example Chinese migrants in Australia and Indian women accountants in Australia.

4. ***Authentic Leadership and Followership: International Perspectives*** **978-3-319-65306-8**
   Editor: Dorianne Cotter-Lockard
   Authentic leadership, albeit controversial, is a well-accepted form of leadership. Given that the characteristics of authentic leadership and followership are largely context specific, this volume explores leader–follower dynamics in different cultural contexts. This volume is divided into two broad themes: global perspectives, including chapters from the Middle East, Latin America, and South Africa; and conceptual perspectives, including chapters ranging from early career relationships to an existential perspective. The foreword to this volume has been written by Prof. William L. Gardner, a foremost expert on Authentic Leadership.
5. ***Leadership and Role Modelling: Understanding Workplace Dynamics*** 978-3-319-69055-1
   Editors: Shruti Vidyasagar and Poornima Hatti
   Presenting role modelling as an independent construct, separate from the other developmental relationships in the workplace, this volume is a deep exploration of role modelling as both a concept and a dynamic process which impacts career development and outcomes. The chapters, consisting of literature reviews and research studies, reflect both academic and practitioner perspectives from across the globe. This volume also has sections on gender diversity and regional diversity (India).

To conclude, this series situates leadership in the eye of the beholder, exploring how followers make sense of leaders and leadership, and the impact this has on follower identity, work relationships, the leader, and the firm. 'Leadership is really not about leaders themselves. It's about a collective practice among people who work together—accomplishing the choices we make together in our mutual work' (Raelin, 2015, p. 96).

Payal Kumar

References

Antonakis, J., House, R. J., & Simonton, D. K. (2017). Can super smart leaders suffer from too much of a good thing? The curvilinear effect of intelligence on perceived leadership behavior. *The Journal of Applied Psychology, 102,* 1003–1021.

Baker, S. D. (2007). Followership: The theoretical foundation of a contemporary construct. *Journal of Leadership & Organizational Studies, 14*(1), 50–60.

Bligh, M. C. (2011). Followership and follower-centered approaches. In A. Bryman (Ed.), *The SAGE Handbook of Leadership* (pp. 425–436). SAGE Publications.

Brown, D. J. (2012). In the mind of follower: Follower centric approaches to leadership. In D. V. Day, & J. Antonakis (Eds.), *The Nature of Leadership* (pp. 331–362). SAGE Publications.

Carsten, M. K., Uhl-Bien, M., West, B. J., Patera, J. L., & McGregor, R. (2010). Exploring social constructions of followership: A qualitative study. *The Leadership Quarterly, 21*(3), 543–562.

Collinson, D. (2006). Rethinking followership: A post-structuralist analysis of follower identities. *The Leadership Quarterly, 17*(2), 179–189.

Dasborough, M. T., Ashkanasy, N. M., Tee, E. Y., & Herman, H. M. (2009). What goes around comes around: How meso-level negative emotional contagion can ultimately determine organizational attitudes toward leaders. *The Leadership Quarterly, 20*(4), 571–585.

Gabriel, Y. (1997). Meeting God: When organizational members come face to face with the supreme leader. *Human Relations, 50*(4), 315–342.

Gottfredson, R. K., & Aguinis, H. (2016). Leadership behaviours and followership performance: Deductive and inductive examination of theoretical rationales and underlying mechanisms. *Journal of Organizational Behaviour.*

Katz, R. L. (1955). Skills of an effective administrator. *Harvard Business, 33*(1), 33–42.

Katz, D., & Kahn, R. L. (1978). *The social psychology of organizations* (Vol. 2). New York: Wiley.

Koonce, R. (2013). Partial least squares analysis as a modeling tool for assessing motivational leadership practices. *International Annual Conference Proceedings of the American Society for Engineering Management, 2013 International Annual Conference, Minneapolis, MN.*

Meindl, J. R. (1995). The romance of leadership as a follower-centric theory: A social constructionist approach. *The Leadership Quarterly, 6*(3), 329–341.

Raelin, J. A. (2015). Rethinking leadership. *MIT Sloan Management Review, 56*(4), 95–96.

Uhl-Bien, M., Riggio, R. E., Lowe, K. B., & Carsten, M. K. (2014). Followership theory: A review and research agenda. *The Leadership Quarterly, 25*(1), 83–104.

Yukl, G. (2012). Effective leadership behavior: What we know and what questions need more attention. *The Academy of Management Perspectives, 26*(4), 66–85.

Contents

Notes on Contributors

Louis Baron is Full Professor in the Department of Organisation and Human Resources, Management School of the Université du Québec à Montréal, Canada. His research interests include leadership development, executive coaching, authentic leadership, and action learning methods. He has a PhD in Industrial/Organisational psychology and a Master's degree in Clinical Psychology. He is a chartered psychologist and certified coach.

Adré B. Boshoff is Extraordinary Professor at the University of the Western Cape and Emeritus Professor of the University of Pretoria, South Africa. He has more than 40 years of teaching experience at various Universities in South Africa and internationally. He is an awarded researcher and supervisor of doctoral students (40+ doctoral students graduated under his guidance). He has received awards such as Excellent Achiever (University of Pretoria), one of the first 500 World intellectual leaders (International Biographical Institute, Cambridge, UK 1990), various best paper awards, and research grants. He has been honoured within South Africa as one of the foremost thinkers in management and leadership studies.

Kim Bradley-Cole is a Chartered Psychologist and an Associate Fellow of the British Psychological Society. She has a PhD in Leadership and Organisational Behaviour from University of Reading, and an MSc in Occupational and Organisational Psychology from University of Surrey. Kim has held marketing and human resources roles in large organisations, as well as working agency-side in market research and as a freelance work psychologist and coach. Her research focuses on the social psychology of organisations and exploring how meanings of phenomena are constructed by individuals and groups through everyday social processes. Kim is also a Lecturer at University of Winchester and a Visiting Fellow at University of Reading, teaching in the fields of work psychology, organisational behaviour, and qualitative research methods.

Susanne Braun is a Professor in Leadership at Durham University Business School, United Kingdom. She received her PhD from Ludwig Maximilian University of Munich in 2011. Her research work addresses the effects of values-oriented leadership styles such as authentic and transformational leadership, as well as the dark side of leadership, including leader narcissism, follower envy, and counter-productivity. Her research has been published internationally, such as *The Leadership Quarterly*, *Journal of Business Ethics*, and *Journal of Management & Organisation*. She has co-edited a comprehensive international volume addressing the theoretical and practical implications of Leadership Lessons from Compelling Contexts, which was recognised with the 2016 Emerald Citations of Excellence Award.

Patricia Bravo is the founder of Bravo For You, a consultancy that helps organisations develop and facilitate leadership programs to accelerate leader capability. In her work, she equips leaders with empathetic leadership techniques which drive team member engagement and increase business results. She uses her organisation development experiences, gleaned at companies such as Starbucks, to shape the leadership landscape of the future. Patricia teaches leadership courses at the University of California Los Angeles Extension and University of California, Irvine Division of Continuing Education. She earned a BA in Psychology from California State University, Fullerton, and an MBA from the University of Notre Dame.

Sharon Davis Brown received a PhD in Human and Organisational Systems from Fielding Graduate University. She holds an MA in Expressive Therapies with a specialisation in dance/movement therapy from Lesley University, is certified as a movement analyst from the Laban Bartenieff Institute for Movement Studies, and certified as an evidence-based coach from Fielding Graduate University. Sharon founded the Art of Business Coaching business to provide executive, business, academic, and life coaching. The Art of Business is an arts-based coaching model to enhance individual and team dynamics. She has taught at Lesley University in the Graduate School of Arts and Social Sciences and provided clinical supervision for university graduate students from both Lesley University and Antioch New England.

Joseph Crawford is a Doctoral Candidate in Leadership and Management at the Tasmanian School of Business and Economics, University of Tasmania. With a First Class Honours degree in Business, his research surrounds understanding and developing ethical behaviours in organisational citizens; especially leaders. Effective leadership development, in his perspective, begins with a holistic approach to leadership – one which recognises the importance of the follower.

Dorianne Cotter-Lockard is a Fellow at the Institute for Social Innovation at the Fielding Graduate University, USA, where she conducts research in the areas of team collaboration, leadership, coaching, music education, and spirituality in the workplace. She also teaches courses in mindful and compassionate leadership at Saybrook University, USA. She earned a PhD in Human and Organizational Systems from Fielding Graduate University and an MBA in Finance from New York University, Stern School of Business. Previously, she served as an executive in a Fortune 100 company, where she was a key member of a divisional C-level leadership team. Dorianne leads a consultancy devoted to mentoring young entrepreneurs to become conscious, collaborative leaders, and has presented papers and facilitated symposia at several international academic conferences, including the Academy of Management, American Psychological Association, and European Sociological Association.

Sarah Dawkins is a Lecturer in Management at the Tasmanian School of Business and Economics, University of Tasmania. Sarah is also a registered Clinical Psychologist and co-leader of the University of Tasmania Work, Health and Wellbeing Network. She earned her PhD from the University of Tasmania, receiving recognition by the Australia and New Zealand Academy of Management with the best doctoral dissertation award in 2014. Her research focuses on the development of positive psychological resources in employees and work teams. Sarah's research has been published in the *Journal of Occupational and Organisational Psychology* and *Human Relations*.

Marieta du Plessis is a Registered Industrial/Organisational Psychologist who has dedicated time to creating healthy Human Resource practices in organisations. She completed her PhD studies in the field of Positive Organisational Behaviour, with a focus on positive leadership. Marieta currently is a faculty member of the Department of Industrial/Organisational Psychology at the University of the Western Cape, South Africa. Her areas of teaching and research include Leadership and Positive Organisational Scholarship, Occupational Counselling, Organisational Behaviour and Psychology. She is also a Section Editor for the *South African Journal of Industrial Psychology* with a focus on Positive Organisational Psychology.

Behice Ertenu lectures at Bogazici University on the Faculty of Management. Along with teaching, she assists for-profit and non-for-profit organisations in the process of change, gives customised executive training, and leadership workshops. She completed her PhD in Organisational Behaviour at Marmara University, an MA in European studies, and BA in Business Administration at Bogazici University. Her move to the academic field was built on a foundation of 25 years of work experience, as a professional and an entrepreneur. Behice has experience in a wide range of business areas, including audit, finance, banking, market research, and human resources. She is also an accredited executive coach. Behice publishes articles in topics such as organisational development, corporate culture, climate change, empowerment, leadership, creativity, work engagement, and social entrepreneurship.

Cloé Fortin is currently pursuing her PhD in Industrial/Organisational Psychology at Université du Québec à Montréal after obtaining a Master's degree in Human Resource Management with honours from the same university. Her research interests include authentic leadership, ACT training and therapy, organisational development and systemic intervention.

John M. Friend received his PhD in political science from the University of Hawai'i at Mānoa. He was a Graduate Degree Fellow with the East-West Centre, a member of the Young Leaders Program at Pacific Forum CSIS, and a visiting research fellow at the Social Development Research Centre, De La Salle University (the Philippines), and Department of Political Science & International Studies, Yonsei University (South Korea). Presently, he is Assistant Professor of Political Science at the College of St. Benedict and St. John's University. Before joining that faculty, he taught in the Shidler College of Business, University of Hawai'i. His current research addresses the sociocultural factors shaping identity, perception, and decision making in the Asia-Pacific region.

William L. Gardner is the Jerry S. Rawls Chair in Leadership and Director of the Institute for Leadership Research in the Rawls College of Business at Texas Tech University. Additionally, he serves as the Editor-in-Chief for *Group & Organisation Management* and an Associate Editor for *The Leadership Quarterly*. He received his Doctorate of Business Administration (DBA) from Florida State University. He has published over 60 peer-reviewed articles in such scholarly outlets as the *Academy of Management Review, Academy of Management Journal, Group & Organisation Management, The Leadership Quarterly, Journal of Management, Journal of Management Studies, Journal of Leadership & Organisational Studies*, and the *Journal of Organisational Behaviour*. The Rawls

College of Business recognised his research contributions in 2013 with the Outstanding Researcher Award and in 2014 with the Distinguished Faculty Research Award. In 2015, Texas Tech recognised him as an "Integrated Scholar," and in 2016 he received the President's Academic Achievement Award.

Zhiyuan He is an international student from Xi'an, China. He is currently completing his bachelor's degree by double majoring in Political Science and Global Business Leadership at St. John's University. Zhiyuan is interested in learning more about international politics, religious conflicts, entrepreneurship, and leadership styles.

Lars Hornuf is an Associate Professor of Law and Economics at the University of Trier. He holds an M.A. in Political Economy (University of Essex, UK) and a PhD in Economics (University of Munich, Germany). He was a Junior Researcher at the Ifo Institute for Economic Research and the Institute for International Law at the University of Munich, as well as a visiting scholar at UC Berkeley, Stanford Law School, Duke University, and Georgetown University. Currently, he is an Affiliated Research Fellow at the Max Planck Institute for Innovation and Competition. Lars' research has been published in journals such as *Frontiers in Psychology* and the *Journal of Cross-Cultural Psychology*. His work has been covered in newspapers like *The Economist* and *Foreign Policy*.

Hayat Kabasakal is Professor of Management and Organisation Studies at the Management Department of Bogazici University, Istanbul, Turkey. She received her PhD in Strategic Management and Organisational Behaviour from the University of Minnesota. She has served as the Associate Dean of the Faculty of Administrative Sciences, Department Chair of the Management Department, and country co-investigator of the GLOBE project. She was the editor of *Bogazici Journal: Review of Social, Economic and Administrative Studies* and on the editorial boards of several journals. Her research focuses on organisational behaviour, including leadership, culture, employee attitudes, and gender. She has published in journals such as the *Journal of Strategic Management*, *Journal of Applied Psychology: An International Journal*, *Journal of World Business*, *International Journal of Social Economics*, and *International Journal of Human Resource Management*.

Gaye Karacay is an Assistant Professor at the Industrial Engineering Department of Istanbul Technical University. Her PhD in Management and Organisation is from Bogazici University with a focus on Organisational

Behaviour and an MBA degree from London Business School. Before her PhD studies, Dr. Karacay worked as a professional at public and private sector institutions in strategic management and public management. Her research interests include leadership, cross-cultural management, organisational culture, human resource management, talent management, and corporate entrepreneurship. She has published in international journals including *Journal of World Business* and *Personnel Review*. She has presented her studies at several international conferences.

Gemma Lewis is a Lecturer in Management at the Tasmanian School of Business and Economics, University of Tasmania. She has a PhD in Collaborative Marketing and Horizontal Networks, and has active research interests in entrepreneurship, inter-organisational relationships, value chain adaptation, and innovation. Gemma's research has been published in *Journal of Strategic Marketing* and *International Journal of Social Research Methodology*.

Angela Martin is an Associate Professor in Management at the Tasmanian School of Business and Economics, University of Tasmania. She received her PhD in Organisational Psychology from Griffith University, Australia. Her research focuses on the management of employee health and well-being. Prior to working as a full-time academic, Angela project-managed an Australian Research Council (ARC) Industry Partnership at the University of Queensland, investigating organisational change within public sector organisations. She has also worked as a policy/research officer in rural health, media and communications, economic development, industrial relations and vocational education. Angela's research has been published in the *Academy of Management: Learning & Education and Human Resource Management*.

Lucas Monzani is a Lecturer in Leadership at the Graduate School of Management of Plymouth University, United Kingdom, and an associate researcher at both the Institute for Organisational Development and Quality of Work Life at the University of Valencia (Spain), and the Centre for Leadership and Behaviour in Organisations at Goethe University (Germany). Lucas holds a PhD in Psychology of Human Resources from the University of Valencia and is an *Erasmus Mundus* Master in Work, Organisational, and Personnel Psychology. His research interests include exemplary leadership, commitment to lead, and other topics bridging neuropsychology with organisational behaviour. Lucas combines his research activities with his professional practice as an executive consultant, for which he contributed to several leadership development projects within the Department of Peacekeeping Operations of the United Nations.

Deborah J. Pembleton received her PhD in Organisational Leadership, Policy, and Development with a focus on International Education from the University of Minnesota. She is an associate professor in the Global Business Leadership Department, where she teaches International Human Resources, International Organisational Behaviour, Global Strategy, and Global Management Principles. In her classes and research, she focuses on the internationalisation of business education and cross-cultural leadership with a particular focus on Southeast Asia. She is a member of several professional organisations including the Academy of Management, the Society for International Education, Training, and Research, and the Organisational Behaviour Teaching Society. Prior to her academic career, she attained 20 years of industry experience with IBM Corporation and 3M Company.

Cécile Renucci is currently completing her PhD in Industrial/Organisational psychology at Université du Québec à Montréal. She holds both a Bachelor's degree in Business Administration with a major in management from HEC Montreal and a Bachelor's degree in Psychology from the University of Montreal. Her primary interests are in leadership development training. Her thesis project is based on innovative training methods, such as meditation & mindfulness in leadership development.

Tara Wernsing is an Associate Professor in Organisational Behaviour at IE Business School in Madrid, Spain, where she teaches MBA and PhD level courses in leadership development and mixed methods research. Her research investigates authentic and ethical forms of leadership based in self-awareness, relational trust, positive psychological capital, and diversity across cultures. She has published in top academic journals including *Journal of Applied Psychology, Journal of Management, Journal of Business Ethics, Journal of Leadership and Organisational Studies, Journal of World Business, Journal of Management Development*, and *European Journal of International Management*. She has more than ten years of full-time work experience in business marketing at Sears and Brunswick/Life Fitness and has conducted consulting projects with Johnson & Johnson, Gateway, Walgreens, Unilever, and the U.S. National Institute of Corrections.

List of Figures

List of Tables

Part I

International Perspectives

1

Leader Self-Awareness and Follower Psychological Empowerment Across Cultures

Tara Wernsing

According to a recent meta-analysis, there have been more than 40 empirical articles on authentic leadership (Hoch, Bommer, Dulebohn, & Wu, 2016). Despite a growing interest in authentic leadership, relatively less research exists on its components, although some scholars argue that the decision to analyze authentic leadership as a single higher-order construct or as four first-order constructs depends on the leader and situation under study. Based on context, the process and effects of authentic leadership may be modeled and understood through its components and "reinforces the potential importance of not assuming that perceived authentic leadership is universally a unitary or higher-order (global) construct" (Neider & Schriesheim, 2011: 1154). Since there is value in studying individual components as causal factors in the leadership process, this chapter begins a deeper investigation of a foundational component of authentic leadership, namely leader self-awareness, and its relationship to followers across cultures. This component was described

T. Wernsing (✉)
IE Business School, IE University, Madrid, Spain

© The Author(s) 2018

D. Cotter-Lockard (ed.), *Authentic Leadership and Followership*, Palgrave Studies in Leadership and Followership, https://doi.org/10.1007/978-3-319-65307-5_1

as underlying the theoretical core to the development of authentic leadership as a self-based model (Gardner, Avolio, Walumbwa, Luthans, & May, 2005: 346), and thus deserves further dedicated theory development and analysis of its explanatory power in predicting follower attitudes and behaviors. Therefore, the primary purpose of this chapter is to examine the effect of leader self-awareness (in the context of authentic leadership and its measurement) and develop theory predicting followers' psychological attitudes, specifically a sense of empowerment at work. Secondly, these relationships will be examined across national cultures to ascertain potential differences in the measurement or structural models across multiple levels of analysis (individual, work group, and national culture). It is beyond the scope of this chapter to explain in theoretical depth the differences that exist country by country, yet potential explanations for work unit and cultural differences in measurement and structural effects will be offered.

This study contributes to the field of authentic leadership in several ways. First, this research builds on prior theoretical explanations of the multidimensional nature of authentic leadership, specifically outlining a framework for leader self-awareness and its development. Although prior definitions exist, there is not a specific framework for leader self-awareness that describes its construct model and corresponding developmental practices. Second, although previous studies find that different measures of self-awareness are positively related to leadership effectiveness, less is known about the impact of leader self-awareness on followers' attitudes at work. Therefore, the current study offers insight into the cross-level relationships between leader self-awareness at the work group level and followers' sense of empowerment at work. Third, the existing survey instrument for authentic leadership contains items for assessing leader self-awareness, but these items have not been evaluated across cultures for measurement invariance. Without deconstructing variance across levels to assess random and systematic sources, differences in mean levels of any construct could be due to numerous factors (Byrne & Watkins, 2003; Jak, 2017). Therefore, evaluation of measurement invariance and differences in the relationship between leader self-awareness and follower empowerment will be examined across national cultures as a third contribution.

Literature Review and Hypotheses

What Is Leader Self-awareness and Why Is It Important?

Leader self-awareness is considered a foundation in leadership development by practitioners and scholars alike (Avolio, 2005; Gardner, Avolio, Luthans, May, & Walumbwa, 2005; George, 2003; Goleman, 1998; London, 1995, 2002; Luthans & Avolio, 2003; McCauley & Van Velsor, 2003). Since sensitivity training emerged in organizations beginning in the 1950s, the idea has prevailed that managers should be more aware of their perceptual biases and potential prejudices in order to be effective interpersonally at work (Katz, 1956; Miles, 1960). More recently, the theory of authentic leadership presents leader self-awareness (LSA) as one of its four primary components (Gardner et al., 2005) explaining that "self-awareness refers to demonstrating an understanding of how one derives and makes meaning of the world and how that meaning making process impacts the way one views himself or herself over time. It also refers to showing an understanding of one's strengths and weaknesses and the multifaceted nature of the self, which includes gaining insight into the self through exposure to others, and being cognizant of one's impact on other people" (Walumbwa, Avolio, Gardner, Wernsing, & Peterson, 2008: 95). Further, they argue that "self-awareness is not an end in itself, but a process whereby one comes to reflect on one's unique values, identity, emotions, goals, knowledge, talents and/or capabilities" (Gardner, Avolio, Luthans, May, & Walumbwa, 2005: 349).

Prior research on LSA found significant positive relationships with leader effectiveness (Church, 1997), charismatic leadership (Sosik, 2001), and follower satisfaction with the leader (Tekleab, Sims, Yun, Tesluk, & Cox, 2007). Leaders who are self-aware tend to possess high levels of self-efficacy and provide orientation for followers (Sosik & Megerian, 1999).

How Does LSA Develop?

Self-awareness arises from the human capacity for self-reflexivity. No other species seems to have the reflexive capacity to observe and evaluate themselves in the same ways that the human species can (Gallup, 1982). Evolutionary perspectives suggest that the brain in humans has developed layers of complexity over time, including the reptilian brain (basal ganglia) governing survival and aggression instincts, the limbic system (paleomammalian) generating emotions motivating social behaviors, and the neocortex regions (neomammalian) responsible for conceptual thinking, abstract reasoning, language, and projecting time into the future and past (MacLean, 1990). "The different brains seem to cooperate like three interconnected biological computers, each of them having its own feeling of subjectivity and its own perception of time, space, and memories" (Wiest, 2012). Humans uniquely possess mental time travel, and can project an image of themselves in their minds out in the future and into the past (Wheeler, Stuss, & Tulving, 1997). The human capacity for self-reflexivity and imaginal mental travel produces a sense of conceptual identity that endures over time and is central to how people view themselves in relation to their work (Albert, Ashforth, & Dutton, 2000), how they relate to others (Sluss & Ashforth, 2007), and how they lead teams (Ellemers, De Gilder, & Haslam, 2004).

To become more aware of each aspect of the self, and how it influences other people and is affected by others, requires attending to inner states as well as developing sensitivity of one's environment and mutual influence with it. In this regard, the long history of prior research in self-awareness provides an initial framework that broadly identifies two forms of self-awareness: private and public (Fenigstein, Scheier, & Buss, 1975) or objective and subjective (Duval & Wicklund, 1972). On one hand, awareness of "private" inner states includes personal thoughts (cognition), emotions (affect), physical sensations (somatic experience), and motivational drives (conation). The focus inward generates attention on the self as an "object" of awareness. On the other hand, "public" self-awareness involves sensitivity to external situations, social dynamics, how one's behaviors influence other people's perceptions and reactions, and vice versa. The focus outward reflects a view from the self as the "subject" or source that is placing attention on external objects.

Therefore, developing self-awareness in the context of authentic leadership derives from both internally and externally focused awareness-generating practices. The internal–external model maps directly onto a fundamental state of leadership as being both an inner-directed and other-focused process (Quinn, 2005). Being inner-directed and other-focused integrates authenticity to the self with the process of leading change that is aligned externally with aspects of the social world. Hence, authentic leadership theory reflects an integration of the inner-directedness of authenticity of the self (Kernis, 2003; Kernis & Goldman, 2006) with the social influence process of leadership and its necessary focus on other people (Avolio & Gardner, 2005).

To develop LSA in these ways, multiple practices must be used to build sensitivity to internal states, relational interactions, and social group dynamics. Based on a review of the literature regarding self-awareness development generally and LSA specifically, three types of practices are central to developing LSA. These include introspection (an internal, private awareness building practice), self-reflection (a hybrid of internally and externally sourced awareness building), and feedback from others (a source of external awareness building). Each type of practice will be briefly reviewed below.

Practices for Developing LSA

A review of research on LSA and developing self-awareness converges on three primary types of practices: introspection, self-reflection, and feedback. The practices for developing LSA can serve as indicators for the construct and assess levels of developmental resources underlying LSA.

Introspection

In the early years of psychology, *introspection* was described as "looking into our own minds and reporting what we there discover" (James, 1890:

185). In modern times, neuroscientists equate introspection with metacognition (Weil et al., 2013) and describe it as a type of thinking about one's own internal experiences. Specifically, introspection is defined as directing attention to internal thoughts and feelings, and reporting on them through self-talk, writing, or verbalizing aloud. Verbal description of inner experience provides the opportunity to linguistically label direct experience, and this transcription process from direct experience to verbalized description can shift unconscious experience to conscious awareness through activating the symbolic representation of language.

Self-reflection

In contrast to introspection, *self-reflection* is evaluating past events and experiences to learn more about the self and prepare for the future (Kolb, 1984). Dewey (1933) defined reflection as a form of thinking that involves "active, persistent and careful consideration of any belief or supposed form of knowledge in light of the grounds that support it and the further consequences to which it leads." (p. 9). Therefore, self-reflection is a type of "after-action review" concerning personal experiences and assumptions from the past. It is an evaluative practice used to gain insight about the self that can inform and change the future.

Feedback

Finally, feedback is a third common practice identified in prior research on self-awareness. Feedback is information provided from external sources and people concerning perceptions, assessments, and evaluations. Ashford and Tsui (1991) explain that feedback provides greater understanding for how people are perceived by others. Feedback helps develop leadership skills because it provides information on the effectiveness of social influence intentions and attempts. Thus, LSA can be enhanced through the exchange of feedback on leadership behaviors from multiple sources (i.e., subordinates, peers, and supervisors; Day & Dragoni, 2015) which can counterbalance the human habit of basing expectations on a "self-referential criterion" (Lee, 1966).

How Can LSA Be Measured?

LSA has been assessed in a variety of ways over the last few decades, most often with a comparison of ratings of leadership between self-ratings and others' ratings as an indicator (Alimo-Metcalfe, 1998; Atwater & Yammarino, 1992; Moshavi, Brown, Dodd, 2003; Van Velsor, Taylor, & Leslie, 1993; Wohlers & London, 1989). A recent trend in the operationalization of LSA placed emphasis on the ability to anticipate the views of others, such as the boss (Sturm, Taylor, Atwater, & Braddy, 2014; Taylor, 2010). A different method for assessing LSA has been through self-report survey measures. For example, Sosik and Dworakivsky (1998) measured private and public self-consciousness as indicators of LSA, and found that private self-consciousness serves as a source of inner-directedness in charismatic leadership.

Another survey instrument, the Authentic Leadership Questionnaire (ALQ; Walumbwa et al., 2008) offered a method for assessing four behavioral components that conceptually define authentic leadership, including specific items concerning LSA. Evidence for the factor validity of the ALQ instrument across some cultures has been demonstrated by numerous authors (Caza, Bagozzi, Woolley, Levy, & Caza, 2010; Peus, Wesche, Streicher, Braun, & Frey, 2012; Rego, Vitória, Magalhães, Ribeiro, & Cunha, 2013). Additionally, the study by Caza et al. (2010) in New Zealand confirmed measurement equivalence for authentic leadership across gender.

As the research field has developed, questions concerning whether to treat authentic leadership as a single-factor model, four-factor model, or higher-order construct have emerged and the conclusion thus far is that the context and leader under study may determine which model is best (Neider & Schriesheim, 2011). In situations where the individual components of authentic leadership are important to distinguish, additional theory and analysis will be needed for each component. This chapter serves that purpose for the component of LSA.

Based on the first measure of authentic leadership called the ALQ, there are four items proposed to reflect the dimension of LSA. Of these four, two items are related to feedback and understanding others' perceptions of the self, one item refers to understanding one's impact on others, and one item implies that self-reflection is used to make a decision to adjust one's beliefs for the future. Therefore, although this short measure may not completely capture the conceptual domains indicated earlier, it may be sufficiently consistent and predictive of follower attitudes, which will be empirically tested in this study:

Hypothesis 1 Leader self-awareness, measured with the ALQ, demonstrates measurement equivalence across the world's major cultures.

How Does LSA Relate to Followers?

Given the nature of LSA described above, there are specific experiences that should be affected by the degree of self-awareness exhibited by the leader of a group, team, or work unit. Based on the evidence for how self-awareness develops in the context of leadership, increased LSA results from enhanced sensitivity to inner states, to relational and social dynamics, and to the influence that occurs between self and other(s). In turn, increased LSA could provide a greater sense of empowerment for the individuals involved in the same work unit due to enhanced sensitivity of these states and dynamics in self and others.

Psychological empowerment refers to intrinsic motivation manifested in four cognitions (meaning, competence, self-determination, and impact) reflecting an individual's orientation to his or her work role (Thomas & Velthouse, 1990). Meaning arises from a fit between one's work and personal values; competence is a belief in one's own capability to do the work effectively; self-determination is a sense of autonomy and choice; and impact is the perceived degree of influence over strategic, administrative, or operating outcomes in the organization (Spreitzer, 1995).

Since enhanced LSA develops from introspection and self-reflection, LSA is likely associated with greater sense of meaning and purpose that comes from aligning personal values with choices at work. Values are guiding principles used to select actions and make evaluations (Schwartz, 1994). Greater awareness of personal values likely results in those principles becoming more salient and central to decision-making (Badaracco, 1998; Ravlin & Meglino, 1987), thus serving as a guide to select leadership roles that align with those values. Leaders whose work responsibilities align with their personal values derive greater meaning and purpose from their work. In turn, a leader's purpose informs the vision they communicate to their work groups. In fact, a compelling vision for the future based on shared values inspires followers to exert extra effort to make the vision a reality, and this form of leadership is positively related to follower empowerment (Jung & Sosik, 2002). Therefore, higher LSA likely translates into a greater sense of meaning and purpose for both the group leader and group members.

LSA is also posited to influence follower's sense of competence, autonomy, and impact at work. As described above, LSA requires attention to inner dynamics (personal thoughts, emotions, and motivations) as well as outer dynamics (interaction and influence of the self with external people, objects, and events). A leader's awareness of personal strengths and weaknesses in social influence would grow more detailed and nuanced based on engaging in introspection, self-reflection, and feedback during and after leadership episodes at work. Increased attention to strengths/weaknesses in leadership interactions would likely result in heightened sensitivity to individual differences among people at work, including people's personalities, strengths, goals, motivations, and cultural values (Earley, 1987; Katz, 1956). Enhanced recognition of strengths and weaknesses of people offers opportunities to leverage the uniqueness of each person involved in a leadership process because heightened sensitivity of individual strengths/weaknesses provides greater knowledge for how to involve people in ways that are more effective and more authentic to their unique differences and the characteristics of the context (van Woerkom & Meyers, 2015). For example, managers who are more tuned-in to their own strengths/weaknesses can rely on co-workers who have complementary strengths/weaknesses, potentially balancing cognitive biases and improving decision quality (Korte, 2003). Therefore, greater LSA prepares a unit leader to more effectively allocate work responsibilities to those people who have the desire and skill for tasks at varying levels of impact, thus providing the opportunity and resources needed for followers to experience a greater sense of competence, autonomy, and impact with their work tasks.

Hypothesis 2 Leader self-awareness is positively related to followers' sense of empowerment at work.

Method

Sample

A survey of over 100,000 employees was conducted within one multinational organization of consumer products. Confidentiality for respondents was assured through use of a third-party independent firm for data collection. The survey had a response rate of 78%. Survey instruments were translated into multiple languages in over 100 countries. The translation of the original English language instrument into each language was done using a back translation methodology (Brislin, 1983). Therefore, the questionnaire was first translated from the original language into the local country language by a bilingual native speaker and a professional translator from a specialized ISO 9001 certified agency. Next, the translated language version was translated back into English by a second bilingualist. Finally, the translated English version was compared with the original and any discrepancies were resolved by mutual agreement between linguists and researchers.

A subsample was used for this study representing ten countries (Brazil, China, Germany, India, Italy, Mexico, Poland, South Africa, Sweden, Turkey, United Kingdom, and United States) one for each of the major world cultures, including Anglo, Arab, Germanic Europe, Latin America, Latin Europe, Eastern Europe, Middle East, Nordic Europe, Sub-Sahara Africa, Confucian Asia, and Southern Asia, based on the GLOBE project (House, Hanges, Javidan, Dorfman, & Gupta, 2004). The total sample size was 48,012 individuals.

Structural equation models were estimated using Mplus 7.0. For the multigroup confirmatory factor analyses, a simple random sample of 200 respondents from the total sample for each country was selected. This random sample provided equal sample size for all countries for the weighted average model statistics to represent the overall effects and because the exact chi-squared test is sensitive to sample size.

Measures

Brief measures were used for this study, and prior research shows that short scales composed of 3–5 items for each factor in cross-cultural analysis and measurement invariance testing can perform adequately (cf. Marsh & Hau, 2003). Methodologists recommend a minimum of 3 items to form a factor (Byrne, 1998; Guilford, 1952; Kline, 2005: 172; MacCallum, 1995). Furthermore, there is evidence that short and even single-item measures of attitudes and perceptions can be valid and reliable (Bergkvist & Rossiter, 2007; for example, see job satisfaction by Wanous & Reichers, 1997, and personality by Gosling, Rentfrow, & Swann, 2003). Most recently, a study of measurement invariance across 26 cultures used a 5-item measure of well-being (Jang et al., 2017).

Leader Self-awareness

Each employee rated their supervisor's level of self-awareness using 4 items from the 16-item survey instrument for authentic leadership (Walumbwa et al., 2008). Items were measured on a five-point Likert scale assessing frequency ranging from not at all (1) to always (5). Specific items in order are: "seek feedback to improve interactions with others," "accurately describe how others view his/her capabilities," "know when it is time to reevaluate his/her position on important issues," and "shows he/she understands how specific actions impact others." The internal reliability of the scales was adequate. Cronbach's coefficient alpha was .85 for the 4-items, and latent factor estimates of reliability were calculated using Mplus syntax provided in supplementary material by Geldhof, Preacher, and Zyphur (2014) for composite reliability (omega) which was estimated at .83 and maximal reliability (H) estimated at .86 for this scale.

Follower Psychological Empowerment

Each employee rated their perception of their empowerment at work based on nine items using a five-point Likert response scale assessing frequency ranging from not at all (1) to always (5). A scale was created for this measure based on Spritzer's (1995) definition and theoretical model for psychological empowerment. Two items for each of sub-dimensions of psychological empowerment were used, except for competence which had three items. Sample items for meaning: "My job provides me with meaningful and challenging work," for competence: "I have the training I need to do my job effectively," for self-determination: "I have the authority I need to get my job done," and for impact: "I can see a clear link between my work and the objectives of my organization." Coefficient alpha for the scale was .84, while the latent factor composite reliability (omega) was estimated at .85 and maximal reliability (H) at .85 (Geldhof, Preacher, & Zyphur, 2014). Further, a confirmatory factor analysis (CFA) was conducted to verify the factor validity of the scale based on Spreitzer's (1995) model of empowerment. A second-order model with four first-order factors was tested with a random sample of 200 employees per country. Based on global fit indices, the sample data provided sufficient evidence for the higher-order latent factor model with a chi-square of 240.944, df = 23, $p < .05$, comparative fit index (CFI) = .964, root mean square error of approximation (RMSEA) = .069, and standardized root mean square residual (SRMR) = .032. See the guidelines below for recommended indices values.

Results

Hypothesis 1: Measurement Equivalence Across National Cultures

Means, standard deviations, and scale reliabilities for each country for each survey instrument scale are shown in Tables 1.1 and 1.2. Additionally, for LSA, the four items' standardized factor loadings are provided for each country, and for the second-order construct of follower psychological empowerment the factor loadings for the four first-order latent construct indicators are shown.

In Tables 1.3 and 1.4, SEM model global fit statistics were used to evaluate structural equation models besides the chi-square statistic and

Table 1.1 Descriptive statistics for LSA by country

Country	Cultural cluster[a]	Mean (SD)	Coefficient α (omega)	IItem 1	IItem 2	IItem 3	IItem 4
Brazil	Latin America	3.31 (.99)	.85 (.84)	.795	.657	.836	.803
China	Confucian Asia	3.43 (.89)	.87 (.85)	.870	.738	.864	.749
Germany	Germanic Europe	3.35 (.88)	.84 (.82)	.772	.711	.793	.775
India	Southern Asia	3.43 (.91)	.80 (.78)	.757	.678	.771	.687
Italy	Latin Europe	3.16 (.96)	.86 (.85)	.809	.703	.855	.785
Poland	Eastern Europe	3.33 (.92)	.85 (.83)	.713	.602	.858	.779
South Africa	Sub-Sahara Africa	3.06 (1.02)	.85 (.83)	.787	.630	.879	.745
Sweden	Nordic Europe	3.15 (.90)	.81 (.78)	.740	.531	.788	.815
Turkey	Arab	3.27 (.94)	.85 (.84)	.772	.685	.783	.718
USA	Anglo	3.31 (1.02)	.88 (.87)	.837	.740	.909	.796

Note: [a]Every major culture based on the GLOBE project (House et al., 2004) is represented by one country

likelihood ratios, namely, the CFI, the RMSEA, and SRMR. Values greater than .90 and .95 are commonly interpreted to represent "acceptable" and "good" fit, respectively, for the CFI (Medsker, Williams, & Holahan, 1994). For the SRMR, values of less than .08 are generally considered acceptable fit (Hu & Bentler, 1999). Concerning the RMSEA, values less than .05 are indicative of good fit, whereas acceptable fit values can range from .06 to .08 (Browne & Cudeck, 1992), however more recent research argues that absolute cutoffs for RMSEA and other fit indices may not be generally useful (Chen, Curran, Bollen, Kirby, & Paxton, 2008; Fan & Sivo, 2005; Steiger, 2007). Chen (2007) recommended acceptable invariance model fit based on the following criteria: change in CFI $\leq$ .01, change in RMSEA $\leq$ .015, and change in SRMR $\leq$ .03 for tests of factor loading invariance and change in CFI $\leq$ .01, change in RMSEA $\leq$ .015, and change in SRMR $\leq$ .01 for tests of intercept and residual invariance.

Table 1.2 Descriptive statistics for follower empowerment by country

Country	Cultural cluster[a]	Mean (SD)	Coefficient α (omega)	Factor 1: meaning	Factor 2: competence	Factor 3: autonomy	Factor 4: impact
Brazil	Latin America	3.78 (.66)	.82 (.82)	.773	.809	.834	.928
China	Confucian Asia	3.60 (.66)	.89 (.89)	.869	.931	.894	.992
Germany	Germanic Europe	3.74 (.62)	.85 (.85)	.832	.850	.856	.936
India	Southern Asia	3.97 (.64)	.82 (.82)	.835	.910	.788	.979
Italy	Latin Europe	3.43 (.75)	.88 (.88)	.870	.862	.846	.958
Poland	Eastern Europe	3.64 (.61)	.81 (.81)	.828	.819	.891	.933
South Africa	Sub-Sahara Africa	3.51 (.75)	.85 (.85)	.801	.885	.852	.963
Sweden	Nordic Europe	3.75 (.59)	.80 (.81)	.810	.808	.852	.957
Turkey	Arab	3.90 (.62)	.85 (.82)	.827	.794	.803	.965
USA	Anglo	3.70 (.68)	.87 (.87)	.800	.859	.867	.976

Note: [a]Every major culture based on the GLOBE project (House et al., 2004) is represented by one country

Table 1.3 Configural invariance for LSA: independent single group model for each country

Country	n	χ^2	df	p	CFI	RMSEA	SRMR
Brazil	200	4.849	2	.20	.993	.084	.015
China	200	2.095	2	.35	.998	.015	.011
Germany	200	5.700	2	.06	.987	.099	.026
India	200	5.620	2	.06	.979	.095	.031
Italy	200	5.296	2	.07	.993	.076	.018
Poland	200	5.088	2	.08	.992	.088	.020
South Africa	200	4.665	2	.09	.993	.082	.021
Sweden	200	3.017	2	.22	.995	.051	.019
Turkey	200	2.811	2	.25	.997	.045	.017
USA	200	3.562	2	.16	.997	.063	.014
Country	n	χ^2	df	p	CFI	RMSEA	SRMR
Brazil	10009	72.263	2	.00	.996	.059	.009
China	3857	64.132	2	.00	.992	.090	.014
Germany	2388	13.185	2	.09	.997	.048	.009
India	15202	38.305	2	.00	.998	.035	.007
Italy	2200	10.510	2	.00	.998	.044	.007
Poland	2073	.249	2	.88	1.00	.000	.001
South Africa	2428	5.305	2	.07	.999	.026	.005
Sweden	470	4.898	2	.09	.995	.056	.013
Turkey	1744	7.465	2	.02	.998	.040	.008
USA	7641	36.460	2	.00	.998	.047	.007

Configural Equivalence

Following the steps outlined by Vandenberg and Lance (2000), configural equivalence was estimated for each country independently based on a CFA for a first-order factor structure (see Table 1.3). Each country-level CFA met minimally borderline acceptable level of model fit based on cutoff values of CFI > .95 and SRMR <= .08, but RMSEA <= .08 was not found for all the countries. In fact, based on a sample of 200 per country, 6 of 10 countries had an RMSEA of .08 to .10 suggesting some model misspecification. However, given the stronger performance of the other model fit statistics, and the RMSEA results in the total sample shown at the bottom of Table 1.3, the conclusion is that the four item indicators of a latent construct for LSA is adequate for each national culture.

Table 1.4 Measurement equivalence for multigroup models

Model	n	χ^2	df	p	CFI	RMSEA	SRMR	Models compared	Δ CFI	Decision
1. Configural invariance baseline	2000	42.863	20	.002	.993	.076	.018			
2. Equal factor loadings (weak metric invariance)	2000	112.727	56	<.001	.983	.071	.132	2 vs 1	.010	(Accept null of equality of groups)
3. Equal item intercepts (strong scalar invariance)	2000	297.453	92	<.001	.924	.106	.188	3 vs 2	.059	(Reject null of equality)
4. Equal error variances (strict residual invariance)	2000	578.431	128	<.001	.833	.133	.235	4 vs 3	.091	(Reject null of equality)

Note: Measurement invariance comparisons were based on a random sample of 200 for each country

Model	n	χ^2	df	p	CFI	RMSEA	SRMR	Models compared	Δ CFI	Decision
1. Configural invariance baseline	48012	252.781	20	>.001	.997	.049	.008			
2. Equal factor loadings (weak metric invariance)	48012	774.639	56	<.001	.991	.052	.086	2 vs 1	.005	(Accept null of equality of groups)
3. Equal item intercepts (strong scalar invariance)	48012	2795.435	92	<.001	.960	.078	.114	3 vs 2	.031	(Reject null of equality)
4. Equal error variances (strict residual invariance)	48012	5477.672	128	<.001	.921	.093	.146	4 vs 3	.039	(Reject null of equality)

Note: Measurement invariance comparisons were based on the total sample available for each country, so the overall result is weighted by sample size

Furthermore, the standardized factor loadings for each of the four items measuring LSA were shown Table 1.1 for each country. The second item, "accurately describe how others view his/her capabilities," had relatively lower weights than the other items, and had the lowest weight in Sweden (.531). The first item "seek feedback to improve interactions with others" was dropped in an analysis conducted by Neider and Schriesheim (2011, p. 1150) due to a "modest" cross-loading. However, for the purpose of the current study, a correlation with another dimension does not present a problem and the item performed adequately and consistently across countries, so it was retained in all analyses in this study.

In order to move forward in the invariance testing procedures and examine the next levels of invariance, the configural model for each country is placed together in one multigroup CFA to be estimated simultaneously, forming the configural baseline model. The results of the model fit for the multigroup configural baseline are shown in the first row of Table 1.4, and demonstrate acceptable fit based on a CFI > .95, SRMR < .05, and RMSEA < .08. Better results are found using the full sample size, shown in the lower portion of Table 1.4. Therefore, a single factor underlying these four items seems to represent the data equally well across national cultures.

Metric Equivalence

Next, metric invariance was examined, which constrains factor loadings to be equivalent across countries. Constraining the items' factor loadings to be equal across ten countries did reduce the model fit, but not significantly (see Table 1.4, model 2). Cheung and Rensvold (2002) recommended that when comparing models with less than or equal to .01 change in CFI, the null hypothesis can be accepted. However, the SRMR, an index of the average of standardized residuals between the observed and the hypothesized covariance matrices, is concerning since it increased over .100 based on the sample size of 200. Hu and Bentler (1999, p. 27) suggest that an SRMR "close to .09" represents a reasonable fit. Given this initial evidence, metric invariance seems marginal, also challenged by the low factor loading on item 2 in Sweden shown in Table 1.1, for example. However, examining the results of the total sample available (shown in bottom of Table 1.4), the change in CFI is lower and the SRMR is also lower, offering support for metric invariance when using the total sample to estimate regression coefficients.

Scalar Equivalence

The next step in measurement invariance is testing the assumption of strong invariance, which investigates if the intercepts of the equations linking indicators and latent factors are the same across groups, in addition to the prior constraints from earlier steps in the sequential process. The results are shown in Table 1.4 Model 3. Based on a random sample of 200 individuals per country, the model fit statistics diminish significantly (i.e., CFI = .924, RMSEA = .106, and SRMR = .188, ΔCFI = .059) suggesting that LSA does not have equal item intercepts (means) across national cultures, and scalar invariance is not supported. The total sample results also show diminished model fit; thus, the latent factor means for LSA cannot be compared if the assumption is that the construct represents exactly the same concept and that its point of origin in each country is similar. Intercept variance could occur due to social desirability, social norms, a propensity to respond more strongly to an item despite having the same latent trait or factor mean, and/or respondents using a different reference point (Chen, 2008). Finally, although the sequential testing process could stop here, since additional equality constraints can only decrease the model fit, a final model provides the results for item-level residual invariance (Table 1.4, Model 4) and as expected, there is no support.

In conclusion, because metric invariance was marginal or fully supported depending on the sample size, researchers can cautiously use latent factor scores for LSA to compare structural relationships (regression slopes) between latent factors across countries. However, comparing means of LSA is likely confounded with other sources of variation due to differences in responding to scales, item meaning, or cultural differences that create a comparison of "chopsticks to forks," as Chen (2008) explains. The lack of invariance indicates something is different across cultures in the point of origin (intercept mean) for each item or indicator for a latent construct. For example, based on the means shown in Table 1.1, one might be tempted to conclude that LSA is higher in China and India than in South Africa. However, a lack of scalar invariance indicates that there are cultural differences in the meaning or responding to the items for this measure, and therefore, we cannot know that LSA as originally defined with the instrument created in the United States in the English language represents the same latent construct conceptually in South Africa, China, and India.

Hypothesis 2: Effects of LSA on Follower Empowerment

Hypotheses 2 was tested using multilevel mixed models in SAS 9.4 given that individual employees were nested within work units within countries. Maximum likelihood was used in estimating model parameters. The significance of fixed effects was evaluated with a Wald ratio (i.e., the z-test of the ratio of each estimate to its standard error), whereas random effects were evaluated via likelihood ratio tests. Overall results with unstandardized coefficients are provided in Table 1.5, and specific effects for level 1 (individuals) and level 2 (units) are shown by country in Table 1.6.

First, an analysis of the nested variance for each factor was conducted by examining the intraclass correlation or ICC (Shrout & Fleiss, 1979). An ICC(1) calculates the proportion of variance that is between units and represents the average correlation among individuals within a work unit (Bliese, 1998). Derived from an empty means, random intercept model, follower empowerment had an ICC of .08 at the work unit level, indicating that 8% of the variance was between work units, and .055 at country level indicating that 5.5% of the variance in empowerment was due to country differences. LSA had an ICC of .0925 at level 2, indicating that 9.25% of the variance was between work units, and ICC of .004 at level 3 indicating that there was almost no variance (.4%) in LSA that can be attributed to country. This suggests the mean levels could be different (as the lack of scalar invariance suggested) but the variance in LSA is due to individual and unit level factors, rather than country. Therefore, two-level modeling was used.

Table 1.5 Multilevel modeling for the effect of LSA on follower empowerment

Level and variable	Model 1: Empty model at L1	Model 2: Empty model at two levels, random intercept for unit	Model 3: Random intercept for unit, fixed slope for LSA L1	Model 4: Fixed slope for L1, fixed slope L2	Model 5: Random slope for L1, fixed slope L2
Level 1					
Intercept	3.78	3.75	3.76	3.75	3.75
LSA within-unit			.388	.389	.386
Level 2					
LSA between-unit mean centered				.470	.464
Variance components					
Within-unit (L1) residual variance	.464	.409	.283	.283	.283
Intercept (L1) variance		.055	.058	.032	.032
Intercept-slope covariance					−.008
−2 log likelihood	99371.7	93973.8	76479.1	76313.6	76048.5

Note: L1 = Level 1, L2 = Level 2
Level 1 n = 48,012 and Level 2 n = 562

Table 1.6 Multilevel model effects of LSA on follower empowerment by country

	Zero-order correlation at Level 1	Level 1 sample size	Level 2 sample size	Effect of within-group variation of LSA (level 1)	Effect of between-group variation of LSA (level 2)
Brazil	.57	10,009	74	.384 (.006)[a]	.342 (.082)
China	.62	3857	52	.422 (.009)[a]	.420 (.082)
Germany	.55	2388	71	.389 (.012)	.281 (.091)[a]
India	.57	15,202	57	.388 (.005)[a]	.598 (.050)
Italy	.68	2200	46	.513 (.013)[a]	.808 (.088)[a]
Poland	.55	2073	28	.369 (.013)	.237 (.101)[a]
South Africa	.56	2428	51	.390 (.013)	.526 (.093)
Sweden	.51	470	19	.313 (.027)	.497 (.094)
Turkey	.51	1744	37	.342 (.014)	.314 (.092)
USA	.56	7614	127	.364 (.007)	.495 (.051)

Note: Standard errors are given in parentheses
All effect sizes were significantly different than zero at $p < .05$
[a]Represents a significant difference (Fisher's z-score greater than 1.96) between that country's effect size compared to USA

Hypothesis 2 proposed that LSA positively relates to follower's level of empowerment. First, the effects of LSA at each level were created (Snijders & Bosker, 1999). The within-unit effect was separated from between-unit effect. The within-unit effect (level 1) is the relative difference of each person within the work unit from the unit's average score for LSA. The between-unit effect (level 2) was represented by the unit mean score for LSA. Including a random intercept for unit was a significant improvement in model fit based on the −2 log likelihood comparison for nested models (see Table 1.5, model 1 versus 2, 99,371–93,973 = 5398, $p > .001$). The within-unit effect of LSA was significant (Model 3), accounting for 31% of the residual variance, and indicated that for each one point increase in the level of assessment of LSA relative to unit mean, there is a corresponding increase of .388 in the level of follower empowerment. Adding a fixed effect for the between-unit effect of LSA was significant and accounted for 45% of the random intercept variance, and indicated that for every one point increase in a unit's LSA mean score, empowerment is expected to be higher by 0.47 points (see Model 4). For the next step, a random slope was evaluated for the within-unit effect of LSA (see Model 5) to see if the relationship between individual level LSA and follower empowerment varies across units. There was a significant improvement to model fit, $-2\Delta LL(2) = 165, p < .05$.

In order to compare separate effect sizes at the individual and work unit levels across cultures, two-level models were estimated for each country separately and shown in Table 1.6 using the total sample. Fisher's z-test was used to compare the regression coefficients between countries, using the United States as the reference group as commonly done (Chen, 2008). Both within-unit effects and between-unit effects for each country were compared to the U.S. Four countries (Brazil, China, India, Italy) had statistically significant higher within-unit effects than the U.S. indicating the relationship with follower empowerment was stronger in these countries. At the unit level, the effect of LSA was higher for Italy, but lower for Germany and Poland, indicating that the variance between the unit mean levels for leader self-awareness had a stronger effect on follower empowerment in Italy than in the United States, but a significantly weaker effect in Germany and Poland.

Discussion

The purpose of this study was to begin investigation into a sub-component of authentic leadership theory, namely LSA, and examine its effects on followers′ attitudes, namely psychological empowerment. The study intended to address two primary research questions: Does the measure of LSA provided in the initial survey instrument developed for authentic leadership (ALQ) display measurement equivalence across national cultures? If so, can LSA predict follower psychological empowerment at multiple levels of analysis?

In this study, a sample of over 40,000 employees within one corporation rated their unit manager's level of LSA as well as their own sense of empowerment in the workplace. The LSA measure demonstrated adequate configural and metric invariance across ten countries. Furthermore, multilevel analysis supported the positive effects of LSA on follower empowerment at the individual and work unit level. Relative perceptions of leader self-awareness for the unit manager as well as average unit-level LSA had positive effects on follower empowerment. Comparisons of the effect sizes were made between the United States and each of the other countries in the sample. Evidence for significant differences between some countries was found, suggesting that in Brazil, China, India, and Italy, the impact of follower's perception of their unit manager's level of LSA is even stronger. Similarly, in Italy there was a stronger effect of LSA on follower empowerment at the work unit level. On the other hand, LSA had smaller effects in Germany and Poland than the U.S. at the work unit level. Caution should be used in drawing conclusions about country comparison, since these differences may be due to unique issues within the source company of the data and the units located in each country, rather than attributing the source solely to cultural differences.

Theoretical and Practical Implications

This study offers empirical support for the usefulness of research focused on components of authentic leadership. Initial theoretical distinctions were integrated from prior research to explain the construct of LSA, and specific practices required for developing LSA were outlined. Introspection, self-reflection, and feedback were defined as distinct domains in developing LSA.

A second implication derives directly from the measurement invariance findings. In terms of empirical support, a brief measure of LSA offers consistent measurement across cultures at the level of metric invariance, which implies that the relationship of each of the measured questionnaire items to the latent construct are similar across national cultures, and that relationships with other factors can be compared across cultures. However, because evidence for scalar invariance was not found, comparing the means of LSA across countries and assuming the construct represents the same concept in each country is not warranted and would be misleading.

A third implication concerns followership in the context of authentic leadership. This study shows significant positive relationships between LSA and follower psychological empowerment. Although further evidence of the positive effects of the components of authentic leadership is demonstrated, this research does not suggest that authentic leadership or LSA is the only source of positive influence on followers′ psychological empowerment. The other components of authentic leadership may be equally predictive, and other leadership factors are likely to be important. For example, the field of psychological empowerment separates the structural components of empowerment (organizational structures, processes, and policies) from psychological components. Each form is likely driven by different factors and mechanisms.

In terms of practical implications from this research, this study supports the practice of authentic leadership in organizations as a path toward greater employee empowerment. Although causal conclusions cannot be made, correlational patterns suggest that perceived self-awareness of unit leaders is positively related to employees' sense of empowerment. Organizations striving to increase employee motivation at work may want to encourage the development of authentic leadership and followership in their people. Although there are multiple ways to increase employee motivation at work, leadership development is a powerful tool for organizations. Specific practices to help employees develop their own skills at introspection, self-reflection, and exchanging feedback, could be offered as programs. Not everyone is ready for in-depth self-awareness development in the context of leadership. Therefore, optional courses and tools in multiple modalities (online, face to face) could be offered.

Limitations and Future Research

Despite the contribution of the research, this study is not without limitations. First, although a large sample of employees and countries was used in this study, all the data came from one organization, and thus features unique to the organization and its internal culture likely affect the data. Explanations of cultural differences that could be due to internal culture of the units within each country were not explained, and yet would be important to interpreting the cause of the differences observed in these analyses. Future research should seek to replicate these findings.

Second, a common limitation of survey research is common source variance. All the data used in these analyses was obtained from employee ratings of themselves and their unit managers. However, the survey responses are not solely self-reported assessments, but also assessments of the unit managers. Furthermore, the use of multilevel modeling offers a way to estimate separate effects at individual and unit levels.

For future research, scholars can further explore the theoretical domain of LSA and the underlying cognitive, affective, and conative processes that cause its emergence and development in individuals and its effects on groups. Additional operationalizations and measurements of LSA can be designed and tested across leadership situations and cultural contexts. Also, since this study did not examine the potential for mutual influence, such as the impact of followers on their unit managers, future research could explore the effects of follower self-awareness on unit leaders' development over time. In any case, this study offers an initial view of the individual and unit effects of LSA on follower empowerment across ten national cultures, and can serve as a foundation for future research on LSA.

References

Albert, S., Ashforth, B. E., & Dutton, J. E. (2000). Organizational identity and identification: Charting new waters and building new bridges. *Academy of Management Review, 25*(1), 13–17.

Alimo-Metcalfe, B. (1998). 360 degree feedback and leadership development. *International Journal of Selection and Assessment, 6*(1), 35–44.

Ashford, S. J., & Tsui, A. S. (1991). Self-regulation for managerial effectiveness: The role of active feedback seeking. *Academy of Management Journal, 34*, 251–280.

Atwater, L. E., & Yammarino, F. J. (1992). Does self-other agreement on leadership perceptions moderate the validity of leadership and performance predictions? *Personnel Psychology, 45*(1), 141–164.

Avolio, B. J. (2005). *Leadership development in balance: Made/born*. Mahwah, NJ: Lawrence Erlbaum Associates.

Avolio, B. J., & Gardner, W. L. (2005). Authentic leadership development: Getting to the root of positive forms of leadership. *Leadership Quarterly, 16*, 315–338.

Badaracco, J. L. (1998). The discipline of building character. *Harvard Business Review, 76*, 114–125.

Bergkvist, L., & Rossiter, J. R. (2007). The predictive validity of multiple-item versus single-item measures of the same constructs. *Journal of Marketing Research, 44*(2), 175–184.

Bliese, P. D. (1998). Group size, ICC values, and group-level correlations: A simulation. *Organizational Research Methods, 1*(4), 355–373.

Brislin, R. W. (1983). Cross-cultural research in psychology. *Annual Review of Psychology, 34*(1), 363–400.

Browne, M. W., & Cudeck, R. (1992). Alternative ways of assessing model fit. *Sociological Methods & Research, 21*(2), 230–258.

Byrne, B. (1998). *Structural equation modeling: Basic concepts, application, and programming*. Mahwah, NJ: Lawrence Erlbaum Associates.

Byrne, B. M., & Watkins, D. (2003). The issue of measurement invariance revisited. *Journal of Cross-Cultural Psychology, 34*(2), 155–175.

Caza, A., Bagozzi, R. P., Woolley, L., Levy, L., & Caza, B. B. (2010). Psychological capital and authentic leadership. *Asia-Pacific Journal of Business Administration, 2*(1), 53–70.

Chen, F. F. (2007). Sensitivity of goodness of fit indexes to lack of measurement invariance. *Structural Equation Modeling, 14*(3), 464–504.

Chen, F. F. (2008). What happens if we compare chopsticks with forks? The impact of making inappropriate comparisons in cross-cultural research. *Journal of Personality and Social Psychology, 95*(5), 1005–1018.

Chen, F. F., Curran, P. J., Bollen, K. A., Kirby, J., & Paxton, P. (2008). An empirical evaluation of the use of fixed cutoff points in RMSEA test statistic in structural equation models. *Sociological Methods and Research, 36*(4), 462–494.

Cheung, G. W., & Rensvold, R. B. (2002). Evaluating goodness-of-fit indexes for testing measurement invariance. *Structural Equation Modeling, 9*(2), 233–255.

Church, A. H. (1997). Managerial self-awareness in high-performing individuals in organizations. *Journal of Applied Psychology, 82*(2), 281–292.

Day, D. V., & Dragoni, L. (2015). Leadership development: An outcome-oriented review based on time and levels of analyses. *Annual Review of Organizational Psychology and Organizational Behavior, 2*(1), 133–156.

Dewey, J. (1933). *How we think: A restatement of the relation of reflective thinking to the educative process.* New York: D. C. Heath and Company.

Duval, S., & Wicklund, R. A. (1972). *A theory of objective self-awareness.* New York: Academic.

Earley, P. C. (1987). Intercultural training for managers: A comparison of documentary and interpersonal methods. *Academy of Management Journal, 30*(4), 685–698.

Ellemers, N., De Gilder, D., & Haslam, S. A. (2004). Motivating individuals and groups at work: A social identity perspective on leadership and group performance. *Academy of Management Review, 29*(3), 459–478.

Fan, X., & Sivo, S. A. (2005). Sensitivity of fit indexes to misspecified structural or measurement model components: Rationale of two-index strategy revisited. *Structural Equation Modeling, 12*, 343–367.

Fenigstein, A., Scheier, M. F., & Buss, A. H. (1975). Public and private self-consciousness: Assessment and theory. *Journal of Consulting and Clinical Psychology, 43*, 522–527.

Gallup, G. G. (1982). Self-awareness and the emergence of mind in primates. *American Journal of Primatology, 2*(3), 237–248.

Gardner, W. L., Avolio, B. J., Luthans, F., May, D. R., & Walumbwa, F. (2005). "Can you see the real me?" A self-based model of authentic leader and follower development. *The Leadership Quarterly, 16*, 343–372.

Geldhof, G. J., Preacher, K. J., & Zyphur, M. J. (2014). Reliability estimation in a multilevel confirmatory factor analysis framework. *Psychological Methods, 19*(1), 72–91.

George, W. (2003). *Authentic leadership: Rediscovering the secrets to creating lasting value.* San Francisco: Jossey-Bass.

Goleman, D. (1998). *Working with emotional intelligence.* New York: Bantam Books.

Gosling, S., Rentfrow, P., Swann, W. (2003). A very brief measure of the Big-Five personality domains. *Journal of Research in Personality, 37*(6), 504–528.

Guilford, J. P. (1952). When not to factor analyze. *Psychological Bulletin, 49*(1), 26–37.

Hoch, J. E., Bommer, W. H., Dulebohn, J. H., & Wu, D. (2016). Do ethical, authentic, and servant leadership explain variance above and beyond transformational leadership? A meta-analysis. *Journal of Management*. https://doi.org/10.1177/0149206316665461.

House, R. J., Hanges, P. J., Javidan, M., Dorfman, P. W., & Gupta, V. (2004). *Culture, leadership, and organizations: The GLOBE study of 62 societies*. Thousand Oaks, CA: Sage.

Hu, L., & Bentler, P. (1999). Cutoff criteria for fit indexes in covariance structure analysis: Conventional criteria versus new alternatives. *Structural Equation Modeling, 6*(1), 1–55.

Jak, S. (2017). Testing and explaining differences in common and residual factors across many countries. *Journal of Cross-Cultural Psychology, 48*(1), 75–92.

James, W. (1890). *The principles of psychology*. New York: Holt.

Jang, S., Kim, E. S., Cao, C., Allen, T. D., Cooper, C. L., Lapierre, L. M., et al. (2017). Measurement invariance of the satisfaction with life scale across 26 countries. *Journal of Cross-Cultural Psychology, 48*(4), 560–576.

Jung, D. I., & Sosik, J. J. (2002). Transformational leadership in work groups: The role of empowerment, cohesiveness, and collective-efficacy on perceived group performance. *Small Group Research, 33*(3), 313.

Katz, R. L. (1956). Human relations skills can be sharpened. *Harvard Business Review, 34*, 61–73.

Kernis, M. H. (2003). Toward a conceptualization of optimal self- esteem. *Psychological Inquiry, 14*, 1–26.

Kernis, M. H., & Goldman, B. M. (2006). A multicomponent conceptualization of authenticity: Theory and research. In M. Zanna (Ed.), *Advances in experimental social psychology* (Vol. 38, pp. 283–357). San Diego, CA: Elsevier.

Kline, R. B. (2005). *Principles and practice of structural equation modeling* (2nd ed.). New York: Guilford Press.

Kolb, D. (1984). *Experiential learning: Experience as the source of learning and development*. Englewood Cliffs, NJ: Prentice-Hall.

Korte, R. (2003). Biases in decision making and implications for human resource development. *Advances in Developing Human Resources, 5*(4), 440–457.

Lee, J. A. (1966). Cultural analysis in overseas operations. *The International Executive, 8*(3), 5–6.

London, M. (1995). *Self and interpersonal insight: how people gain understanding of themselves and others in organizations*. New York: Oxford University Press.

London, M. (2002). *Leadership development: Paths to self-insight and professional growth*. Mahwah, NJ: Erlbaum.

Luthans, F., & Avolio, B. J. (2003). Authentic leadership: A positive developmental approach. In K. S. Cameron, J. E. Dutton, & R. E. Quinn (Eds.), *Positive organizational scholarship* (pp. 241–261). San Francisco: Barrett-Koehler.

MacCallum, R. C. (1995). Model specification: Procedures, strategies, and related issues. In R. H. Hoyle (Ed.), *Structural equation modeling: Concepts, issues, and applications* (pp. 16–36). Thousand Oaks, CA: Sage.

MacLean, P. D. (1990). *The triune brain in evolution: Role in paleocerebral functions*. New York: Plenum.

Marsh, H. W., & Hau, K.-T. (2003). Big-fish – Little-pond effect on academic self-concept: A cross-cultural (26-country) test of the negative effects of academically selective schools. *American Psychologist, 58*(5), 364–376.

McCauley, C., & Van Velsor, E. (2003). *The center for creative leadership handbook of leadership development*. San Francisco: Jossey-Bass.

Medsker, G. J., Williams, L. J., & Holahan, P. J. (1994). A review of current practices for evaluating causal models in organizational behavior and human resources management research. *Journal of Management, 20*(2), 439–464.

Miles, M. (1960). Human relations training: Processes and outcomes. *Journal of Counseling Psychology, 7*(4), 301–306.

Moshavi, D., Brown, F. W., & Dodd, N. G. (2003). Leader self-awareness and its relationship to subordinate attitudes and performance. *Leadership & Organization Development Journal, 24*(7), 407–418.

Neider, L. L., & Schriesheim, C. A. (2011). The authentic leadership inventory (ALI): Development and empirical tests. *The Leadership Quarterly, 22*, 1146–1164.

Peus, C., Wesche, J., Streicher, B., Braun, S., & Frey, D. (2012). Authentic leadership: An empirical test of its antecedents, consequences, and mediating mechanisms. *Journal of Business Ethics, 107*, 331–348.

Quinn, R. (2005). Moments of greatness: Entering the fundamental state of leadership. *Harvard Business Review, 83*, 74–83.

Ravlin, E. C., & Meglino, B. M. (1987). Effect of values on perception and decision making: A study of alternative work values measures. *Journal of Applied Psychology, 72*(4), 666–673.

Rego, A., Vitória, A., Magalhães, A., Ribeiro, N., & e Cunha, M. P. (2013). Are authentic leaders associated with more virtuous, committed and potent teams? *The Leadership Quarterly, 24*, 61–79.

Schwartz, S. H. (1994). Are there universal aspects in the structure and contents of human values? *Journal of Social Issues, 50*(4), 19–45.

Shrout, P., & Fleiss, J. (1979). Intraclass correlations: Uses in assessing rater reliability. *Psychological Bulletin, 86*(2), 420–428.

Sluss, D. M., & Ashforth, B. E. (2007). Relational identity and identification: Defining ourselves through work relationships. *Academy of Management Review, 32*(1), 9–32.

Snijders, T., & Bosker, R. (1999). *Multilevel analysis: An introduction to basic and advanced multilevel modeling*. Los Angeles, CA: Sage.

Sosik, J. J. (2001). Self-other agreement on charismatic leadership: Relationships with work attitudes and managerial performance. *Group & Organization Management, 26*(4), 484–511.

Sosik, J. J., & Dworakivsky, A. C. (1998). Self-concept based aspects of the charismatic leader: More than meets the eye. *Leadership Quarterly, 9*(4), 503–526.

Sosik, J. J., & Megerian, L. E. (1999). Understanding leader emotional intelligence and performance. *Group & Organization Management, 24*(3), 367–390.

Spreitzer, G. M. (1995). Psychological empowerment in the workplace: Dimensions, measurement, and validation. *Academy of Management Journal, 38*(5), 1442.

Steiger, J. H. (2007). Understanding the limitations of global fit assessment in structural equation modeling. *Personality and Individual Differences, 42*(5), 893–898.

Sturm, R. E., Taylor, S. N., Atwater, L. E., & Braddy, P. W. (2014). Leader self-awareness: An examination and implications of women's under-prediction. *Journal of Organizational Behavior, 35*(5), 657–677.

Taylor, S. N. (2010). Redefining leader self-awareness by integrating the second component of self-awareness. *Journal of Leadership Studies, 3*(4), 57–68.

Tekleab, A. G., Sims, H. P., Yun, S., Tesluk, P. E., & Cox, J. (2007). Are we on the same page? Effects of self-awareness of empowering and transformational leadership. *Journal of Leadership & Organizational Studies, 14*(3), 185–201.

Thomas, K. W., & Velthouse, B. A. (1990). Cognitive elements of empowerment: An "interpretive" model of intrinsic task motivation. *Academy of Management Review, 15*(4), 666–681.

Van Velsor, E., Taylor, S., & Leslie, J. B. (1993). An examination of the relationships among self-perception accuracy, self-awareness, gender, and leader effectiveness. *Human Resource Management, 32*(2–3), 249–263.

van Woerkom, M., & Meyers, M. C. (2015). My strengths count! *Human Resource Management, 54*(1), 81–103.

Vandenberg, R. J., & Lance, C. E. (2000). A review and synthesis of the measurement invariance literature: Suggestions, practices, and recommendations for organizational research. *Organizational Research Methods, 3*(1), 4–70.

Walumbwa, F. O., Avolio, B. J., Gardner, W. L., Wernsing, T. S., & Peterson, S. J. (2008). Authentic leadership: Development and validation of a theory-based measure. *Journal of Management, 34*(1), 89–126.

Wanous, J. P., & Reichers, A. E. (1997). Overall job satisfaction: How good are single-item measures? *Journal of Applied Psychology, 82*(2), 247–252.

Weil, L. G., Fleming, S. M., Dumontheil, I., Kilford, E. J., Weil, R. S., Rees, G., et al. (2013). The development of metacognitive ability in adolescence. *Conscious Cognition, 22*(1), 264–271.

Wheeler, M. A., Stuss, D. T., & Tulving, E. (1997). Toward a theory of episodic memory: The frontal lobes and autonoetic consciousness. *Psychological Bulletin, 121*, 331–354.

Wiest, G. (2012). Neural and mental hierarchies. *Frontiers in Psychology, 3*(516), 1–8.

Wohlers, A. J., & London, M. (1989). Ratings of managerial characteristics: Evaluation difficulty, co-worker agreement, and self-awareness. *Personnel Psychology, 42*, 235–261.

2

Follower Gender and Authentic Leadership: Perspectives from the Middle East

Gaye Karacay, Behice Ertenu, and Hayat Kabasakal

In the current era, there has been an increasing loss of trust towards leaders in business and political arenas. This loss of trust, in return, has shifted the definition of leader effectiveness. From the societal level to the corporate level around the world, people search for leaders whom they can trust. Such a change in follower expectations consequently has directed researchers to study new leadership approaches that build and nurture follower trust. In previous studies, authentic leadership was found to be associated with follower trust towards leaders (Avolio & Gardner, 2005; Avolio, Gardner, Walumbwa, Luthans, & May, 2004; Bass & Steidlmeier, 1999). Authenticity involves having one's actions in line with one's thoughts and feelings (Harter, 2002, p. 382). At the core of authenticity lies the harmony of one's self and behaviour

G. Karacay (✉)
Department of Industrial Engineering, Istanbul Technical University, Macka, Istanbul, Turkey

B. Ertenu • H. Kabasakal
Department of Management, Bogazici University, Bebek, Istanbul, Turkey

© The Author(s) 2018
D. Cotter-Lockard (ed.), *Authentic Leadership and Followership*, Palgrave Studies in Leadership and Followership, https://doi.org/10.1007/978-3-319-65307-5_2

(Gardner, Avolio, Luthans, May, & Walumbwa, 2005). This implies that reflections of one's own life experiences may help an individual to get closer to expressing the genuine self.

According to Gardner et al. (2011) authenticity involves a series of behavioural and cognitive processes that are related with self-development. During these processes, people discover and reach their genuine selves. Kernis (2003) indicated that authenticity is about operating as one's true or core self in daily life. Since authenticity is not an either/or condition, people can be described as being more or less authentic or inauthentic (Erickson, 1995). This gives leaders and followers to have an opportunity for self-development. Accordingly, the importance of self-development as a component of authenticity has been explicitly mentioned by other researchers in the field (Walumbwa, Avolio, Gardner, Wernsing, & Peterson, 2008).

In addition to self-development, several researchers proposed that authentic leaders focus on building followers' strengths and developing associates into leaders themselves (Gardner et al., 2005; Ilies, Morgeson, & Nahrgang, 2005; Luthans & Avolio, 2003). Luthans and Avolio (2003) stated that "the authentic leader does not try to coerce or even rationally persuade associates, but rather the leader's authentic values, beliefs, and behaviours serve to model the development of associates" (p. 243). Likewise, Gardner and associates (2005) stated that "positive modelling is the basic means whereby leaders develop authentic followers" (p. 347).

Most researchers define authentic leaders as being true to themselves and displaying high levels of moral integrity (Luthans & Avolio, 2003). As pointed out by Avolio and Gardner (2005), authentic leaders' moral integrity becomes established when their espoused values align with their behaviours in the course of time and across varying situational challenges.

In addition to the above conceptualizations, Begley (2001) posits that authentic leadership implies "a genuine kind of leadership – a hopeful, open-ended, visionary and creative response to circumstances" (p. 354). In this sense, having a vision which is shared and trusted by the intellects, hearts, and souls of people also becomes important for authentic leadership (Bhindi & Duignan, 1997).

By setting an open and honest communication context, authentic leaders become able to develop honest and genuine connections with their followers (George & Sims, 2007; Walumbwa et al., 2008) which foster positive relationships (Gardner et al., 2005; Kernis & Goldman, 2006; Whitehead, 2009). Through such open and truthful relationships, followers build trust in authentic leaders (Goldman & Kernis, 2002; Ilies et al., 2005; Spitzmuller & Ilies, 2010).

In summary, authentic leadership is a process which relates to developing a genuine self and principles through a moral perspective. This genuineness applies to relationships via open and honest communication with followers. A leader's authenticity is set up by knowing both oneself and one's followers, as well as by focusing on the development of both oneself and one's followers. That's why authentic leaders have a propensity for setting up common ground with their followers, usually through the connections to their roots (Goffee & Jones, 2005). Accordingly, authentic leadership is defined as genuine leadership reflecting on vision and values, resulting in greater self-awareness together with fostering positive development (Begley, 2001; Luthans & Avolio, 2003).

Previous research on authentic leadership empirically validated its significant consequences mainly on positive follower responses such as perceived trustworthiness of the leader, identification with the leader, and positive social exchanges in addition to positive work outcomes (Avolio & Gardner, 2005; Avolio et al., 2004; Gardner et al., 2011). While these research findings reinforce the importance of authentic leadership for today's organizations in all parts of the world, they are much more vital in the Middle East region since in this part of the world trust in leaders within all layers of society is quite low (World Economic Forum, 2016). The Global Competitiveness Report 2016–2017 by the World Economic Forum (2016) explicitly stated that for economic competitiveness of the Middle East, there is a critical need for reforms that aim to strengthen the private sector: promoting competition, reducing red tape, and making labour markets more flexible (p. 23). The starting point for these reforms should be successful transformation of organizations which requires leaders who can successfully execute these transformation processes by generating positive outcomes and building trust (Zahra, 2011).

A leader's action is perceived as genuine provided there is relational authenticity, i.e., two-sided authenticity wherein both a leader's action and the identification of it by followers mutually constitute authenticity (Eagly, 2005). Therefore, investigating leader authenticity requires understanding the different viewpoints and expectations of followers. Similarly, Uhl-Bien, Riggio, Lowe, and Carsten (2014) suggested that the follower–leader relationship is socially constructed as result of cognitive and attributional complexities, as well as the social identity of followers. With a parallel perspective, in the current study we analysed the follower aspect with respect to a leadership construction.

Although studies on authentic leadership need to be grounded in a well-developed follower ontology due to its relational aspect, previous research has largely overlooked follower characteristics, and especially ignored the possibility of variations in the perception of leadership resulting from individual cognitive processes. Some of the studies on implicit leadership theories pointed out that, over and above societal culture, a subordinate's self-concept represents a cognitive constraint in leader categorization processes (Lord, Brown, Harvey, & Hall, 2001). Gender identity, by being one of the most influential layers of self-identity, is likely to shape individual perceptions, evaluations, and behaviours (Betz & Fitzgerald, 1987).

In the current study, we claim that followers' self-concepts have significant impact on the cognizance of authentic leadership by shaping followers' perspectives through their expectations which are rooted in their gender identities. Accordingly, the aim of the study is to explore how perceptions of female and male followers differ regarding their emphasis on different attributes of authentic leadership. By adopting a qualitative methodology, the data of the study was collected during the 2009–2016 time period by conducting in-depth interviews with 105 male and female employees in 10 Middle East countries, namely; Egypt, Iran, Iraq, Jordan, Lebanon, Morocco, Saudi Arabia, Syria,[1] Turkey; and the United Arab Emirates.

The main contributions of the current study derive both from its data being collected from the Middle East region, and also its particular focus for integrating both female and male perspectives in perceptions of authentic leadership. The Middle East region is the least researched area in leadership studies, and has relatively higher gender inequality in terms of societal cultural norms compared to the other parts of the world (Kabasakal & Bodur, 2002). Therefore, the Middle East region, distinctively, constitutes an interesting area to analyse gender-based differences in perceptions of leadership.

The Cultural Context of the Middle East

Previous research showed that the countries included in the current study, i.e., Egypt, Iran, Iraq, Jordan, Lebanon, Morocco, Saudi Arabia, Syria, Turkey, and the United Arab Emirates share some similar societal cultural values like high power distance and low individualism (Hofstede, 2001). High power distance practices are characterized by a hierarchical decision making mechanism, and inequality in the distribution of resources as well as decision power. Kabasakal and Bodur (2002) showed that societies in the GLOBE's Middle Eastern Cluster, are highly in-group oriented and hierarchical. The established in-group collectivist cultural aspects of the region merge with high worth attached to family members. As the head of the family, the father figure is usually the most respected and he stands at the top of the hierarchy (Kagitçibasi, 1994). Middle Eastern societies have relatively low levels of gender egalitarianism as a societal cultural norm (Barakat, 1993; Kabasakal, Dastmalchian, Karacay, & Bayraktar, 2012; Moghadam, 1993) leading them to be labelled as masculine societies which are not willing to reduce the differences in societal roles and status of women and men. These societal norms have roots in the common historical, religious, and socio-cultural characteristics of the countries in the region (Barakat, 1993; Bill & Leiden, 1979; Kabasakal et al., 2012). Islam, by being the prevailing religion in the Middle East, creates a shared culture that provides guidance, rules, and common values about personal lives, community relations, and ways of doing business (Kabasakal & Bodur, 2002; Zahra, 2011).

In addition to the above mentioned societal cultural norms, the Middle Eastern countries are identified by their unique public and economic problems, including unemployment among the youth, underutilization of educated people, and gender imbalance in the workforce with very small numbers of working women, which derives from the traditions that give men higher status and power over women in public and professional lives. Further, several Arab countries face problems of corruption control, accountability, and transparency of government services (World Economic Forum, 2013). Managing and overcoming these problems in an effective and peaceful way may require these societies to build trust and confidence toward leaders. The importance of authentic leadership for the Middle East region derives especially from its effect on follower responses of feeling trust and identification with leaders. These are activated by accepting the leader's internalized ethical and moral perspectives as genuine (Walumbwa, Wang, Wang, Schaubroeck, & Avolio, 2010). For that reason, understanding perceptions of authentic leadership in this part of the world is important. In view of this context, this study explores the differences in female and male followers' perceptions of authentic leadership in the Middle Eastern context.

Authentic Leadership Perspectives in the Middle East

Societal culture, by its definition, i.e. "shared motives, values, beliefs, identities; and interpretations or meanings of significant events that result from common experiences of members of communities, and are transmitted across age generations" (House, Hanges, Javidan, Dorfman, & Gupta, 2004, p. 15) provides guidelines for categorizing and understanding individual viewpoints by referring to norms of larger groups. Within this framework, we expect that the depth of the meaning attributed to authentic leadership is linked to the common understanding and interpretation of "what constitutes authenticity" in the Middle East area.

A few studies have assessed authentic leadership and its influence in the Middle East (Erkutlu & Chafra, 2013; Ertenu, Karacay, Asarkaya, & Kabasakal, 2011; Özkan & Ceylan, 2012; Senam, Rashid, Sarkawi, & Zaini, 2014; Tabak, Polat, Cosar, & Turkoz, 2013). Among them, the study of Ertenu and colleagues showed that attributes of authentic leadership are expected to be manifested not only by etic factors, but also by some emic elements which are directly linked with the collectivist cultural norms of the region.

Followers' Gender Identity in Cognizance of Authentic Leadership

Self-concept is important because it is central to an individual's perceptions, evaluations, and behaviours (Geertz, 1975; Markus & Kitayama, 1991; Triandis, 1989). Self is accepted as a reflexive concept since it can be categorized, classified, or named in specific ways in relation to social groups or categorizations (Stets & Burke, 2000). Through such a process of *self-categorization* (Tajfel & Turner, 1979) and/or *identification* (Burke, 1980), individual identities are formed (Stets & Burke, 2000).

Individuals have multiple identities through which they operationalize different impressions of themselves within different social situations (Tajfel, 1981). Accordingly, individuals are likely to put emphasis on one identity over the other in different social circumstances. Stryker and Serpe (1982) asserted that the more committed an individual is to an identity, the more activated (salient) an identity becomes in a given situation. Yet, one's gender provides an implicit background identity (Ridgeway, 1997, p. 231) such that interactions between the gender identity and other identities are often based on internalized beliefs about one's gender and appropriate behaviour for that gender (Stets & Burke, 1996). Consequently, these interactions sustain the gender system as a whole by maintaining the stability of human behaviour that is gendered (Ridgeway & Smith-Lovin, 1999). Previous research has indicated statistically that throughout human life, gender becomes one of the most important sources of one's identity as it bears on individual's perceptions, evaluations, and behaviours (Brewer & Lui, 1989).

Socio-cultural norms function as root forces that shape individual's identity, including gender identity, by defining socially expected gender roles (Shweder & Bourne, 1984). According to Markus and Kitayama (1991), societal level cultural division of individualism-collectivism can also be found in one's self-identification. Based on the findings of the study by Markus and Kitayama, Cross and Madson (1997) conducted research to investigate the reflections of self-construal within gender groups by arguing that females and males differ in the ways they view themselves, and their self-construal provides the fundamental basis for regulating and influencing their behaviours. More specifically, Cross and Madson (1997) suggested that men tend to be more independent, while women tend to be more interdependent; and such differences are reflected as gender differences in their affect, motivation, and cognition.

The main reason for men and women to have divergent self-construal, that is men being more independent while women are more interdependent, drives back to their different socialization experiences (Eagly, 1987; Maccoby, 1990). Individuals initially learn about acceptable behaviours linked to gender roles from their primary groups who are closest to them during initial socializations (Ridgeway & Smith-Lovin, 1999). On this subject, Chodorow's (1978) model of gender differences in the development of identity pioneered extant research by claiming that while girls continue to define themselves within the context of their initial socialization with their mothers, boys feel the need to separate themselves in order to develop as males. Men's identity formation, then, results in independence and detachment, while women's identity formation results in interdependence and attachment. Accordingly, women and men develop different ways of knowing compared with each other (Belenky, Clinchy, Goldberger, & Tarule, 1986). Likewise, developmental theories draw attention to the differences in primary and secondary socialization experiences of boys and girls that lead to separate identity formations.

These primary and secondary socialization experiences also shape one's moral identity which represents an individual's self-conception organized around a set of moral traits (Aquino & Reed, 2002). Moral identity reflects the organization of self-related information brought together according to the principles of moral consistency; therefore, moral identity functions as a distinct mental image of how a moral person is prone to think, feel, and behave (Kihlstrom & Klein, 1994). As a result, it becomes part of the self-definition. Gilligan (1982) highlighted the association between the definition of self and one's morality development; and pointed to the differences in the ways males and females define themselves which are reflected in their approaches while resolving dilemmas involving others. Gilligan (1987) based her assertions on the identification theory, that is, identity formation of women being rooted in relatedness, whereas identities of men are rooted in autonomy; and argued that these different self-identification patterns are reflected in the moral orientations of men versus women. Women's moral action derives from care, responsibility, intimacy, and relationships (i.e., *ethics of care*), while men's moral action depends on the capacity to be an autonomous, objective and impartial agent in making verifiable and reliable decisions based on universal rules and principles (i.e., *ethics of justice*).

Given that leadership is socially constructed among leaders and followers by cognitive and attributional complexities (Uhl-Bien et al., 2014), cognizance of a leader's authenticity necessitates relational authenticity, i.e., a mutual existence of leader's authenticity, and its identification by followers (Eagly, 2005). For that reason, investigating authentic leadership requires understanding different viewpoints and expectations of followers. In the current study, we analysed a conception of leadership from the follower perspective by focusing particularly on followers' gender.

In reference to identity theories, we proposed that male and female followers would have differences in their perceptions about authentic leadership in accordance with their gender identities which are believed to shape their expectations about relationships (Brewer & Lui, 1989; Ridgeway, 1997; Ridgeway & Smith-Lovin, 1999). Particularly, we expected that female followers would focus more on leader's interdependence, while male followers would concentrate more on leader's independence. We also claim that such differences in gender-based expectations are likely to be much more evident in the Middle East context due to the prevalent societal cultural norm of high gender inequality, which nurtures gender roles being polarized among men and women.

Methodology

As an exploratory study, qualitative research methodology was applied by conducting in-depth interviews with 105 participants from 10 Middle Eastern countries. Qualitative data collection was made via face-to-face interviews (85), and if necessary Skype and email communication (20). The researchers conducted interviews with the participants, mainly in the English language, without making deliberate effort to have matching genders. The sample consisted of employees with professional careers as well as self-employed entrepreneurs working in various sectors; 43 of which were from Turkey, 16 from Iran, 12 from Lebanon, 9 from Saudi Arabia, 8 from Egypt, 7 from Jordan, 4 from Syria,[2] 3 from United Arab Emirates, 2 from Iraq; and 1 from Morocco. While 42.9% of total participants were female, with an average age of 35 years and 13 years of work experience, 57.1% of them were male, with an average age of 38 years and 15 years of work experience. The composition of the research sample is consistent with the general demographic structure of the Middle East region where there is a male dominance within business life.

Each in-depth interview was started with an open-ended question, through which the participants were asked to make comments on the traits of leaders whom they would define to be "genuine or true." Followed by this opening question, the participants were directed to elaborate on the criteria for being a "genuine/true leader." Whenever the term "authentic" was explicitly mentioned by the participants, the researcher asked for a specific definition of authentic leadership as well as their personal expectations from an authentic leader. While asking about their perceptions of authentic leaders, the participants acknowledged that the gender of the leader was an irrelevant issue; that is to say, an authentic leader's gender can be either male or female. In the last part of the interview, the participants were questioned for their related feelings and reactions towards authentic leaders.

Each of these interviews was recorded and then redacted in order to be content-analysed. From the redaction of 105 interviews, totalling 954 narratives, each of them representing at least one idea articulated within one or more phrases, were documented. Then, the researchers progressively categorized the documented narratives.

As a first step, the researchers went over the 954 narratives, and identified 67 separate descriptions of concepts about authentic leadership that were either existing in the authentic leadership literature or new depictions of authentic leadership given for the first time in these narratives. In this procedure, each separate idea was assigned to only one description. In a later stage, the researchers agreed by consensus on categorization of these 67 items into nine attributes of authentic leadership which are mutually exclusive and jointly bring a holistic construction of authentic leadership. All verbatim quotes were classified under these nine categories, and also matched to the gender of the respondents in order to exhibit the gender distribution of these items. As a final step, verbatim quotes under nine categories were linked with the main conceptualizations of authentic leadership. The final four categories that emerged from the data matched with key aspects of authentic leadership that was mentioned in the existing literature.

In order to check the reliability of the results of the content analysis, the inter-judge reliability method was used. For that purpose, two judges independently re-coded all 954 reported narratives according to the commonly agreed nine authentic leadership attributes. Consistency between the assessments of the judges was checked, and compared with that of the researchers. Cases of disagreement were discussed among judges and, if possible, consensus was reached. For the few cases of disagreement where consensus could not be obtained, the related items were dropped from the final analyses. The inter-judge reliability score was calculated by Krippendorff's alpha, which is used as the standard reliability measure in content analysis (Hayes & Krippendorff, 2007). Found at 85%, the inter-judge reliability is shown to be at acceptable levels (Krippendorff, 2004, p. 242).

Findings

In reference to the development theories and gender identity theory, the main assertion of the study was that perceptions and expectations about authentic leadership would vary based on follower gender. While male followers would expect authentic leaders primarily to be autonomous and independent by presenting a solid standing that verifies their uniqueness, female followers would prefer authentic leaders to show nurturance and care by being interdependent. This proposition would be particularly valid for authentic leadership rather than for generic leadership due to the fact that authenticity is about knowing and developing oneself, and behaving in accordance with thoughts and beliefs that define the true self (Harter, 2002), and therefore linked to self-identity. For this reason, authentic leadership was expected to be strongly linked with gender identity, which derives from self-identity.

In order to explore whether perceptions and expectations about authentic leadership vary based on follower gender, the narratives derived from the interviews were content-analysed, and by means of a progressive grouping, nine attributes that jointly relate to the different aspects of authentic leadership were identified. These nine attributes were further merged under four dimensions, which are linked with the main conceptualizations of authentic leadership mentioned in the existing literature. The nine categories as well as the related four main dimensions of authentic leadership derived from these analyses are found to be as follows:

Development of self and others:

- Being autonomous, unique, and decisive
- Mentoring, coaching and counselling followers
- Being aware of weaknesses and strengths

Moral perspective in terms of ethics of justice and care:

- Fairness and integrity
- Caring and empathy for needs of others
- Prioritization of collective interest and team welfare

Openness in outgoing and incoming communication:

- Open, honest and trustworthy communication
- Listening and understanding others' points of view

Visionary and equipped:

- Being competent, visionary, and equipped in business life by seeing the bigger picture

Table 2.1 summarizes the findings of the content analysis regarding authentic leadership attributes classified under nine categories by providing a comparative distribution based on the gender of respondents. The frequency level of each attribute was calculated as a percentage of total narratives of female (370 narratives), and total narratives of male respondents (584 narratives). The overall findings of the study shown in Table 2.1 indicated that although female and male respondents share some common convictions about the attributes necessary to acknowledge a leader as authentic, there were some key differences both in the strength as well as in the scope of some attributes expected from authentic leaders by female versus male respondents.

Exhibited in Table 2.1, both female and male respondents expected authentic leaders to show attributes related with development, moral integrity, open communication, and vision. These findings support the assertions of the previous research that conceptualises authentic leadership as a process which relates to developing a genuine self and principles through a moral perspective and reflecting this genuineness in their open

Table 2.1 Authentic leadership attributes mentioned by female and male followers

Expected attributes from authentic leaders	Female respondents	Male respondents
Development (self & others)	Frequency level	Frequency level
Being autonomous, unique, and decisive ("to be oneself")	< 1%	31.3%
Mentoring, coaching, and counselling followers	19.7%	< 1%
Being aware of weaknesses and strengths	1.8%	7.2%
Moral perspective (ethics of justice & ethics of care)	Frequency level	Frequency level
Fairness and integrity	13.5%	22.9%
Caring and empathy for needs of others	15.2%	< 1%
Prioritization of collective interest and team welfare	17.5%	< 1%
Openness in communication (outgoing & incoming)	Frequency level	Frequency level
Open, honest and trustworthy communication	12.1%	20.5%
Listening and understanding others' points of views	9.9%	8.4%
Visionary and equipped	Frequency level	Frequency level
Being competent, visionary, and equipped in business life by seeing the bigger picture	10.3%	9.6%

and honest communication with followers (George & Sims, 2007; Luthans & Avolio, 2003; Walumbwa et al., 2008). Existing literature indicates that a leader's authenticity is shaped by knowing both oneself and one's followers, as well as self-development and contributing to the development of others (Gardner et al., 2005; Goffee & Jones, 2005; Ilies et al., 2005; Luthans & Avolio, 2003). Moreover, setting a vision by reflecting on values which are shared and trusted by the intellects, hearts and souls of people becomes important for authentic leadership (Bhindi & Duignan, 1997). Consequently, authentic leaders' truthful relationships foster follower trust in them (Goldman & Kernis, 2002; Ilies et al., 2005; Spitzmuller, & Ilies, 2010; Whitehead, 2009).

The comparative findings below show the expectations of female versus male respondents from authentic leaders: while male and female respondents exhibited some common convictions about authentic leaders, they also had major differences in their expectations of authentic leaders.

Development (Self and Others)

In relation to the "development" dimension of authentic leadership, while female respondents primarily expect authentic leaders to mentor, coach and counsel followers so as to bring the best out of each employee (19.7%), male respondents rarely mentioned this aspect (< 1%). As an example of this attribute, a female participant stated:

> Authentic leaders should genuinely be interested in others – their career goals, professional development, personal issues etc.; and should not just do "tick box exercise" or go through the motions of pretending to care. (Anonymous participant)

In contrast, male respondents gave a significantly higher importance to being unique, autonomous and decisive, in developing the true self (31.3%), and awareness of strengths and weaknesses (7.2%), whereas these aspects of authentic leadership were quite insignificant for women (< 1% and 1.8%, respectively) in explaining their perceptions of authentic leadership. With the highest frequency, men stated that in order to accept a leader as being authentic, they expect that leader to have a solid depiction of "being oneself"; that is in general explained as, "having a solid, autonomous and inspirational standing; which becomes factual by the actions, decisions, and speeches of the authentic leader; all reflecting his/her personal principles rooted in objective criteria." Some examples for male participants' narratives regarding development of the true self are as follows:

> Talks the talk and walks the walk, acts what he/she preaches.
>
> An authentic leader can be different than others, be unique without being afraid of criticism.
>
> I expect an authentic leader to recognize his/her own mistakes.

The findings reported in Table 2.1 show that female respondents give higher importance to development of followers and associates by coaching and counselling, in line with their interdependent self-construal. On the other hand, male respondents focused more on developing a genuine self by being autonomous and being aware of their strengths and weaknesses.

Moral Perspective (Ethics of Care and Ethics of Justice)

In terms of the moral aspect of authentic leadership, women mentioned prioritization of the collective interest and paying attention to cooperation within the work environment (17.5%) and caring and having empathy for the needs of others (15.2%) as important aspects of authentic leadership. On the other hand, men did not mention these attributes at a significant level (< 1% for both items), while they focused on fairness and integrity more frequently (22.9%) compared to women (13.5%). The fact that women concentrated on care, sensitivity to needs of others, and prioritization of collective welfare is in line with the female identity that has been shown by previous researchers to be connected to *ethics of care* (Gilligan, 1987). Some examples for female participants' narratives regarding ethics of care are as follows:

> I expect authentic leaders to take ownership for their teams, boost them and take the best out of them, authentic leaders should definitely be a peoples' person.
>
> S/he needs to be understanding, empathetic, always supportive, and have attention to detail and to what matters to me; s/he needs to be willing to fight for me and for her/his team, and go the extra mile for us.

In contrast to women, men highly emphasized fairness and integrity which is in line with making verifiable and reliable decisions based on universal rules and principles, indicating that male identity is more closely associated with *ethics of justice* (Kohlberg, 1969). For instance; a male participant stated: "I expect an authentic leader to be driven by principles – he/she must stick to what are his/her core values."

Women also mentioned importance of principles and justice as a component of authentic leaders at a relatively lower frequency. These findings suggest that while both men and women expect to see fairness and principles in the actions and decisions of authentic leaders, women in addition focus on the care and nurturance aspect of morality to a great extent indicating the importance of relationships and interdependence in their moral understanding.

Openness in Communication (Outgoing and Incoming)

Both men and women indicated that openness in communication was an important aspect of authentic leadership. They mentioned a two-way openness in communication, indicating that they expect authentic leaders to be honest by providing correct information as well as being keen to listen and understand diverse points of view. Both women and men seemed to agree on the importance of listening and understanding others' points of view (9.9% and 8.4%, respectively). Respondents made the following comments:

> Have an open-door policy in terms of being open to communication from employees. Be open to ideas, concerns and criticisms. (Male respondent)
>
> Should be willing to listen to team members and take their discussions into consideration. (Female respondent)

On the other hand, men to a greater extent than women seemed to emphasize the openness and trustworthiness of authentic leaders in communicating with others (20.5% vs. 12.1%). For instance, a man said: "Authentic leaders should avoid high secrecy and failing to deliver on promises."

Visionary and Equipped

Both female and male respondents indicated the importance of authentic leaders to set a vision which is built on solid knowledge, accumulated experience, and business acumen. They mentioned the significance of competence and ambition in individual business profession by seeing the bigger picture rather than focusing on small issues (10.3% for women, and 9.6% for men). Some examples of female and male participants' narratives are as follows:

> Authentic leaders need to understand their business well so they're credible and deliver what they say they'll do. Set a vision and a plan for the business so we know the goal. (Male respondent)

> For me, authenticity is a vibe/ feeling you get from a person that is very difficult to verbalize or quantify, but some associated attributes include: being competent and knowledgeable – has to feel credible and be not an imposter who is pretending to know what he/she is talking about or only in a leadership position due to the position in the hierarchy. (Female respondent)

In addition to the attributes of authentic leadership derived from expectations of female versus male respondents, respondents also indicated their attitudes and feelings towards authentic leaders. While telling their stories, all respondents, both men and women, indicated that they respect and trust authentic leaders. Authentic leadership initiates followers' admiration and respect, through which followers become much more motivated to trust leaders who satisfy followers' core expectations of having genuine qualities. Some examples of female and male participants' quotes from the interviews are as follows:

> I would respect the authentic leader and potentially aspire to become like him/her one day. (Female respondent)
>
> I would feel trust, respect and honour. (Male respondent)

To sum up, regarding followers' cognizance of authentic leadership, the findings of the current study showed that followers' own gender plays a role in shaping some perceptions and evaluations of authenticity. The results clarified that female respondents, by their more communal point of view as well as their tendency for having interdependent self-construal, more frequently expected authentic leaders to have a relational perspective by deliberately focusing on the development of followers through coaching and mentoring them, prioritizing collective interests and caring, and having empathy for followers' needs. On the other hand, according to male participants, the self-development of an authentic leader would be more evident in "being one's-self," which indeed points to leader's independence and a higher emphasis on fairness and integrity in conduct. Integration of the expectations of female and male respondents points to an important fact that although male and female expectations may differ in some points, it is necessary that authentic leaders fill expectations of both male and female followers.

Concluding Remarks

The current study showed that authentic leadership is an important concept for the Middle East region, since the sample population perceived that authenticity brings a morality perspective to leaders' conduct. Accordingly, they mentioned that in this part of the world authenticity is highly respected, and people of this region trust leaders whom they find to be authentic. Previous research on authentic leadership validated the significant consequences of authentic leadership in the western part of the world by showing that authenticity increases perceived trustworthiness of the leader and identification with the leader (Avolio et al., 2004; Avolio & Gardner, 2005; Walumbwa et al. 2008). The findings of the current study showed similar results for the outcomes of authentic leadership for today's organizations in the Middle East. Since trust is relatively lower in this region (World Economic Forum, 2016), authenticity on the part of leaders is a highly valued quality for building trust and solving problems in a peaceful and effective way.

The interviews conducted with followers from the Middle East region show that they have many common convictions about authentic leaders. They addressed a holistic construction of authentic leadership by focusing on diverse and mutually exclusive aspects of authentic leadership. In this regard, interviewees indicated their expectations of development, moral perspective, open communication, and providing vision derived from experience. On the other hand, in line with the main assertion of our study, there are also some significant differences between perceptions and expectations of men and women about authentic leaders. We based our proposition on the idea that the follower–leader relationship is socially constructed through cognitive and attributional complexities as well as social identity processes of followers (Eagly, 1987, 2005; Uhl-Bien et al., 2014). Signifying the validity of this assertion, the findings of the current study make an initial and focused contribution to authentic leadership literature, explicitly by showing that identity formation on the basis of gender identity can have influential effects on the expectations and perceptions of male and female followers concerning authentic leaders. In other words, in the cognizance of authentic leadership, followers' own gender identities shape their related perceptions regarding authenticity.

The findings of the study show that expectations of women and men regarding authentic leaders may differ in terms of importance and strength of different attributes. While women indicated mentoring, coaching and counselling of followers as the most important aspects of authentic leadership, none of the male respondents talked about these attributes as expectations from authentic leaders. However, men predominantly mentioned the importance of being oneself, i.e., having a unique, autonomous and independent standing driven by personal and objective principles. On the other hand, independence and uniqueness were not mentioned by female respondents as a required aspect of authenticity in any of their stories. The general theme in the stories of women consisted of interdependent and communal aspects of authentic leadership, whereas the stories of men had a general emphasis on being independent. This major difference in the expectations of respondents based on their gender identities suggests that women respondents gave more importance to the *nurturing* aspect of authentic leadership, while male respondents suggested the importance of *being one's true self* as a part of authentic identity.

Middle Eastern societies are characterized by high power distance and low gender egalitarianism practices (Kabasakal & Bodur, 2002; Kabasakal et al., 2012). In line with the hierarchical nature of society, organizations are highly centralized and have very powerful organizational and political leaders. The high power distance practices lead to authoritarian decision making practices, which detach the leaders and managers from the input of employees (Kabasakal & Bodur, 2002). In describing their expectations, respondents in the current study indicated a desire to have authentic leaders who listen and take into consideration different viewpoints. This finding suggests a willingness to voice their viewpoints and be heard by the leaders. Thus, open communication, listening, and understanding employee viewpoints should be considered as a tool to balance the high power distance practices prevalent in this region.

Due to the highly masculine culture of the Middle Eastern region, there are some differences between gender roles and status of men and women, and a great gender imbalance in the workforce with very small numbers of working women in both public and private sectors. Indeed, increasing employment levels of women in the workforce would be significantly beneficial for the economic prosperity of the region

(World Economic Forum, 2015). Total number of women in the workforce is relatively limited in this region, thus meeting expectations of women workers might be particularly important for organizational leaders to support their presence in the work environment by coaching and mentoring them.

Although the findings of the study represent a general view regarding the expectations of the followers within the Middle East region, a limitation of the study is that there might be differences among the Middle East countries that could not be reflected in the current study. By extending the scope of the sample representation, a more rigorous depiction may be possible.

The current study showed that gender identity, by being one of the most dominant aspects of self-identity, shaped individual perceptions and expectations regarding authentic leadership via bringing a cognitive restraint and disparity in leader categorization processes (Lord et al., 2001). More qualitative and empirical research investigating authentic leadership from a follower perspective is needed to better understand the intricate and complex dimensions of follower–leader relationships in different parts of the world, especially in regions like the Middle East where research on leadership is scarce (Zahra, 2011). Future research on authentic leadership needs to consider and integrate other characteristics of followers. In addition to gender, the attributes of age, education, and social background of followers might impact the cognitive and attributional complexities as well as social identity processes of followers. Additionally, the gender of the leader can be also integrated as a variable in future research.

Notes

1. From Syria, the last data collection was in 2010.
2. The interviews continued to be conducted up until 2016 with the respondents from the nine Middle East countries, except Syria, from where the last data collection was in 2010.

References

Aquino, K., & Reed, A. (2002). The self-importance of moral identity. *Journal of Personality and Social Psychology, 83*, 1423–1440. https://doi.org/10.1037/0022-3514.83.6.1423.

Avolio, B. J., & Gardner, W. L. (2005). Authentic leadership development: Getting to the root of positive forms of leadership. *The Leadership Quarterly, 16*(3), 315–338. https://doi.org/10.1016/j.leaqua.2005.03.001.

Avolio, B. J., Gardner, W. L., Walumbwa, F. O., Luthans, F., & May, D. R. (2004). Unlocking the mask: A look at the process by which authentic leaders impact follower attitudes and behaviours. *The Leadership Quarterly, 15*(6), 801–823. https://doi.org/10.1016/j.leaqua.2004.09.003.

Barakat, H. (1993). *The Arab world: Society, culture, and state.* Berkeley, CA: University of California Press.

Bass, B. M., & Steidlmeier, P. (1999). Ethics, character, and authentic transformational leadership behaviour. *The Leadership Quarterly, 10*(2), 181–217. https://doi.org/10.1016/S1048-9843(99)00016-8.

Begley, P. T. (2001). In pursuit of authentic school leadership practices. *International Journal of Leadership in Education, 4*(4), 353–365. https://doi.org/10.1080/13603120110078043.

Belenky, M., Clinchy, B., Goldberger, N., & Torule, J. (1986). *Women's ways of knowing: The development of self, voice, and mind.* New York: Basic Books.

Betz, N. E., & Fitzgerald, L. F. (1987). *The career psychology of women.* Orlando, FL: Academic Press.

Bhindi, N., & Duignan, P. (1997). Leadership for a new century: Authenticity, intentionality, spirituality, and sensibility. *Educational Management and Administration, 25*(2), 117–132. https://doi.org/10.1177/0263211X97252002.

Bill, J. A., & Leiden, C. (1979). *Politics in the Middle East.* Boston: Little, Brown and Company.

Brewer, M., & Lui, L. (1989). The primacy of age and sex in the structure of person categories. *Social Cognition, 7*(3), 262–274. https://doi.org/10.1521/soco.1989.7.3.262.

Burke, P. (1980). The self: Measurement implications from a symbolic interactionist perspective. *Social Psychology Quarterly, 43*(1), 18–29. https://doi.org/10.2307/3033745.

Chodorow, N. (1978). *The reproduction of mothering.* Berkeley, CA: University of California Press.

Cross, S., & Madson, L. (1997). Models of the self: Self-construals and gender. *Psychological Bulletin, 122*(1), 5–37. https://doi.org/10.1037/0033-2909.122.1.5.
Eagly, A. H. (1987). *Sex differences in social behaviour: A social-role interpretation*. Hillsdale, NJ: Erlbaum.
Eagly, A. H. (2005). Achieving relational authenticity in leadership: Does gender matter? *The Leadership Quarterly, 16*(3), 459–474. https://doi.org/10.1016/j.leaqua.2005.03.007.
Erickson, R. J. (1995). The importance of authenticity for self and society. *Symbolic Interaction, 18*(2), 121–144. https://doi.org/10.1525/si.1995.18.2.121.
Erkutlu, H., & Chafra, J. (2013). Effects of trust and psychological contract violation on authentic leadership and organizational deviance. *Management Research Review, 36*(9), 828–848. https://doi.org/10.1108/MRR-06-2012-0136.
Ertenu, B., Karacay, G., Asarkaya, C., & Kabasakal, H. (2011). Linking the worldly mindset with an authentic leadership approach: An exploratory study in a middle- eastern context. In S. Turnbull, P. Case, G. Edwards, D. Schedlitzki, & P. Simpson (Eds.), *Worldly leadership: Alternative wisdoms for a complex world* (pp. 206–222). Basingstoke, UK: Palgrave Macmillan.
Gardner, W. L., Avolio, B. J., Luthans, F., May, D. R., & Walumbwa, F. O. (2005). Can you see the real me? A self-based model of authentic leader and follower development. *The Leadership Quarterly, 16*(3), 343–372. https://doi.org/10.1016/j.leaqua.2005.03.003.
Gardner, W. L., Cogliser, C. C., Davis, K. M., & Dickens, M. P. (2011). Authentic leadership: A review of the literature and research agenda. *The Leadership Quarterly, 22*(6), 1120–1145. https://doi.org/10.1016/j.leaqua.2011.09.007.
Geertz, C. (1975). On the nature of anthropological understanding. *American Scientist, 63*(1), 47–53. Retrieved from http://www.jstor.org.contentproxy.phoenix.edu/stable/27845269?pq-origsite=summon&seq=1#page_scan_tab_contents
George, W., & Sims, P. (2007). *True north: Discover your authentic leadership*. San Francisco: Jossey-Bass.
Gilligan, C. (1982). *In a different voice*. Cambridge, MA: Harvard University Press.
Gilligan, C. (1987). Moral orientation and moral development. In E. Kittay & D. Meyers (Eds.), *Women and moral theory*. Totowa, NJ: Rowman & Littlefield.
Goffee, R., & Jones, G. (2005). Managing authenticity. *Harvard Business Review, 83*(12), 85–94.
Goldman, B. M., & Kernis, M. H. (2002). The role of authenticity in healthy functioning and subjective well-being. *Annals of the American Psychotherapy*

Association, *5*(6), 18–20. Retrieved from http://www.biomedsearch.com/article/role-authenticity-in-healthy-psychological/95844662.html

Harter, S. (2002). Authenticity. In C. R. Snyder & S. Lopez (Eds.), *Handbook of positive psychology* (pp. 382–394). Oxford, UK: Oxford University Press.

Hayes, A. F., & Krippendorff, K. (2007). Answering the call for a standard reliability measure for coding data. *Communication Methods and Measures, 1*(1), 77–89. https://doi.org/10.1080/19312450709336664.

Hofstede, G. (2001). *Culture's consequences: Comparing values, behaviours, institutions, and organizations across nations*. Thousand Oaks, CA: Sage.

House, R. J., Hanges, P. J., Javidan, M., Dorfman, P. W., & Gupta, V. (2004). *Leadership, culture and organizations: The Globe study of 62 societies*. Thousand Oaks, CA: Sage.

Ilies, R., Morgeson, F. P., & Nahrgang, J. D. (2005). Authentic leadership and eudaemonic well-being: Understanding leader–follower outcomes. *The Leadership Quarterly, 16*(3), 373–394. https://doi.org/10.1016/j.leaqua.2005.03.002.

Kabasakal, H., & Bodur, M. (2002). Arabic cluster: A bridge between east and west. *Journal of World Business, 37*(1), 40–54. https://doi.org/10.1016/S1090-9516(01)00073-6.

Kabasakal, H., Dastmalchian, A., Karacay, G., & Bayraktar, S. (2012). Leadership and culture in the MENA region: An analysis of the GLOBE project. *Journal of World Business, 47*(4), 519–529. https://doi.org/10.1016/j.jwb.2012.01.005.

Kagitçibasi, C. (1994). A critical appraisal of individualism and collectivism. Toward a new formulation. In U. Kim, H. C. Triandis, C. Kagitçibasi, S.-C. Choi, & G. Yoon (Eds.), *Individualism and collectivism: Theory, method, and applications* (pp. 52–65). Thousand Oaks, CA: Sage.

Kernis, M. H. (2003). Toward a conceptualization of optimal self-esteem. *Psychological Inquiry, 14*(1), 1–26. https://doi.org/10.1207/S15327965PLI1401_01.

Kernis, M. H., & Goldman, B. M. (2006). A multicomponent conceptualization of authenticity: Theory and research. In M. P. Zanna (Ed.), *Advances in experimental social psychology* (Vol. 38, pp. 283–357). San Diego: Academic Press.

Kihlstrom, J., & Klein, S. (1994). The self as a knowledge structure. In R. S. Wyer Jr. & K. Thomas (Eds.), *Handbook of social cognition* (Vol. 1, pp. 153–208). Hillsdale, NJ: Erlbaum.

Kohlberg, L. (1969). Stage and sequence: The cognitive-development approach to socialization. In D. Goslin (Ed.), *Handbook of socialization theory and research*. Chicago, IL: Rand McNally & Company.

Krippendorff, K. (2004). *Content analysis: An introduction to its methodology*. Thousand Oaks, CA: Sage.

Lord, R. G., Brown, D. J., Harvey, J. L., & Hall, R. J. (2001). Contextual constraints on prototype generation and their multilevel consequences for leadership perceptions. *The Leadership Quarterly, 12*(3), 311–338. https://doi.org/10.1016/S1048-9843(01)00081-9.

Luthans, F., & Avolio, B. J. (2003). Authentic leadership: A positive developmental approach. In K. S. Cameron, J. E. Dutton, & R. E. Quinn (Eds.), *Positive organizational scholarship* (pp. 241–261). San Francisco: Barrett-Koehler.

Maccoby, E. (1990). Gender and relationships. A developmental account. *The American Psychologist, 45*(4), 513–520. https://doi.org/10.1037/0003-066X.45.4.513.

Markus, H., & Kitayama, S. (1991). Culture and the self: Implications for cognition, emotion, and motivation. *Psychological Review, 98*, 224–252.

Moghadam, V. M. (1993). *Modernizing women: Gender and social change in the Middle East*. Boulder, CO: Lynee Rienner Publishers.

Özkan, S., & Ceylan, A. (2012). Multi-level analysis of authentic leadership from a Turkish construction engineers perspective. *South East European Journal of Economics and Business* (Online), *7*(2), 101–114. https://doi.org/10.2478/v10033-012-0018-2.

Ridgeway, C. (1997). Interaction and the conservation of gender inequality: Considering employment. *American Sociology Review, 62*(2), 218–235. https://doi.org/10.2307/2657301.

Ridgeway, C., & Smith-Lovin, L. (1999). The gender system and interaction. *Annual Review of Sociology, 25*, 191–216. https://doi.org/10.1146/annurev.soc.25.1.191.

Senam, M., Rashid, K., Sarkawi, A., & Zaini, R. (2014). Construction project leadership from the perspective of Islam. *International Journal of Islamic Thought, 6*, 46–56. Retrieved from http://www.ukm.my/ijit/IJIT%20Vol%206%202014/IJIT%20Vol%206%20Dec%202014_5_46-56.pdf

Shweder, R., & Bourne, E. (1984). Does the concept of person vary cross-culturally? In R. A. Shweder & R. A. LeVine (Eds.), *Culture theory: Essays on mind, self, and emotion* (pp. 158–199). Cambridge, MA: Cambridge University Press.

Spitzmuller, M., & Ilies, R. (2010). Do they [all] see my true self? Leader's relational authenticity and followers' assessments of transformational leadership. *European Journal of Work and Organizational Psychology, 19*(3), 304–332. https://doi.org/10.1080/13594320902754040.

Stets, J., & Burke, P. (1996). Gender, control, and interaction. *Social Psychology Quarterly, 59*(3), 193–220. https://doi.org/10.2307/2787019.

Stets, J., & Burke, P. (2000). Identity theory and social identity theory. *Social Psychology Quarterly, 63*(3), 224–237. https://doi.org/10.2307/2695870.

Stryker, S., & Serpe, R. (1982). Commitment, identity salience, and role behaviour: A theory and research example. In W. Ickes & S. Eric (Eds.), *Personality, roles, and social behaviour* (pp. 199–218). New York: Springer.

Tabak, A., Polat, M., Cosar, S., & Turkoz, T. (2013). A research on the consequences of authentic leadership. *Bogazici Journal Review of Social, Economic, and Administrative Studies, 27*(2), 63–82. 10.21773/boun.27.2.4.

Tajfel, H. (1981). *Human groups and social identity*. Cambridge, UK: Cambridge University Press.

Tajfel, H., & Turner, J. (1979). An integrative theory of intergroup conflict. In W. G. Austin & S. Worchel (Eds.), *The social psychology of intergroup relations* (pp. 33–47). Monterey, CA: Brooks-Cole.

Triandis, H. C. (1989). The self and social behaviour in differing cultural contexts. *Psychological Review, 96*(3), 506–520. https://doi.org/10.1037/0033-295X.96.3.506.

Uhl-Bien, M., Riggio, R. E., Lowe, K. B., & Carsten, M. K. (2014). Followership theory: A review and research agenda. *The Leadership Quarterly, 25*(1), 83–104. https://doi.org/10.1016/j.leaqua.2013.11.007.

Walumbwa, F., Avolio, B., Gardner, W., Wernsing, T., & Peterson, S. (2008). Authentic leadership: Development and validation of a theory-based measure. *Journal of Management, 34*(1), 89–126. https://doi.org/10.1177/0149206307308913.

Walumbwa, F. O., Wang, P., Wang, H., Schaubroeck, J., & Avolio, B. J. (2010). Psychological processes linking authentic leadership to follower behaviours. *The Leadership Quarterly, 21*(5), 901–914. https://doi.org/10.1016/j.leaqua.2010.07.015.

Whitehead, G. (2009). Adolescent leadership development: Building a case for an authenticity framework. *Educational Management Administration and Leadership, 37*(6), 847–872. https://doi.org/10.1177/1741143209345440.

World Economic Forum. (2013). *The Arab world competitiveness report*. Cologny, Geneva, Switzerland. Retrieved from http://www3.weforum.org/docs/WEF_AWCR_Report_2013.pdf

World Economic Forum. (2015). *Global gender gap report*. Cologny, Geneva, Switzerland. Retrieved from http://www3.weforum.org/docs/GGGR2015/cover.pdf

World Economic Forum. (2016). *The global competitiveness report 2016–2017*. Cologny, Geneva, Switzerland. Retrieved from http://www3.weforum.org/docs/GCR2016-2017/05FullReport/TheGlobalCompetitivenessReport2016-2017_FINAL.pdf

Zahra, S. A. (2011). Doing research in the (new) middle east: Sailing with the wind. *Academy of Management Perspectives, 25*(4), 6–21. https://doi.org/10.5465/amp.2011.0128.

3

Empathy as a Vehicle to Authentic Leadership and Followership in Latin America: A Practitioner Perspective

Patricia C. Bravo

Despite the current interest in empathy, existing research about empathy related to authentic leadership is limited, and generally connected to the broader topic of emotional intelligence. While a large body of knowledge about empathy exists, the literature rarely targets the role of empathy in the workplace. By extension, the connection between empathy and authentic leadership, particularly in Latin America, has not been thoroughly investigated. Trends gauging movement over time suggest the current landscape of employee engagement in Latin America continues to remain stagnant (AON Hewitt, 2016). In my experience as a leadership development practitioner, employees often cite tension around leaders who focus on profit over people. This inspired me to wonder if leaders can effectively engage followers using empathy and how empathy relates to authentic leadership. Existing research also indicates there is an opportunity to further extend research by exploring the cultural nuances within and between cultural contexts as it relates to authentic leadership (Walumbwa, Avolio, Gardner, Wernsing, &

P.C. Bravo (✉)
Bravo for You, LLC, Seattle, WA, USA

© The Author(s) 2018
D. Cotter-Lockard (ed.), *Authentic Leadership and Followership*, Palgrave Studies in Leadership and Followership, https://doi.org/10.1007/978-3-319-65307-5_3

Peterson, 2008). The background that follows will provide a definition of authentic leaders and followers, describe how empathy relates to authentic leadership, and explain the benefit of incorporating a global perspective with a focus on Latin America.

What Are Authentic Leaders?

Authentic leadership has recently gained popularity as an effective means of leadership in organizations. Persons who practice authentic leadership have been defined as leaders who have achieved high levels of authenticity in that they know who they are, what they believe, what their values are, and can act upon those values and beliefs while transparently interacting with others (Avolio, Gardner, Walumbwa, Luthans, & May, 2004). Four major attributes of authentic leadership have been put forward: internalized regulation, balanced processing of information, relational transparency, and authentic behavior (Gardner, Avolio, Luthans, May, & Walumbwa, 2005). This collective set of behaviors attracts followers. The relational transparency attribute, which refers to leaders who present themselves to followers in a genuine manner, is particularly relevant. This is the attribute most likely to link empathy to authentic leadership because empathy is about genuinely relating to others by demonstrating understanding of their experiences and responding in a congruent manner.

Followership Related to Authentic Leadership

Followers are individuals in the workplace motivated to follow leaders. In this chapter, I will refer to followers as those who follow leaders who demonstrate core elements of authentic leadership. Gardner, Fischer, and Hunt (2009) posited that individuals who choose to follow the leader may or may not be members of the leader's formal organization. In organizational settings, followers can appear as team members of a leader with a formal reporting relationship, as part of a project, as prior direct reports, or as admirers. In addition, followers who admire and are motivated to follow the leadership of authentic leaders often do so partly because they have a personal connection with the leader's values (Burns, 1978; Yukl, 2002). I will refer to followership as the process of individuals actively following the leader.

Empathy Related to Authentic Leadership

Empathy has several possible links to authentic leadership via emotional intelligence. As defined by Goleman in his groundbreaking book *Emotional Intelligence* (1995), empathy is "the ability to understand the emotional make-up of other people" and "the skill in treating people according to their emotional reactions" (Goleman, Boyatzis, & McKee, 2002, p. 50). They described empathy as a critical competency to what they call "social awareness" which allows for "resonance" with their followers. Further, Kellett, Humphrey, and Sleeth (2006) described emotionally intelligent leadership as the creation of a bond between the leader and the follower. It's possible to infer that empathy, as a component of social awareness via the skill of responding to others based on their emotions, contributes to this bond. Empathy may also link to authentic leadership through the relational transparency attribute.

A Global Perspective

In Western cultures, we know followers are more engaged, voluntarily offer discretionary work effort, and increase productivity if they feel their manager is supportive of their work (Shuck, Rocco, & Albornoz, 2011). In their highly regarded book *Primal Leadership,* Goleman et al. (2002) stated that, "empathy makes a leader able to get along well with people of diverse background or from other cultures" (p. 255). Yet, 98% of leadership theory hails from research conducted in the United States (House & Aditya, 1997), so an opportunity exists to extend research into less economically developed regions and regions with diverse cultures, such as Latin America.

Focus of the Study

Through this research study, I explore whether the commitment of followers in Latin America is affected when leaders use empathy as one element of authentic leadership and whether the Latin American culture influences the use of empathy. I will identify key themes and trends about empathy as they relate to authentic leadership using an interpretative qualitative approach to understand the leader and follower's actual experiences in the workplace, along with context from my experiences as a leadership development practitioner. I will bring to life existing research findings while identifying opportunities for further research.

My key research question aims to discover the following: Do leaders in Latin America use empathy as a vehicle to authentic leadership, does empathy affect their followership and followership commitment and what are the cultural implications? As it relates to authentic leadership, my research specifically explores the following in Latin America:

- What is the role of empathy?
- Does the national culture influence adoption of empathy?
- What similarities and differences across Latin American country culture exist when empathy is used?
- Do leaders increase followership and followership commitment by using empathy?

The following sections describe the interview approach and findings along with the benefits and drawbacks of this approach. The final section offers recommendations for future research.

Interview Approach

I conducted semistructured one-on-one interviews with 11 leaders and 22 of their followers from multiple organizations, industries, and geographies across Latin America. In advance of each interview, I provided a written overview of the research project, a definition of authentic leadership and empathy, and a set of open-ended questions to initiate dialogue. I began each interview with open-ended questions, listened to responses and probed for further information or detail based on the leader's or follower's response.

Leaders and followers represented the following countries: Argentina, Brazil, Chile, and Colombia. Most of the leaders currently hold leadership roles in well-known Fortune 500 organizations, and a majority of the followers formally reported to one of these leaders. The leader interviews were all conducted in English, and the follower interviews were conducted both in English and Spanish, depending on the language preference of the follower. I reviewed and analyzed the data that emerged from these interviews and identified key themes. In several instances, leader quotes contain unedited grammatical errors to preserve the integrity of the comments because English is not the leader's primary language.

Findings

The findings suggest there appears to be a relationship in which empathy serves as a vehicle for authentic leadership in Latin America. When leaders use empathy, they open a window to understanding. This expands the relationship with the follower, most frequently through a deepening of trust and greater understanding of the follower. When a follower feels understood and has a more trusting relationship with the leader, the follower is more willing to follow the leader.

An overwhelming majority of the leaders interviewed reported they regularly use empathy as part of their leadership. While only half of the leaders indicated they have followers that follow them because of their use of empathy, an overwhelming majority of the followers indicated the leader's use of empathy made them want to follow the leader.

Key Themes Emerging from Research Questions

Several themes arose from the leader and follower interviews. The following sections explore the themes in each of the focus areas of the study.

Empathy Has a Role as Part of Authentic Leadership

The findings surfaced examples where empathy played a role when it comes to authentic leadership. Specifically, themes emerged around working relationships, communication, and trust with a connection to improved work or business results. In addition, leaders indicated followership and follower commitment occurred when using empathy, even when the organization operated incongruently.

Most leaders used empathy regularly within their everyday interactions with followers, and as an intervention, when needed. In contrast, leaders who indicated they used empathy on a periodic basis described its use primarily as an intervention. Empathy was most frequently described in a way indicating it serves as a compass to guide leader responses. Most leaders also indicated they self-initiated their investment in empathetic behaviors and were self-motivated to do so.

Empathy appears to serve as a container where deeply collaborative relationships thrive. As a result, these relationships were reported as translating to increasingly effective and efficient business outcomes. Leaders indicated the elements of the empathetic container include approaches for deepening trust, creating partnerships, placing a greater focus on results, encouraging a willingness to embrace change, increasing motivation, increasing engagement, and affecting both direct and indirect relationships. When mixed with the other attributes of authentic leadership, empathy may serve as a springboard to strengthen relationship outcomes of authentic leadership.

The use of empathy relates to relational transparency, a core attribute of the authentic leader. While a leader may be designated as an authentic leader within the context of other attributes such as competence, reliability, concern for followers, and standards of performance (Fields, 2007), empathy was not assigned any specific contextual attributes. However, leaders did acknowledge empathy must be used in an authentic way to achieve improved relationship or business outcomes. When asked about the connection to authentic leadership, Carolina (participant names are pseudonyms) highlighted, “I think people respond to that. They admire when you truly care and you cannot care without empathy.” Rafael described an inauthentic attempt to practice empathy: “You can use it fake, but it doesn't come from inner, and over time it shows up that you didn't really care. It shows up in a transactional environment. If you think about long-term relations, it has to be used in an authentic way."

Within this empathetic container, several empathetic leadership approaches stood out. The most frequently cited result included a deepening of trust. This appeared in a variety of ways, from the leader actively taking trust into consideration, to using emotion to develop or enhance mutually trustworthy relationships.

In a study by Avolio et al. (2004), they defined trust as a critical element in the efficiency of the leader. In my experience as a leadership development practitioner, I've routinely observed trust emerge through relationship development between the leader and the follower in a variety of contexts. In my research, many followers suggested the leaders they follow use empathy to contribute to a solid foundation of trust. This trust results in extending the relationship beyond that of a leader into a long-term trusted advisor. Phyllis described her interaction with her leader: "I feel so comfortable to work with her and I trust her. Not just on the project, but I trusted her help me to contribute with other topics. I could share similar situations. If the situation is not good at the company and if I feel something is not going well and I need someone to trust and share an opinion, she always has an answer."

Followers described empathy leading to an increase in the depth of trust. Miguel stated: "I made a connection with her. Our connection started to be more emotional. I used to tell her everything. When we have an open conversation, everything got better." Myrna described the relationship bond: "He shows closeness. He is not by the book. He is human."

These deeper levels of trust may be established or enhanced using empathy. Leaders described the deepening of trust as supporting and anchoring a more effective partnership. They noted the more the leader used empathy, the greater the trust. This translated to a better partnership between leader and follower because followers felt as though they could put forth their best effort without feeling as if they were simply doing as they were told or being manipulated to do additional work.

Communication arose as a theme. Through communication, empathy played a role in increasing motivation and inspiring the willingness of the follower to embrace change and increase engagement. This occurred in multiple ways. First, empathy opened up greater willingness to receive communication from the leader. This can affect the receptivity to explore a change, motivate an action, or increase engagement. One leader, Claudio, explained: "When you use empathy, it's like you transmit a message that you are someone who stands on the same position to the other person, even without being there."

Secondly, leaders claimed that balanced dialogue was key. While there was often a formal reporting relationship between a leader and a follower, several leaders reported they eschewed hierarchy. As a result, followers reportedly felt a power balance in which the dialogue was between colleagues, rather than between leader and subordinate. Parry used empathy to tease apart a subtle difference between viewing employees as a vehicle to complete work and viewing employees as individuals. He shared: "I like to see employees as a person with unique emotions and a way of seeing the world. I am not trying to see them as an instrument."

Followers appeared to favorably receive this approach. A follower, Maureen, explained how her leader led her to feel a balance of power because her leader used empathy to treat her like a peer and colleague. Maureen shared this about her leader: "His door is open; he is not hierarchical."

Finally, followers who were recipients of empathetic communication indicated they were more willing to follow and, together with their leader, crack open a space for a deeper working relationship. One follower shared that the commitment to her leader was not solely her own willingness to follow, it extended to the broader team as well. Her team symbolically referred to the leader as the "company logo" – something they looked up to – and it represented the type of willingness they had to follow her.

Jorge expressed his approach like this: "I try to establish communication. The empathy is something really, really important. If I don't understand the other side, I will not reach the best result." Empathy further served to guide leader responses and to influence productive results. One leader identified multiple positive results when using empathy. Rene said: "When I use empathy, I can see more participation in the decisions, more motivation in the team, embracing change, focus on results, team work cross functionally." Another leader described the results achieved when using empathy. Marcela shared:

> The District Managers were working out of fear with previous leaders. When you sit down and hear what the employees feel, it's easier to identify how to help them and put yourself in their shoes. You might identify how to create confidence, or if motivation is lacking.

It was not just the leaders who identified these results. Followers described very similar results. Manolo described it like this: "It is important to have empathy, and my result regarding engagement and results to bring new business increased."

Leaders indicated some of the ways they differentiated themselves as authentic leaders is by using empathy for career development, conflict management, or as an intervention. Carolina communicated: "I gravitate to developing people, and there's a certain amount of empathy to use to stretch them, but not let them crack."

Several leaders described employing empathy as an intervention in specific situations to engage a follower in a challenging conversation such as managing performance or navigating conflict or organizational change. In those circumstances, they intentionally planned an empathetic dialogue or conversation in advance. Jaime explained: "I tend to use empathy the most for organizational change especially. I try to put myself in their position first, before talking to them." Jaime described his approach in action:

> The Human Resources Manager is always trying to be the short-term winner and be on the good side of everyone. I need this guy to function. I spoke to him privately. It was empathetic, but planned. He's afraid that he doesn't win. I decided to be just as honest. Having done that, I created a loyalty needed to get out of the slump and make appropriate business decisions.

Rafael empathized with a follower to coach them on their performance. This follower happened to be a leader, trying to drive organizational change. Rafael noticed the follower was taking a less effective approach. The follower was engaging with one of his own followers to drive toward a result. He offered some advice on the follower's performance using empathy. Rafael described making his follower aware that when he takes a particular approach, he solves the business problem but simultaneously reveals that someone was not performing. This results in increased support from his leadership but decreases support from followers. He explained: "By using empathy, I was able to successfully coach the leader and help them understand that when trying to drive change, they can do it in a constructive or destructive manner." Rafael also voiced that he used empathy in times of conflict to help him examine the other perspective and then turn the mirror on himself. He discovered that often during times of conflict, the responsibility was his, stating:

> I like to use it in conflict management. One thing that I have in my assumption is people do things in the wrong way but not with the wrong intent. 90% of the time I think that I was wrong because I didn't have the full picture.

Lastly, Carolina expressed an example of her use of empathy as a situational lever. She read the situation and determined the degree of empathy warranted and adjusted accordingly. She described using empathy as a radar, stating: "Situationally, I might tighten it more as a volume lever. If someone is going through a tough time, my radar gets broader. Certain times, it has to get higher."

The National Culture Influences Adoption of Empathy

Use of empathy as part of authentic leadership may be influenced by national culture. Leaders differed in their opinion of whether they were influenced by the national culture. Some leaders indicated the national culture directly or indirectly influenced their use of empathy while others indicated no influence whatsoever. What emerged is an early indication the national culture may influence the leaders' use of empathy based upon the specific cultural norms of the respective Latin American country. For example, leaders based in Brazil overwhelmingly indicated the elements of their national culture influenced their use of empathy in their leadership. Jorge, a Brazil-based leader stated: "The Brazilian culture affects the way I do things. We are very informal and close to everyone. This part of the culture helps me to be more open in any discussion."

Julia, another Brazilian leader shared: "In Brazil, we are very open and accept that people approach us. People give you the space so you can connect at a different level than the business itself."

Conversely, in Chile, the opposite may be in effect. Leaders in Chile indicated a preference for large power distance, as described by Hofstede's (1984) model of cultural dimensions. They also indicated that hierarchy and competition are highly valued. These two areas might appear diametrically opposed to using empathy as part of authentic leadership. Jaime, a leader based in Chile, declared the hierarchy as "a class system." Another Chile based leader, Parry, stated that the culture in Chile is: "…very competitive. Not empathetic at all. That's why I am a little different."

While both countries are in Latin America, it appears the national culture influences use of empathy in a somewhat polarized way. Another perspective arose where meaningful connections could be derived using empathy. Regardless of the national culture, leaders opined that empathy can be used to make connections to break through cultural barriers and even build a bridge between cultures. Julia expressed: "You are able to use empathy to connect, especially with the different cultures." Marcela explained that the use of empathy is culture-agnostic, stating: "It's regardless of what country I'm in because we work with human beings." Another leader shared that in Latin America the balance between emphasizing both the professional and personal is important, a leader must be mindful of erring on the side of too much business conversation. The incorporation of inquiries about personal interests into conversations is another way to use empathy. Rafael used the popular Latin American pursuit of soccer as an example: "Building the bridge is part of empathy – asking about soccer is important."

Lastly, one leader based in Chile raised the use of empathy within the context of the Hofstede masculinity–femininity dimension. This dimension refers to societal adoption of gender roles. Within societies, behavior trends toward either masculine or feminine dimensions. Parry described his behavior as leaning toward the masculine dimension by identifying his paternalistic experience related to trust, sharing: "When you start being empathetic, you are a father to the rest of the company. They feel support that is not technical, but emotional. They trust me. It is more of an affective response."

Similarities and Differences Across Latin American Country Culture Exist When Empathy Is Used

When empathy is used, similarities and differences exist across national country cultures in Latin America. I will highlight the similarities reported, along with notable differences.

Leaders overwhelmingly indicated a preference for consistently leading with empathy across the four Latin American country cultures included in this research. Followers across Latin American cultures overwhelmingly reported the leader's use of empathy specifically made them want to follow the leader.

Leaders reported similarities in the positive benefits and business outcomes because of using empathy. They collectively described creating an environment where people can be themselves, can work more efficiently and therefore more productively, and are more responsive and engaged, resulting in higher degrees of trust and commitment to both the work and the leader.

Followers across cultures consistently reported feeling comfortable in their relationship with the leader because of the leader's use of empathy. Cristobal reported: "It makes it a lot easier when you feel comfortable, I can ask for guidance instead of holding to yourself and hoping for the best. In other cases, I hold back because fear of punishment."

Differences between Latin American cultures can be noted. While trust was similar between Latin American cultures, how it emerged differed across country cultures. Additionally, while leaders regularly used empathy as a vehicle for authentic leadership, their motivation and context for using empathy differed. For example, one leader in one country described using empathy to discover differences, while a leader in another country described using empathy to bring people together. It is unclear whether these differences are due to differences in Latin American culture, context, leader preference or some other factor, such as the organization's industry.

Leaders Increase Followership Using Empathetic Leadership

Consistent with the existing research about the direct effect and indirect effect of authentic leadership on followers (Avolio et al., 2004), both leaders and followers reported direct and indirect follower effects from using empathetic leadership. This Included both an increase in the number of followers and an increase in follower commitment to the leader.

While trust came up as one of the most common effects, it was mentioned as both an antecedent and an outcome of using empathy related to increased followership. Julia shared: "Once you are at a more emotional level you can fulfill the work. Having the connection and then you start building trust." Rafael described trust as an outcome related to better understanding follower intent. He articulated:

> Trust is a long-term benefit. Think about how you use empathy to understand why someone did what they did and the facts. Did they have an intent? Were they distracted? Empathy helps you identify intent over time, and that helps you help people.

Followers observed leaders' use of empathy translated directly into action. In one instance, a leader put people ahead of business results by recognizing the team for their hard work in the face of disappointing business results. Sylvia described this scenario:

> Last time we are in [location redacted] our results were not great. At the end of the meeting, no one expected anything. Marcela arrived with champagne to celebrate. That is the way that she finds to thank us because of our results. It was incredible.

In addition, followers described the impact leaders had upon them when they experienced extremely difficult circumstances. Multiple followers described difficult and poignant personal circumstances that directly impacted their work or would likely impact them in the future. They shared that in those circumstances, the leader put the follower's needs over business results. Their examples included circumstances ranging from medical difficulties during a pregnancy, to fighting life-threatening illnesses, to experiencing a death in the family. Followers explained how the leader, using empathy, understood the seriousness and responded in a way that both supported the follower and brought the follower some measure of relief from the difficulty.

Followers further described leaders as gleaning information through empathetic conversations that influenced the leaders to balance people with results in the business. This description serves as another possible indicator that leaders who use empathy to glean information that influences their actions are embracing the relational transparency attribute of authentic leadership. Followers indicated leaders who allowed themselves to be appropriately influenced by information gleaned from them through empathetic conversations increased their commitment. Klint explained his leader's approach: "He always says that we focus on people and not on product. It's about human relationships. We try to treat them as human beings. Empathy is a great part of that. We are concerned with how people are."

Leaders responded to information gained through empathy by staying true to their beliefs about the best way to solve a problem, even if it pushed a boundary. One follower, Angela, was overloaded by work. Her leader had no budget for additional resources, and she described his empathetic response: "I saw him bend the rules to find a creative way to hire. He has the angle of doing what's right for people and business."

Followers described their loyalty and commitment to leaders as one which would cause them to follow them to another position, company, or even location because of their empathetic leadership. One follower stated she worked with her leader at a previous organization and followed him to the current organization. Another followed their leader three different times. Manuel explained he had a lot of mentees and they told him they would go so far as to resign if he left his role. He said: "People have told me if I relocate, they will leave the company."

Several followers indicated that they experienced emotional distress when their leaders were no longer their leader or even anticipating they would no longer be their leader. This impact may partially indicate the degree of commitment felt by these followers. Phyllis said she reacted when her leader transferred to another role in the company: "I cried when she transferred."

Most followers noted the leader they described was one of the best leaders they ever had. Many leaders described that followers, previously members of their team, now come back to them for career advice. The leaders explained one way they recognized they were known for their use of empathy was when followers outside of the formal reporting channels followed them and sought them out for advice in lieu of their own leader or another designated resource such as a human resource professional. Myrna took the description of the commitment to another level. She said: "I wouldn't just follow him; he is giving an important message. I have the same responsibility to pay it forward to others." Leader motives for using empathy varied, but it is clear it helped to achieve the same outcome; an increase in follower commitment, and in this case, the formation of future empathetic leaders by the example of their empathetic leader.

Followers indicated they committed to authentic leaders who used empathy, even if the organization operated incongruently. Leader descriptions of their internal leadership and organizational culture varied dramatically. In some larger organizations, the organization was described as containing leadership subcultures with their own unique elements. Regardless of these subcultures, in most cases, the cultural leadership orientation of the organization did not directly influence the leader's choice to use empathy.

Followers responded to leaders who used empathy regardless of the expected cultural, organizational, or leadership norms. The leaders even appeared to stand out. Many followers indicated their leader was "different" or "quite different" and distinguished themselves uniquely in their organization by leading with empathy. Marcela declared empathetic leadership as being a part of herself. She said: "It's part of my regular DNA. You use empathy to create the link."

A few leaders indicated their organization advocates and supports the use of empathy in leadership. Of those few, even fewer said they were directly or indirectly influenced by this. In these cases, it's possible the leader was using empathy as a vehicle for authentic leadership. Many followers stated that leaders who used empathy, even if the organization was operating incongruently, was a factor in their followership commitment. Klint explained not only his own commitment as a follower but his observations of other followers' commitment stating: "Other colleagues look for him because he has this environment created at work."

Discussion

Empathy as a Vehicle for Authentic Leadership

My research indicates that if a leader applies empathy as part of authentic leadership, they will be able to more effectively motivate followers and create stronger working relationships. Leaders who regularly use empathy accelerate the development of effective relationships resulting in greater follower willingness to engage, produce, or offer discretionary effort. Thus, investing in using empathy up front while building relationships may free up leader time in the long run. In my work, I've observed multiple occurrences where the use of empathy generates two-way transparent communication as the norm and followers learn to count on support from their leader. Spurred by this enhanced foundation of trust, leaders save time in interactions. By using relationship shortcuts such as an established understanding of expectations and quality standards, preferred approaches for execution, and fewer and brief updates they take advantage of the bond that emerges in developed relationships. A leadership advantage through an increase in follower engagement, productivity, commitment, leader and organizational loyalty and discretionary effort occurs as a result (see Fig. 3.1).

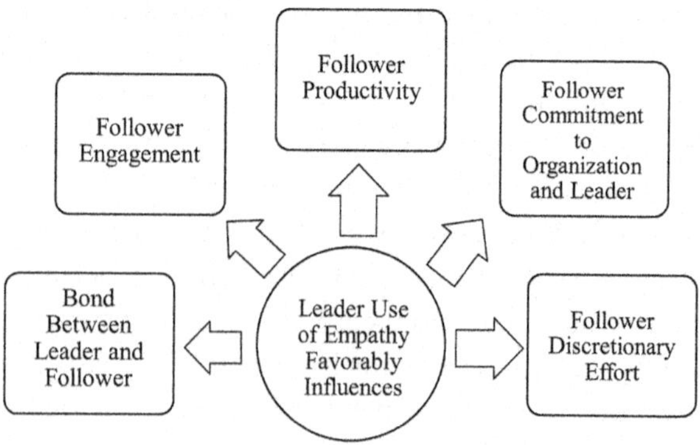

Fig. 3.1 Leadership advantage of using empathy

In this study, leaders across the Latin American cultures indicated their use of empathy influenced follower work engagement as well as commitment. This finding was not wholly unexpected for numerous reasons. Research suggests Authentic Leadership predicts positive work engagement (Aviolo, Gardner, Walumbwa, Luthans, & May, 2004; Rego, Sousa, Marques, & Pina e Cunha, 2012; Walumbwa, Hartnell, & Oke, 2010), so it follows that if empathy is a vehicle for authentic leadership, it may have the potential to influence work engagement. In my view, empathy is then most closely connected to the relational transparency attribute of authentic leadership, and has the potential to influence work engagement through this vehicle. It may be the underlying mechanism responsible for the observations made by leaders across Latin American cultures; their use of empathy influenced follower work engagement as well as commitment.

By leading with empathy, leaders can establish closer relationships (George, 2003). Both leaders and followers described how empathy helped them build a deeper sense of trust and forged a tighter bond between the leader and follower, creating a closer relationship. In many cases, leaders nourished the relationship by continuing to nurture the trust developed through empathy to achieve greater outcomes of engagement. Leaders described the use of empathy and its positive impact on communication, conflict management, organizational change, and decision-making. These findings mirror existing research that indicates empathy may be instrumental in not only building bonds with followers but in effective communication, problem-solving, decision-making, and performance (Kellett et al., 2006).

In some cases, leaders modeled leading with empathy, which fostered the development of empathy in followers and paying it forward for followers to emulate. This finding supports research which indicates that through positive modeling, authentic leaders foster the development of authenticity in followers (Avolio & Gardner, 2005).

While my research suggests empathy can serve as a vehicle for authentic leadership and an increase in follower commitment, additional research is necessary to determine the specific contextual and environmental factors that allow follower commitment to emerge and thrive in Latin American business organizations.

Benefits and Drawbacks of This Research Approach

My interest in deeply understanding the descriptive answers to the research question led me to utilize interviews with leaders and followers. The interviews provided a narrative of specific experiences, and I discovered nuances through follow-up questions, which offered clarification and additional insights. Interviews with followers helped to complete the narrative about the leader's approach and uncover some credible conclusions to examine.

However, this research has some drawbacks, such as limitations in geography and sample size. Data comprised only 4 out of 20 countries in Latin America. The sample size is small, was based on my direct and indirect network, and the study was carried out across a small set of organizations. In addition, the intention of conducting interviews was to draw out specific experiential examples. However, leaders and followers self-reported and could have been influenced by other factors in their responses. Further research is necessary to reach a point of saturation to explore a more direct correlation between empathy and authentic leadership. Despite these drawbacks, the research suggests there is a possible relationship where empathy serves as a vehicle for authentic leadership in Latin America.

Opportunities for Further Exploration

Research tells us leaders with high emotional intelligence can empathize with followers (Gardner et al., 2009). Existing research claims that leaders who have high self-monitoring skills are closely attuned to the situational cues of others and more sensitive to follower's emotions, thus allowing them to demonstrate more empathy (Gardner et al., 2009). Both areas warrant further exploration, considering the findings of this study.

Goleman (1995), in his book *Emotional Intelligence,* explains that empathy is a key attribute of emotional intelligence. While none of the leaders interviewed explicitly used the words "emotional intelligence" in their descriptions, their examples consistently described emotion, how they felt, and how they wanted their followers to feel. Followers also used emotional descriptors. Future research can explore additional intersections between empathy, emotions, and leadership, within leader-follower relationships.

Commitment to leaders who use empathy in their leadership, even though their organizations may be operating incongruently, impacts follower's commitment. However, study participants provided varying degrees of context. Therefore, it is unclear to what degree the leader's use of empathy within this organizational context is a factor in follower's commitment. Because it may be weighted more or less than other factors related to the leaders' use of empathy, there would be a benefit to exploring this further.

Followers reported that the more the leader used empathy as part of their leadership, the more they increasingly counted on consistency and predictability in the actions of the leader. It may be advantageous to explore whether empathetic leadership, consistency, and predictability are correlated.

In describing their leaders, followers often made comparisons between the leader they were describing and a leader who did not demonstrate empathy as part of their leadership. Depersonalization emerges as the possible behavior of a leader who does not demonstrate empathy. Further comparative exploration by comparing the behaviors of empathetic and nonempathetic leaders may offer some additional insight into the impact of empathy on followers as an element of authentic leadership.

Application to Organizations

The research indicates leaders who adopt empathy as part of their leadership approach in the workplace achieve greater positive, collaborative working relationships, and increase follower commitment. This, in turn, leads to greater productivity and work engagement. Empathy is a significant predictor of leadership emergence (Bruch & Walter, 2007; Kellett et al., 2002, 2006). If empathy predicts leadership emergence and could serve as a vehicle for authentic leadership, implementing programs to strengthen empathy as an element of authentic leadership will improve an emerging leader's effectiveness early in their leadership journey.

Organizations can invest in programs to support existing leaders who use this empathetic leadership approach, while training and encouraging emerging and future leaders to adopt empathy as part of their leadership.

Lastly, organizations that intentionally create and maintain an organizational climate where empathy is valued as a part of authentic leadership stand to gain multiple advantages, including increased engagement and productivity.

Conclusions

As described at the outset of this research study, I set out to explore whether empathy serves as a vehicle for authentic leadership. I discovered that empathy may serve as a vehicle to access and engage the relational transparency attribute of authentic leadership, and this may in turn affect leader followership and corresponding commitment of their followers. By using empathy to foster understanding, empathy contributes to creating or increasing a bond between a leader and the follower. This appears to be the key role of empathy as a part of authentic leadership. Empathy results in influencing the development of collaborative relationships based on the deepening of trust and in influencing outcomes that increase in follower engagement, productivity, commitment, leader and organizational loyalty, and discretionary effort. Followers appear to commit to authentic leaders who use empathy even if the organization operates incongruently. In addition, the findings from both leader and follower interviews highlighted that empathy may serve as a springboard to strengthen relationship outcomes of authentic leadership. However, it is unclear whether different national cultures influence adoption of empathy. While there are similarities and differences in Latin American national cultures relating to empathy, the findings indicate that different national cultures may achieve the same outcome, which is an increase in follower commitment, even when leaders' motives for using empathy vary.

References

AON Hewitt. (2016). *Talent thought leadership*. Retrieved from http://www.aon.com/human-capital-consulting/thought-leadership/talent/2016-Trends-in-Global-Employee-Engagement.jsp

Avolio, B. J., & Gardner, W. L. (2005). Authentic leadership development: Getting to the root of positive forms of leadership. *The Leadership Quarterly, 16*(3), 315–338. https://doi.org/10.1016/j.leaqua.2005.03.001.

Avolio, B. J., Gardner, W. L., Walumbwa, F. O., Luthans, F., & May, D. R. (2004). Unlocking the mask: A look at the process by which authentic leaders impact follower attitudes and behaviors. *The Leadership Quarterly, 15*(6), 801–823. https://doi.org/10.1016/j.leaqua.2004.09.003.

Bruch, H., & Walter, F. (2007). Leadership in context: Investigating hierarchical impacts on transformational leadership. *Leadership & Organization Development Journal, 28*(8), 710–726. https://doi.org/10.1108/01437730710835452.

Burns, J. M. (1978). *Leadership*. New York: Harper & Row.

Fields, D. L. (2007). Determinants of follower perceptions of a leader's authenticity and integrity. *European Management Journal, 25*(3), 195–206. https://doi.org/10.1016/j.emj.2007.04.005.

Gardner, W. L., Avolio, B. J., Luthans, F., May, D. R., & Walumbwa, F. (2005). Can you see the real me? A self-based model of authentic leader and follower development. *The Leadership Quarterly, 16*, 343–372. https://doi.org/10.1016/j.leaqua.2005.03.003.

Gardner, W. L., Fischer, D., & Hunt, J. G. (2009). Emotional labor and leadership: A threat to authentic? *The Leadership Quarterly, 20*(3), 466–482. https://doi.org/10.1016/j.leaqua.2009.03.011.

George, B. (2003). *Authentic leadership: Rediscovering the secret to creating lasting value*. San Francisco: Jossey-Bass.

Goleman, D. (1995). *Emotional intelligence*. New York: Bantam Books.

Goleman, D., Boyatzis, R., & McKee, A. (2002). *Primal leadership: Realizing the power of emotional intelligence*. Boston: Harvard Business School Publishing.

Hofstede, G. (1984). Cultural dimensions in management and planning. *Asia Pacific Journal of Management, 1*(2), 81–99. https://doi.org/10.1007/BF01733682.

House, R. J., & Aditya, R. N. (1997). The social scientific study of leadership: Quo vadis? *Journal of Management, 23*(3), 409–473. https://doi.org/10.1177/014920639702300306.

Kellett, J. B., Humphrey, R. H., & Sleeth, R. G. (2002). Empathy and complex task performance: Two routes to leadership. *The Leadership Quarterly, 13*(5), 523–544. https://doi.org/10.1016/S1048-9843(02)00142-X.

Kellett, J. B., Humphrey, R. H., & Sleeth, R. G. (2006). Empathy and the emergence of task and relations leaders. *The Leadership Quarterly, 17*(2), 146–162. https://doi.org/10.1016/j.leaqua.2005.12.003.

Rego, A., Sousa, F., Marques, C., & Pina e Cunha, M. (2012). Authentic leadership promoting employees' psychological capital and creativity. *Journal of Business Research, 65*(3), 429–437. https://doi.org/10.1016/j.jbusres.2011.10.003.

Shuck, M. B., Rocco, T. S., & Albornoz, C. A. (2011). Exploring employee engagement from the employee perspective: Implications for HRD. *Journal of European Industrial Training, 35*(4), 300–325. https://doi.org/10.1108/03090591111128306.

Walumbwa, F. O., Avolio, B. J., Gardner, W. L., Wernsing, T. S., & Peterson, S. J. (2008). Authentic leadership: Development and validation of a theory-based measure. *Journal of Management, 34*(1), 89–126. https://doi.org/10.1177/0149206307308913.

Walumbwa, F. O., Hartnell, C. A., & Oke, A. (2010). Servant leadership, procedural justice climate, service climate, employee attitudes, and organizational citizenship behavior: A cross level investigation. *Journal of Applied Psychology, 95*(3), 517–529. https://doi.org/10.1037/a0018867.

Yukl, G. A. (2002). *Leadership in organizations* (5th ed.). Upper Saddle River, NJ: Prentice Hall.

4

The Role of Workplace Authentic Leadership on Followership Behaviour and Psychological Capital in a South African Context

Marieta du Plessis and Adré B. Boshoff

Confidence in contemporary business leadership has decreased following unethical actions on the part of the leaders and resultant business failure (Kets de Vries & Balazs, 2011; Treviño & Brown, 2007). This is seen in the international context, but also more specifically in the South African context. From a South African business perspective, evidence of unethical actions by business leaders has been prevalent. The range of unethical incidents spans from acts of collusion, bribery, and price-fixing in the private sector, to corruption in the public sector (Schoeman, 2012). A recent survey done by the Ethics Institute of South Africa indicated that 9.7% of South African

This work is based on research supported in part by the National Research Foundation of South Africa. Any opinion, finding, conclusion or recommendation expressed in this material is that of the authors, and the NRF does not accept any liability in this regard.

M. du Plessis (✉) • A.B. Boshoff
Department of Industrial/Organizational Psychology, University of the Western Cape, Bellville, South Africa

© The Author(s) 2018

D. Cotter-Lockard (ed.), *Authentic Leadership and Followership*, Palgrave Studies in Leadership and Followership, https://doi.org/10.1007/978-3-319-65307-5_4

employees felt pressured into compromising their organisation's ethical standards. This pressure emanated mainly from instructions received from management to compromise such standards. What compounded this dilemma was that 39% of employees felt uncomfortable to question their managers, and 35% of employees felt uncomfortable to share bad news with their managers (Groenewald, 2016). These statistics may indicate that the followers either do not question their leaders or do not have the voice or power to do so.

Furthermore, the multicultural demographic composition of the South African population (commonly referred to as the Rainbow Nation) presents a number of management and leadership challenges. This nation in development has a history of considerable strife, culminating in a democratic state coming into being during the 1990s. A large part of the members of the new democracy perceived themselves and their forebears as having been disadvantaged during the Apartheid era. Feelings of entitlement because of previous experiences may result. The current population of 55 million contains a substantial group of individuals (25%) who are between 20 and 34 years of age. A large part of this group came through an education system that functioned ineffectively, resulting in many younger people who are ill-equipped for working in sophisticated modern organisations, yet who expect to share in the benefits of democracy. The complexity of the situation highlights the need for leadership, and specifically the type of leadership that aims to grow and develop followers to be successful in life, business and society. Authentic leadership provides a possible solution to the challenge of diverse value systems, as authentic leaders influence employees beyond bottom-line success (Avolio, Gardner, Walumbwa, Luthans, & May, 2004; George, 2003) by addressing organisational and societal problems.

According to Hofstede's (2014) cultural dimensions, South Africa has a masculine culture where managers and leaders are expected to be decisive and assertive. Moreover, the South African workplace leadership is historically male-dominated—this emanates from traditional gender hierarchies that exist within cultural, religious, and family traditions (Martin & Barnard, 2013). Thus, despite gender equality and empowerment of women in the workplace, the household structure has a traditional hierarchy that assumes the dominant gender to be male; this assumption then becomes entrenched in organisational culture (Hartmann, 2010).

The theory of authentic leadership emphasises positive and developmental interactions between leaders and followers (Woolley, Caza, & Levy, 2011). Avolio et al. (2004) proposed a theoretical framework that links authentic leadership to the attitudes and behaviours of followers. According to Avolio et al. (2004), authentic leaders influence their followers' attitudes and behaviours by creating a sense of personal and social identification, using role-modelling behaviours and setting high moral values and standards. However, it is important to examine whether followers identify more with their leaders if they are male, because the traditional male-dominated leadership remains prevalent in the South African context.

Rationale for the Study

One of the lacunas in leadership research is the absence of discussions around followership and its impact on leadership outcomes (Avolio, Walumbwa, & Weber, 2009). To understand the influence of the leader on work outcomes and desired workplace behaviour, the mediating role of followership characteristics should be taken into account (Woolley et al., 2011). Shamir (2007) suggests that leadership effectiveness results from good followers just as much as it results from good leadership. South Africans to a large extent accept hierarchical order, and based on the power distance between the leaders and the followers, the followers expect to be told what to do (Hofstede, 2014). According to the Hofstede Centre, the ideal leader in the South African context is the benevolent autocrat (Hofstede, 2014). Similarly, in a culture where critical thinking is not valued as a followership trait, the followers would be discouraged from such behaviours owing to the negative consequences. Context therefore plays a critical role in the relationship between leaders and followers.

Greyvenstein and Cilliers (2012) concluded that followers' views of leadership indicate the existence of immature relationships in South African organisations today. These authors indicate that the boss–subordinate relationship mirrors the child–parent dynamic, which causes high levels of anxiety among followers. This may be because the leaders are not attending to the followers' needs or are not role models of leadership behaviour. What the leaders must provide and the followers want may be quite different from what is expected in other populations. Individuals in leadership roles are in many cases part of Eurocentric groups with the assumptions favoured in such cultures. Approaches that in one population group may be seen as authentic behaviour may well be seen as weakness by members of a different group. Similarly, followership behaviour may well be seen as either appropriate or as seeking favours.

South Africa differs significantly from Western countries in terms of language, geography, social and economic indicators and political perspectives (Joshanloo, Wissing, Khumalo, & Lamers, 2013). As most previous studies on authentic leadership were conducted from a Western perspective (Van der Vaart, Stander, & Rothmann, 2015), the need for research on authentic leadership in the South African context is indicated. Cultural differences are important in the South African context, as it has been found that White people are considered to be more individualistic and favouring personal growth attributes, whereas Black people are considered to be more collectivistic and favouring social-relational attributes (Valchev et al., 2012).

Considering the multicultural framework of South African business, it can be concluded that the relationship between leaders and followers is complex. However, building on the idea of authentic leadership as a root construct of leadership, Avolio et al. (2004) state that the leader can be directive, authoritative, or participative, and that displaying these common leader behavioural styles would not indicate whether the leader is authentic or inauthentic. Rather, the leader's ability to act in accordance with their own values, to build credibility and respect in the eyes of followers, to actively encourage diverse points of view and to foster relational transparency would be deemed authentic (Avolio et al., 2004).

The previous decade has produced numerous research articles in the field of authentic leadership. However, more empirical research is needed to understand the impact of authentic leadership on outcome variables within an organisational setting (Muchiri, 2011). To this extent, this study sought to understand the relationship between authentic leadership and followership. Furthermore, the relationship between authentic leadership and psychological capital (PsyCap) was explored.

Literature Review

Authentic leadership has been included in the categorisation of positive forms of leadership (Avolio & Gardner, 2005; George, 2003; Luthans & Avolio, 2003), and recent research results have provided evidence of the positive relationship between authentic leadership and positive workplace outcomes (Avolio & Mhatre, 2012). In the following sections, authentic leadership will briefly be discussed in relation to followership behaviours as well as PsyCap of the follower.

Authentic Leadership

The proponents of authentic leadership define authentic leaders as those who have clear and definite knowledge about themselves in all respects (including beliefs, preferences, strengths and weaknesses) and who behave in a way that is consistent with this self-knowledge (Gardner, Avolio, Luthans, May, & Walumbwa, 2005). Authentic leaders are described as leaders who embody four behavioural tendencies, namely self-awareness, relational transparency, balanced processing and internalised moral perspective (Luthans & Avolio, 2003).

The authentic leadership process suggests that authentic leadership is linked to the followers' attitudes and behaviours (Avolio et al., 2004), and that the most important outcomes of authentic leadership are those for individual followers (Caza & Jackson, 2011). The authentic leader's influence is created through a sense of personal and social identification between the leader and the follower (Avolio et al., 2004). For instance, authentic leaders use role-modelling to display high moral standards to their followers in order that followers' values and beliefs may gradually converge with those of the leader (Gardner et al., 2005). Another example would be the leader and follower's transparent discussion of the leader's vulnerabilities, thereby constantly focusing on the development of the follower as well as the leader (Avolio et al., 2004).

Although the potential value of adopting an authentic leadership approach in an organisation has been demonstrated in a number of studies in other countries, limited empirical work has been done in South Africa. Stander, De Beer, and Stander (2015) found that authentic leadership is related to higher levels of follower optimism, as well as follower trust in the organisation in the South African public healthcare sector (N = 633). Coxen, Van der Vaart, and Stander (2016) reported that authentic leadership influenced trust at three levels, namely trust in the organisation, trust in the manager, and trust in the co-worker. Kotzé and Nel (2015) looked at trait emotional intelligence as an antecedent of authentic leadership and found that empathy (an element of emotional intelligence) explained the biggest proportion of the variance in authentic leadership. These studies did not comment on any differences in authentic leadership based on the demographic characteristics of the leader or the follower. However, interest in the authentic leadership variable in the South African context is growing, as observed in a number of unpublished theses and dissertations.

Followership

The leader of an organisation is responsible for charting a vision and the direction of the company, developing strategies for success, managing change, and influencing others to achieve a common goal (Northouse, 2004). Thus, leadership is critically important to achieve organisational success. However, as the ratio between the leaders and the followers in an organisation is usually characterised by a majority of the followers, the achievement of the goals and accomplishments of the organisation is more dependent on the followers in the group. Researchers have proposed that studies should examine how the influence of the leaders is mediated through the followers they work with to better understand the dynamics of the leadership process (Avolio & Luthans, 2006; Woolley et al., 2011).

To a large extent, the literature about the leadership and followership process is viewed from a leader-centric lens (Bjugstad, Thach, Thompson &

Morris, 2006; Kelley, 2008). Meindl, Ehrlich, and Dukerich (1985) introduced and developed a follower-centric perspective on leadership which directed the attention to the importance of followers' processes of attribution and sense-making in organisations, without disregarding the importance of the leaders. Kelley's (1988) seminal article, *In Praise of Followers*, was published at approximately the same time as the reflections of Meindl et al. (1985) and sought to refocus attention on followership, rather than relegating it to a peripheral leadership component (Kelley, 2008).

Kelley's (1992) conceptualisation of followership is one of the few positive views of followership (Blanchard, Welbourne, Gilmore, & Bullock, 2009). Kelley (1988) explains good followers as sharing the following qualities: (1) they manage themselves well; (2) they are committed to the organisation and are individualists who courageously and honestly pursue their own meaning in life, rather than follow norms and societal goals such as money, status and position; (3) they build competence and exert a focused effort in task completion and (4) they are honest, courageous and credible individuals. These good followers would also not compete for leadership or power, but rather they would cooperate to accomplish goals.

Kelley (1992) further conceptualised followership in relation to the behaviours that are associated with good followers. He categorised these behaviours into the dimensions of independent critical thinking and active engagement. The ideal follower, based on Kelley's (1988) theory, would be the follower who has a high level of active engagement and independent critical thinking. These individuals are self-starters, are focused and committed to the goals of the organisation, and have strong organisational networks. Furthermore, such followers would take the initiative, give constructive criticism, think for themselves and continually increase their value to the organisation.

Authentic leadership theory gives emphasis to positive and developmental interactions between leaders and followers (Woolley et al., 2011). The followers who are led by authentic leaders feel more empowered and take greater ownership of their work (George, 2003; Ilies, Morgeson, & Nahrgang, 2005). George (2003) argues that authentic leaders motivate followers by modelling a deep sense of purpose and an ethical work ethos. Effective followers are committed to a purpose and derive personal satisfaction from their work (Potter & Rosenbach, 2006) and, therefore, their self-perception of their own characteristics can have a positive effect on their work engagement (Zhu, Avolio, & Walumbwa, 2009). It was therefore envisaged that authentic leadership would have a positive relationship with followership.

Psychological Capital

Using positive psychology and positive organisational behaviour (POB) as foundation, Luthans, Youssef, and Avolio (2007b) developed PsyCap as a core construct of POB that could be measured and developed for performance impact. After reviewing the literature, Luthans, Youssef, and Avolio (2007a) determined that the positive constructs that met the inclusion criteria for POB consisted of self-efficacy (confidence and belief about succeeding at challenging tasks), hope (persevering towards goals and, when necessary, redirecting paths to goals to succeed), resilience (bouncing back from problems and adversity to attain success) and optimism (being positive about succeeding now and in the future). Apart from the importance of each of the four constructs, the synergistic phenomenon of overall PsyCap has been shown to have a higher correlation with performance outcomes than any of the four individual constructs (Luthans, Avolio, Avey, & Norman, 2007).

Recent studies have emphasised the role of the leader in enhancing employees' levels of PsyCap (Walumbwa, Peterson, Avolio, & Hartnell, 2010). Leaders who have a high level of PsyCap display more positive attitudes and higher performance levels, while at the same time serving as role models for their followers. Leader PsyCap was found to have a significant relationship with follower PsyCap (Avey, Avolio, & Luthans, 2011).

Viewing the impact of leadership on PsyCap from a positive leadership position, Gardner and Schermerhorn (2004) suggested the possible impacts of authentic leadership on follower PsyCap. These authors state that authentic leaders are likely to develop and influence their followers by energising them with positive psychological states. Studies that tested this assertion found a significant positive relationship between authentic leadership and follower PsyCap (Caza, Bagozzi, Woolley, Levy, & Barker Caza, 2010; Rego, Sousa, Marques, & Pina e Cunha, 2012).

Research Hypotheses

Effective leaders enable their followers to contribute to the success of an organisation (Baker, Mathis, & Stites-Doe, 2011). Gardner et al. (2005) argue that authentic leaders produce heightened levels of follower self-awareness and self-regulation and that this, in turn, leads to positive follower development and outcomes. Walumbwa et al. (2010) state that authentic leadership plays an important role in the extent to which followers feel psychologically empowered. Therefore, our first hypothesis is **H1: The leader's perceived level of authenticity explains a significant proportion of the variance in follower behaviour.**

Authentic leadership and PsyCap have been found to interrelate while both may facilitate employee creativity (Rego et al., 2012). In a sample of 828 working adults, authentic leadership was found to be positively related to followers' PsyCap development (Woolley et al., 2011). In a South African context, Munyaka (2012), too, found a substantial relationship between authentic leadership and follower PsyCap. Our second hypothesis is **H2: There is a statistically significant relationship between authentic leadership and PsyCap.**

Chan, Hannah, and Gardner (2005) proposed that the meaning and effect of authentic leadership may vary depending on the context in which it is measured. For instance, the effects of authenticity may vary by gender (Harter, Waters, Whitesell, & Kastelic, 1998). Woolley et al. (2011) reported that comparable authentic leadership behaviours produced different outcomes among male and female followers in their sample of the New Zealand general population. Eagly (2005) suggested that apart from gender, differences such as ethnicity, occupational level, social class (Gardiner, 2011) and education may also be important in explaining the experience of authenticity and authentic leadership. Finally, we hypothesised **H3: There are statistically significant differences between socio-demographic characteristics of respondents in relation to authentic leadership.**

Methodology

The study was undertaken to determine the following:

1. Configural equivalence of questionnaires to measure authentic leadership, followership, and PsyCap when applied to a South African sample.
2. Relationship between authentic leadership and followership; and authentic leadership and PsyCap.
3. Differences of scores on authentic leadership of biographic/ demographic groups.

Participants

The mean age of respondents was calculated as 45 years (*SD* = 8.08 years), with a minimum age of 25 years and a maximum of 63 years. The average work experience of individuals was 23 years, with an average tenure in the organisation of 11 years (*SD* = 6 years). The mean reporting period to the current manager was calculated as 4 years (*SD* = 4 years). The minimum reporting period that was captured was less than 1 year, with the maximum reporting period to the current manager being 25 years. The frequency distribution of the demographic characteristics of the sample is presented in Table 4.1.

Measuring Instruments

The authentic leadership questionnaire (ALQ) developed by Avolio, Gardner, and Walumbwa (2007) was used to measure the level of authentic leadership. The questionnaire consists of 16 items measuring four dimensions (self-awareness, relational transparency, internalised moral perspective, and balanced processing) which were identified by the authors of the questionnaire as constituting authentic leadership. Responses are captured by way of a 5-point Likert scale ranging from 0 = *not all* to 4 = *frequently*. Walumbwa, Avolio, Gardner, Wernsing, and Peterson (2008) found that the ALQ scale manifested both convergent

Table 4.1 Frequency distribution of the demographic characteristics of the sample

Group	Sub-group	Frequency	Percentage
Gender	Male	126	22.6
	Female	501	77.4
Occupational level	Generally trained office worker/secretary	1	.2
	Vocationally trained craftsperson, technician, IT specialist, nurse, artisan or equivalent	13	2.0
	Academically trained professional or equivalent (but not a manager of people)	71	11.0
	Manager of one or more subordinates (non-managers)	362	56.0
	Manager of one or more managers	162	25.0
	Other	38	5.9
Home language	Afrikaans	426	65.8
	English	145	22.4
	Afrikaans and English	22	3.4
	North Sotho	7	1.1
	Sepedi	6	.9
	Zulu	6	.9
	Tswana	6	.9
	Setswana	5	.8
	Others: German, Russian; Xhosa, Ndebele, Oshikwanyama, Shona, Tsonga, Venda and other indigenous languages	24	3.8
Educational level	Secondary school	2	.3
	Matric or equivalent	26	4.0
	Post-school certificate or diploma	242	37.4
	University degree	179	27.7
	Postgraduate degree	162	25.0
	Other	36	5.6
Manager gender	Male	275	42.5
	Female	372	57.5

and discriminant validity when applied alongside other leadership constructs such as transformational and ethical leadership. The researchers reported a Cronbach's alpha of .91 for the ALQ scale. The results of confirmatory factor analysis (CFA) indicated that the four-factor structure fitted the data well. Through psychometric evaluation, it was established that the ALQ is reliable for use in a South African context (Kotzé & Nel, 2015; Roux, 2010; Stander et al., 2015).

For the purposes of this study, permission was requested and granted from Mindgarden to use the ALQ, and the respondents reported their perceptions of their immediate superiors' authentic leadership behaviour.

PsyCap was measured by means of the PsyCap questionnaire (PCQ) developed by Luthans et al. (2007). Dawkins, Martins, Scott, and Sanderson (2013) conclude that the four-factor structure has been found to be quite consistent. This was confirmed in studies on South African samples (Görgens-Ekermans & Herbert, 2013; Simons & Buitendach, 2013). Du Plessis and Barkhuizen (2011) found that a three-factor structure provided a better fit when applied to 131 respondents.

Luthans, Norman, Avolio, and Avey (2008) reported scale reliabilities of .89, .89 and .91 in three different studies. In later studies (Görgens-Ekermans & Herbert, 2013; Simons & Buitendach, 2013) on South African samples, similar findings were reported with Cronbach's alpha values of .91 for the PCQ and a range of .67 to .90 for the subscales of the PCQ. The PCQ was used as a self-report instrument; the respondents assessed their own level of PsyCap.

Kelley's 1998 20-item questionnaire was used to measure followership. The items in the questionnaire were responded to on a 7-point Likert scale, ranging from 1 = *rarely* to 7 = *almost always*. The items were grouped into two subscales (active engagement and independent critical thinking). Participants were asked to assess their own levels of followership.

Baker (2006) stated that there is a dearth of published research reporting on the factor structure and psychometric characteristics of the instrument. Two studies, Tanoff and Barlow (2002) and VanDoren (1998), respectively, reported reliability coefficients of .68 and .74 for the independent thinking subscale and .84 and .87 for the active engagement subscale. Colangelo (2000) reported a study in which four instead of two factors were found. Blanchard et al. (2009) applied the Kelley instrument to 331 members of the faculty of a large university in the south-east of the United States. Factor analysis yielded three instead of the two factors found by Kelley. Two of the factors corresponded closely to the original factors in Kelley's questionnaire. Blanchard et al. (2009) suggested that researchers needed to validate the instrument when using it. This was done as part of the data analysis in this study in which the instrument was used as a self-report measure.

Data Gathering

Data were gathered electronically. A pilot study was carried out to reduce possible problems when the questionnaire was used in electronic form. Thirty professional and semi-professional individuals who conformed to the specifications for participants in the main study were asked to complete the questionnaire in electronic form. Furthermore, we conducted a Pearson analysis of relationships between PsyCap, followership, and authentic leadership. The relationship between these variables and social desirability was also completed. The Social Desirability Scale-17 (SDS-17) consists of 17 items that measure a person's general tendency to act in a socially desirable manner. Stöber (2001) reported that the SDS-17 is a reliable and valid measure that can be used for adults 18–80 years of age. Based on the results of the pilot study, it was concluded that the PsyCap, followership, and authentic leadership measuring instruments were not related to and hence, probably not affected by social desirability bias. As a result, social desirability did not seem to cause a common method variance problem in this study. The final form of the questionnaire was loaded on an independent research website (Qualtrics).

After consulting the top management of the organisation, permission was obtained for the study to be carried out. The requirements for participation in the study included that respondents' job levels needed to be at a Patterson grading C5 level and above (thus, typically, the sample held middle, senior and executive management positions in the organisation); respondents needed to have access to a computer and the Internet and respondents needed to be equipped with an acceptable level of English literacy, as the questions required them to differentiate between fine nuances of behaviour described in words. Employees from all branches of the organisation were included. As many as 855 people in the organisation met these criteria and were invited to respond to the survey.

Potential respondents individually received the composite questionnaire, including the three measuring instruments and items aimed at eliciting demographic and biographical information, by e-mail. The questionnaire was completed anonymously. To further safeguard respondents from releasing private information unwillingly, the completion of the biographical information section was not compulsory. No password or identifying link was required to access the questionnaire. Informed consent was obtained, and assurances of confidentiality and anonymity were provided. Potential participants were informed in the introduction to the questionnaire about the purpose of the study and had to indicate—by marking 'yes' or 'no'—their willingness to participate. If 'no' was marked, the individual could not access the remainder of the questionnaire. In spite of having consented to complete the questionnaire, an individual could, at any stage of reacting to the instrument, decide not to continue doing so.

A final date was set for submission of responses, and two follow-up messages were sent to all potential respondents. After the process of data gathering, 670 responses were recorded. However, some of these responses were incomplete and had to be excluded from the sample. Therefore, the survey response rate of usable responses was calculated at 76% ($N = 647$).

Data Analysis

The statistical package for the social sciences (SPSS, Version 21) was used to provide the descriptive and inferential statistics. In addition, AMOS software (Version 21) was used to conduct CFA.

Results

In terms of the first aim of the study, CFA was carried out on how well the structures of the three measuring instruments used in the study fitted the data. The fit indices were evaluated for goodness of fit, as per the suggestions of Hair, Black, Babin, and Anderson (2010).

Item parcelling was carried out in cases where more than four items were present in a subscale of an instrument. Item parcelling was done by adding the items with the highest and lowest factor loading, and then the second highest and lowest factor loading. We acknowledge that there has been much debate in academic literature on the feasibility of item parcelling (Little, Cunningham, Shahar, & Widaman, 2002; Meade & Kroustalis, 2005). Most proponents agree that item parcelling is useful when the purpose is mainly to test whether factors fit the model, or when testing various structural models. As the current study dataset has numerous observed variables combined with a large sample size, the choice was made to utilise item parcelling and report the process rigorously. For the ALQ, parcels were created for the transparency dimension. The parcels were allocated as follows: [3, 5, 4] + [2, 1]. For the PCQ, the parcels were created as follows: efficacy [4, 5, 2] + [3, 6, 1]; hope [11, 7, 10] + [8, 9, 12]; resilience [17, 13, 14] + [18, 15, 16] and optimism [21, 24, 19] + [22, 20, 23]. Finally, the parcels for the followership instrument consisted of active engagement [10, 2, 3] + [9, 7, 15] + [6, 4, 13, 8] and independent thinking [12, 1, 16] + [5, 17, 19] + [11, 18, 14, 20]. The indices obtained are shown in Table 4.2.

The fit indices in Table 4.2 indicate that in the case of the ALQ the four-factor structure fitted the data reasonably well, although the values

Table 4.2 Results of confirmatory factor analysis on original structures of measuring instruments

Index	Authentic leadership questionnaire	PsyCap questionnaire	Followership	Followership revised
Chi-square	351.680	30.110	165.200	153.304
df	59	14	8	26
p	.000	.070	.000	.000
Chi-square/*df*	5.961	2.150	20.650	5.896
AIC	415.680	74.110	191.200	191.304
RMSEA	.088	.042	.174	.087
RMR	.063	.097	.567	.087
NFI	.949	.987	.920	.929
CFI	.957	.993	.924	.940

Note. *df* degree of freedom, *p* level of significance, *AIC* Akaike information criteria, *RMSEA* root mean square error of approximation, *RMR* root mean square residual, *NFI* normed fit index, *CFI* comparative fit index for chi-square/degree of freedom (*df*) (which ideally should have been between 2 and 5; Hair et al., 2010) and root mean square error of approximation (RMSEA) were somewhat higher than desirable (acceptable fit would have been <.8; Hair et al., 2010). With the exception of the value for root mean square residual (RMR), the indices indicated that the fit of the PCQ can be regarded as good. The indices for the fit of the two-factor followership questionnaire were, with the exception of the incremental indices (normed fit index [NFI] and comparative fit index [CFI]), unsatisfactory. It was decided to examine the structure by means of exploratory factor analysis (EFA). During the EFA analyses, items that did not load at least .30 on any factor were left out of further analysis. Items loading .30 or higher on more than one factor with the two loadings differing less than .25 were similarly left out of further analyses. During the first round of EFA, an attempt was made to replicate the two-factor structure identified by Kelley (1992). The Kaiser–Meyer–Olkin (KMO) statistic amounted to .939, indicating that it would be feasible to carry out EFA on the data. Three eigenvalues (7.73, 1.77 and 1.26) greater than 1 were obtained, together predicting 53.77% of the total and, respectively, 71.9%, 16.4% and 11.7% of the common variance. Items 14 and 16 cross-loaded on all three factors and, according to the stated rules, were eliminated from a further round of EFA. Four more rounds of EFA had to be carried out before a structure in which all the remaining items loaded satisfactorily were obtained. The results of the last four rounds of EFA are summarised in Table 4.3.

From Table 4.3, it can be seen that after the EFA processes, 9 of 20 items could no longer be seen as part of the followership questionnaire when applied to the present sample. A two-factor structure consisting 11 items was obtained. The final two-factor structure (organised by factor loading) is shown in Table 4.4.

Table 4.3 Results of the last four rounds of exploratory factor analysis on followership data ($N = 647$)

Round	Eigenvalue > 1	% of total variance	Items left out
2	3	54.97	3, 5, 6, 7, 14, 15
3	3	59.22	2
4	3	62.61	1, 18
5	2	60.46	None

Table 4.4 Final structure of Kelley's followership instrument ($N = 647$)

	Factor	
Item	1	2
10	.786	.224
9	.763	.221
11	.760	.286
12	.741	.391
8	.684	.375
13	.662	.284
20	.434	.708
19	.131	.677
17	.272	.384

From Table 4.4, it can be seen that all the retained items now met the criteria that were stated earlier. In the new structure, factor 1 consisted of six items and factor 2 of three items. Factor 2 was made up of items that were included in the independent thinking dimension of the original measurement model and this factor was retained as independent thinking. Items 8, 9, 10 and 13 from the original active engagement dimension and items 11 and 1 from the original independent thinking dimension formed factor 1. These items focused on independent actions, doing more than was expected, championing new ideas, and helping colleagues. The items highlighted the notion of stepping forward and acting independently. This was conceptually distinct from the independent thinking dimension that was more focused on challenging the leader and asserting own views. The factor was therefore named 'initiative'. The new followership measure had a Cronbach's alpha of .793 for the total scale, and .872 (initiative) and .591 (independent thinking) for the respective subscales. The revised followership measure indicated acceptable fit indices (refer to the fit statistics for followership revised in Table 4.1). The instrument was used in its revalidated form in further analyses in this study.

In relation to the first aim of the study, the results presented indicate that the ALQ and PCQ can be regarded as measuring equivalent to the original structure of the instruments when applied to the present large South African sample. Kelley's followership measure had to be modified to be used in further analysis as the original factor structure of the instrument could not be duplicated in this study.

In pursuance of the second aim of the study, the bivariate relationships between the three constructs (authentic leadership, PsyCap, and followership) and their dimensions were calculated by means of Pearson product-moment correlation. The correlation results are shown in Table 4.5.

In Table 4.5, it can be seen that the scale scores of authentic leadership and PsyCap correlated with each other ($r = .34$), representing a common variance of 11.56% between the variables. This is regarded as a low correlation, indicating a small relationship. The correlations between the subscales of the ALQ and the subscales of the PCQ, varying between .13 and .35 (between 3.9% and 12.25% common variance) are regarded as negligible to low relationships. The same can be said of the relationships between the total score on ALQ and the subscales of the PCQ.

It was concluded that the relationships between the scores on the ALQ and on the PCQ are not strong, but can be described as definite, but small. Next, a multiple regression analysis was performed to establish the proportion of variance in PsyCap that was explained by the authentic leadership dimensions.

Table 4.6 indicates that the dimensions of authentic leadership explain a combined 11% of the variance in the total PsyCap score ($R^2 = .11$, $F(4, 642) = 20.55$, $p < .01$). When consulting the beta

Table 4.5 Results of correlational analysis between the dimensions of authentic leadership and PsyCap ($N = 647$)

Variable	1	2	3	4	5	6	7	8	9
Authentic leadership									
1. Transparency	—								
2. Moral/ethical	.78	—							
3. Balanced processing	.75	.78	—						
4. Self-awareness	.80	.76	.82	—					
5. Authentic leadership total	.92	.90	.90	.93	—				
PsyCap									
6. Efficacy	.35	.31	.29	.30	.34	—			
7. Hope	.24	.20	.19	.24	.24	.59	—		
8. Resilience	.13	.16	.16	.13	.16	.44	.49	—	
9. Optimism	.30	.30	.27	.29	.32	.49	.56	.46	—
10. PsyCap total	.32	.31	.29	.30	.34	.79	.84	.74	.80

Table 4.6 Results of multiple regression analysis with PsyCap total as dependent variable

Independent variables	β	$SE\ \beta$	t	p	R	R^2
(Constant)	4.37	.07	61.41	.00	.34	.11
Transparency	.09	.04	2.19	.03		
Moral/ethical	.06	.04	1.62	.11		
Balanced processing	.02	.04	.40	.69		
Self-awareness	.04	.04	1.04	.30		
$F(4, 642) = 20.55$; $p < .01$; std error of estimate: .482						

Note. *SE* standard error

Table 4.7 Results of correlational analysis between the dimensions of authentic leadership and followership ($N = 647$)

Variable	11	22	33	44	55	66	77
Authentic leadership							
1. Transparency	—						
2. Moral/ethical	.78	—					
3. Balanced processing	.74	.78	—				
4. Self-awareness	.80	.76	.82	—			
5. Authentic leadership total	.92	.90	.90	.93	—		
Followership							
6. Initiative	*.05*	.08	*.06*	*.06*	*.07*	—	
7. Independent thinking	*.01*	*.05*	*.01*	*.01*	*.01*	.35	—
8. Followership total	*.03*	.08	*.04*	*.05*	*.05*	.87	.76

Note. Italicised correlations are not statistically significant at the .01 level. Underlined correlations are statistically significant at the .05 level

coefficients, it can be seen that only the transparency dimension of authentic leadership ($\beta = .09$) explains a unique statistically significant proportion of the variance in PsyCap (at the $p < .05$ level).

The bivariate correlations between the scores on the ALQ and the Kelley followership instrument and their subscales are shown in Table 4.7.

From Table 4.7, it can be seen that the scale and subscale scores of followership and authentic leadership had negligible relationships with each other. This was confirmed in the multiple regression analysis reported in Table 4.8, which indicated that the authentic leadership dimensions explained only 1% of the variance in followership. The explained variance was not statistically significant. Only the moral/ethical dimension of authentic leadership had a significant beta weight ($\beta = .132$) at the $p < .05$ level.

Table 4.8 Results of multiple regression analysis with followership total as dependent variable

Independent variables	β	SE β	*t*	*p*	*R*	R^2
(Constant)	4.506	.108	41.753	.000	.09	.01
Transparency	−.069	.061	−1.130	.259		
Moral/ethical	.132	.060	2.210	.027		
Balanced processing	−.041	.058	−.711	.477		
Self-awareness	.025	.057	.430	.667		
$F(4, 642) = 1.583$; $p = .177$; std error of estimate: .731						

Note. *SE* standard error

Table 4.9 Results of the t-tests for gender differences for the authentic leadership variable

	M					
Dimensions	Male	Female	*t*	*df*	*p*	Cohen's *d*
Transparency	2.94	2.74	2.45	645	.57	
Moral/ethical	3.15	2.99	1.90	645	.92	
Balanced processing	3.05	2.70	4.44	282.99	.00	.44
Self-awareness	2.78	2.54	2.51	645	.06	
Authentic leadership total	2.97	2.75	2.88	645	.46	

Note. *df* degree of freedom

The third aim of the study was to determine whether respondents from different demographic and biographic groups differed in their assessments of the levels of authentic leadership displayed by their superiors. One-way analysis of variance (ANOVA) and product-moment correlation was used as an appropriate means to determine whether such relationships existed. No relationships were found between the scores of occupational groups, educational levels, and English proficiency, on one hand, and ALQ total and subscale scores, on the other.

As indicated in Table 4.9, a significant difference was found between the scores of the two gender groups on the balanced processing subscale of the ALQ. Male respondents perceived their managers as having higher scores on this subscale.

Furthermore, as indicated in Table 4.10, male managers were perceived by the respondents as displaying higher levels of transparency, balanced processing, and self-awareness than female managers.

Table 4.10 Results of the t-tests for manager's gender differences on the authentic leadership variable

	M					
Dimensions	Male	Female	*t*	*df*	*p*	Cohen's *d*
Transparency	2.90	2.70	2.92	623	.01	.23
Moral/ethical	3.14	2.95	2.78	645	.70	
Balanced processing	2.94	2.66	3.93	631	.00	.31
Self-awareness	2.71	2.51	2.54	621	.04	.20
Authentic leadership total	2.92	2.71	3.21	645	.10	

Note. *df* degree of freedom

No significant correlation was found between the age of respondents and ALQ scale or subscale scores allocated to their managers. These findings should be interpreted with care, as the large sample will tend to increase the number of significant differences and correlations.

Discussion

Discussion Relating to the Measurement Equivalence of the Measurement Instruments

The reliability coefficients of the ALQ and dimensions in this study are aligned with the results from previous studies. The internal reliability of the composite ALQ measure was high at α = .953, with the coefficients for the dimensions ranging between .810 and .904. In a South African study, Roux (2010) reported α = .92 for the composite ALQ, and coefficients for the dimensions ranging from .69 (balanced processing) to .85 (self-awareness).

It may be concluded that the ALQ shows configural equivalence between the original instrument and the South African healthcare industry sample used in this study. This is consistent with the findings of Kotzé and Nel (2015) and Stander et al. (2015). Nonetheless, the lack of evidence for configural equivalence found by Munyaka (2012) needs to be taken into account. The ALQ has not been extensively used in South Africa, and further studies should include validation of the construct until such time as its factor structure can be repeatedly confirmed in the South African context. Furthermore, qualitative approaches should be used to truly understand leadership authenticity from the multicultural South African perspective. It may be found that South Africans attribute more characteristics to authentic leaders, such as those that have been found in another African country, namely Ghana (Owusu-Bempah, 2012: 39), examples being 'god-fearing' and 'objectivity and justice'. Similarly, the predominant traditional leadership prototype of males may lead to the addition of further male-specific authentic leadership characteristics in the South African context, or to a decrease in focus on characteristics such as transparency (which is viewed by some as a weakness).

The results indicate that the PCQ measurement instrument can confidently be used in the South African context owing to the good fit of the sample data on the original structure of the instrument. The PCQ measuring the respondents' levels of PsyCap maintained its original four-dimensional factor structure (Luthans et al., 2007) in this study. This is consistent with international findings (Avey, Wernsing, & Luthans, 2008; Caza et al., 2010), as well as South African findings (Görgens-Ekermans & Herbert, 2013; Simons & Buitendach, 2013). The results of the reliability analysis were in agreement with the analyses reported in US and non-US samples.

The followership instrument, as developed by Kelley (1992), consists of a two-factor structure with the dimensions of active engagement and independent critical thinking. In this study, a two-dimensional factor structure was found for the instrument. EFA advocated the loss of 11 of the 20 items of the questionnaire. Furthermore, responses of the members of the sample did not yield the factors as presented in the original factor structure. Therefore, one of the factors was renamed 'initiative' to describe the themes of doing more than is expected, championing new ideas, and helping colleagues. The new factor structure still included the minimum number of items (i.e. three or more items per dimension). The newly conceptualised factor structure did demonstrate acceptable fit statistics for the sample.

As an organisational consultant and facilitator, Kelley administered the followership instrument to large numbers of convenience samples (VanDoren, 1998). VanDoren (1998) reported personal communication with Kelley during which Kelley indicated that the questionnaire was developed for exploratory purposes. Hence, there is a need to determine the reliability and validity of the instrument.

This study attempted to validate Kelley's (1992) followership instrument by not only utilising EFA as per previous research but also confirming the factor structure with CFA. An interpretable factor structure was found that demonstrated acceptable levels of fit for the healthcare industry sample. However, more than half of the items were deleted, and therefore the original factor structure of the instrument could not be confirmed. Schein (2015) warns against measuring complex constructs that may not be fully understood with only a limited number of items. Hence, it appears that the followership instrument would need to reconceptualise the construct and its dimensions to clearly discern followership behaviour from follower affect and attitude. This also suggests a need—in relation to authentic leadership research—for an authentic followership questionnaire to be developed.

Discussion Relating to the Correlates of Authentic Leadership

Avolio et al. (2004) suggested that authentic leadership is linked to followers' attitudes and behaviours. Empirical research has confirmed this link, and statistically significant relationships between authentic leadership and PsyCap have been reported (Avolio & Luthans, 2006; Avolio et al., 2004; Caza et al., 2010). With regard to the sequential relationship between authentic leadership and PsyCap, standardised path coefficients were reported for the structural equation models as .67 (Rego et al., 2012) and .37 (Amunkete & Rothmann, 2015).

The findings of this study confirm the reported relationship between authentic leadership and PsyCap. The correlation coefficient (r = .34) indicated a small, statistically significant correlation. The relationships between the dimensions of the variables mostly fell within the low correlation category (r = .13 to .34). Furthermore, the dimensions of authentic leadership explained a combined 11% of the variance in PsyCap, with transparency explaining the biggest proportion of the variance. Munyaka (2012) reported that 20.4% of the variance in PsyCap was explained by authentic leadership.

The results of this study indicated that authentic leadership and the measure of followership were not associated at the $p < .01$ level. The slight variance explained in followership was as a result of the moral/ethical dimension of authentic leadership behaviour. This is consistent with Sergiovanni's (1992) view that the moral component of leadership brings out the best in followers. As the sample size of this study is quite large, correlation coefficients smaller than 0.20, such as those found between authentic leadership and followership, were not considered to have useful statistical or practical significance.

Conceptually, it can be expected that there would be a relationship between leadership and followership behaviour. George (2003) stated that followers who are led by authentic leaders feel more empowered and take greater ownership of their work—both behaviours that are seen as part of exemplary followership. However, authors have suggested that specific leadership styles may be more effective for some followers than others (Conger & Kanungo, 1998; Pillai & Meindl, 1998) and hence, the follower's characteristics would act as a moderator of the influence of the leader. On the other hand, Zhu et al. (2009) found that the perceptions of the qualities, attributes, and characteristics of followers by the leader and the follower may have an impact on the effectiveness of leadership.

This study, quite contrarily, found no support for the statement of Avolio et al. (2004) that authentic leadership is linked to the followers' attitudes and behaviours. There may be various explanations for this finding, possibly including the impact of the follower characteristics on the followers' perceptions of authentic leadership (Leroy, Anseel, Gardner, & Sels, 2015; Shamir, 2007), the situational context in which authentic leadership behaviours are displayed (Avolio et al., 2004; Chan et al., 2005) or personal and social identification with the leader (Snyder, Irving, & Anderson, 1991). Furthermore, the absence of a significant association between authentic leadership and followership may also be attributed to the conceptualisation of the followership construct and instrument. Further studies utilising different conceptualisations of followership may need to be conducted to examine this finding further.

Discussion Relating to the Biographical and Demographic Differences Relating to Authentic Leadership

With respect to age, tenure in the organisation and working experience, this study found no relationship with perceived authentic leadership behaviour. There was also no significant relationship between the respondents' reporting period to their current manager and their perceptions of the manager's authentic leadership behaviours.

With regard to gender, male respondents perceived a higher level of balanced processing behaviour in their leaders than did female respondents. Stereotypical perceptions of men include that they value objectivity and rational, thoughtful perspectives. It may therefore be that men are more aware of the leader's balanced processing abilities and place more value on these abilities than females do, and therefore would provide a higher rating for this dimension. Another noteworthy finding is that male leaders were rated by the respondents as having higher levels of transparency, balanced processing, and self-awareness. Where male leaders were found to display higher levels of authentic leadership behaviours, the finding may have been influenced by South African cultural values that tend to value the male role and masculinity in leadership slightly more than the female role (Booysen & Van Wyk, 2008).

Limitations of the Study

The respondents were from only one organisation and answered the questionnaire at one point in time. The cross-sectional nature of the data therefore limited the causal inferences that could be made about the relationships between the variables. For that reason, these relationships remained exploratory and could be studied further with repeated measures, including other latent variables such as peer reports, or longitudinal research designs. As the research questionnaire included in excess of 60 items, mono-method response bias may have influenced the participant reactions. The researchers endeavoured to limit this by including reverse-scored items. In addition, as recommended by Podsakoff, MacKenzie, Lee, and Podsakoff (2003), the data analysis included an EFA to determine how the items group together. The relatively normal distributions of the data and relatively different distribution of the responses obtained to the different questionnaires also suggest that response bias may have been limited.

Conclusion

In South African organisations, new ways of thinking and management are needed to assist in creating healthy and productive environments for employees (Du Plessis & Barkhuizen, 2011; Luthans, Van Wyk, & Walumbwa, 2004). This study provides an understanding of the relationship between authentic leadership and followership behaviours, a first for South African research. This relationship has not been explored before and hence, the finding that there is only a slight relationship between these two variables offers opportunities for further research.

The results of this study indicated that the followership construct and instrument, as conceptualised by Kelley (1988, 1992), may not be a fully reliable and valid measure of followership behaviour in the workplace. When the items of the followership instrument were subjected to an informal expert review, the experts perceived that the instruments measured components of initiative, personality factors, proactivity, critical thinking and other behaviours. However, it was not clear to the experts how these components linked together to accurately describe followership behaviours in the workplace.

With regard to the differences in authentic leadership based on biographical and demographic variables, this study found only slight differences. The slight differences can be interpreted to be consistent with the male-oriented leadership culture in South Africa. However, these differences can be explored in further studies in relation to personality and cultural factors. This can be especially valuable in South Africa and multicultural international organisations.

References

Amunkete, S., & Rothmann, S. (2015). Authentic leadership, psychological capital, job satisfaction and intention to leave in state-owned enterprises. *Journal of Psychology in Africa, 25*(4), 271–281.

Avey, J. B., Avolio, B. J., & Luthans, F. (2011). Experimentally analyzing the impact of leader positivity on follower positivity and performance. *The Leadership Quarterly, 22*(2), 282–294.

Avey, J. B., Wernsing, T. S., & Luthans, F. (2008). Can positive employees help positive organizational change? Impact of psychological capital and emotions on relevant attitudes and behaviors. *The Journal of Applied Behavioral Science, 44*(1), 48–70.

Avolio, B. J., & Gardner, W. L. (2005). Authentic leadership development: Getting to the root of positive forms of leadership. *Leadership Quarterly, 16*, 315–338.

Avolio, B. J., Gardner, W. L., & Walumbwa, F. O. (2007). *Authentic leadership questionnaire (ALQ)* [Measurement instrument]. Retrieved from http://www.mindgarden.com

Avolio, B. J., Gardner, W. L., Walumbwa, F. O., Luthans, F., & May, D. R. (2004). Unlocking the mask: A look at the process by which authentic leaders impact follower attitudes and behaviors. *The Leadership Quarterly, 15*, 801–823.

Avolio, B. J., & Luthans, F. (2006). *The high impact leader: Moments matter in accelerating authentic leadership development.* New York: McGraw-Hill.

Avolio, B. J., & Mhatre, K. H. (2012). Advances in theory and research on authentic leadership. In K. S. Cameron & G. M. Spreitzer (Eds.), *The Oxford handbook of positive organizational scholarship* (pp. 773–783). New York: Oxford University Press.

Avolio, B. J., Walumbwa, F. O., & Weber, T. J. (2009). Leadership: Current theories, research and future directions. *Annual Review of Psychology, 60*, 421–449.

Baker, S. D. (2006). *The effect of leader-follower agreement on team effectiveness.* Unpublished doctoral dissertation, George Washington University, Washington, DC.

Baker, S. D., Mathis, C. J., & Stites-Doe, S. (2011). An exploratory study investigating leader and follower characteristics at US healthcare organizations. *Journal of Managerial Issues, XXIII*(3), 341–363.

Bjugstad, K., Thach, E., Thompson, K., & Morris, A. (2006). A fresh look at followership: A model for matching followership and leadership styles. *Journal of Behavioral and Applied Management, 7*(3), 304–319.

Blanchard, A. L., Welbourne, J., Gilmore, D., & Bullock, A. (2009). Followership styles and employee attachment to the organization. *The Psychologist-Manager Journal, 12*, 111–131.

Booysen, L. A. E., & Van Wyk, M. W. (2008). Culture and leadership in South Africa. In J. S. Chhokar, F. C. Brodbeck, & R. J. House (Eds.), *Culture and leadership across the world: The GLOBE book of in-depth studies in 25 societies* (pp. 431–474). London: Lawrence Erlbaum Associates.

Caza, A., Bagozzi, R. P., Woolley, L., Levy, L., & Barker Caza, B. (2010). Psychological capital and authentic leadership: Measurement, gender, and cultural extension. *Asia-Pacific Journal of Business Administration, 2*(1), 53–70.

Caza, A., & Jackson, B. (2011). Authentic leadership. In A. Bryman, D. Collinson, K. Grint, M. Uhl-Bien, & B. Jackson (Eds.), *The SAGE handbook of leadership* (pp. 352–364). London: Sage.

Chan, A. Y. L. H., Hannah, S. T., & Gardner, W. L. (2005). Veritable authentic leadership: Emergence, functioning, and impacts. In W. L. Gardner, B. J. Avolio, & F. O. Walumbwa (Eds.), *Authentic leadership theory and practice: Origins, effects, and development* (Vol. 3, pp. 3–41). New York: Elsevier.

Colangelo, A. J. (2000). *Followership: Leadership styles.* Unpublished doctoral dissertation, The University of Oklahoma, Norman, OK.

Conger, J. A., & Kanungo, R. N. (1998). *Charismatic leadership in organizations.* Thousand Oaks, CA: Sage.

Coxen, L., Van der Vaart, L., & Stander, M. W. (2016). Authentic leadership and organisational citizenship behaviour in the public health care sector: The role of workplace trust. *SA Journal of Industrial Psychology/SA Tydskrif vir Bedryfsielkunde, 42*(1), a1364.

Dawkins, S., Martins, A., Scott, J., & Sanderson, K. (2013). Building on the positives: A psychometric review and critical analysis of the construct of psychological capital. *Journal of Occupational and Organisational Psychology, 86*(3), 348–370.

Du Plessis, Y., & Barkhuizen, N. (2011). Psychological capital, a requisite for organisational performance in South Africa. *South African Journal of Economic and Management Sciences, 15*(1), 16–30.

Eagly, A. H. (2005). Achieving relational authenticity in leadership: Does gender matter? *The Leadership Quarterly, 16*(3), 459–474.

Gardiner, R. A. (2011). A critique of the discourse of authentic leadership. *International Journal of Business and Social Science, 2*(15), 99–104.

Gardner, W. L., Avolio, B. J., Luthans, F., May, D. R., & Walumbwa, F. (2005). 'Can you see the real me?' A self-based model of authentic leader and follower development. *The Leadership Quarterly, 16*, 343–372.

Gardner, W. L., & Schermerhorn, J. R. (2004). Unleashing individual potential: Performance gains through positive organizational behavior and authentic leadership. *Organizational Dynamics, 33*, 270–281.

George, W. (2003). *Authentic leadership: Rediscovering the secrets to creating lasting value*. San Francisco, CA: Jossey-Bass.

Görgens-Ekermans, G., & Herbert, M. (2013). Psychological capital: Internal and external validity of the psychological capital questionnaire (PCQ-24) on a South African sample. *SA Journal of Industrial Psychology, 39*(2), 12 pages.

Greyvenstein, H., & Cilliers, F. (2012). Followership's experiences of organisational leadership: A systems psychodynamic perspective. *SA Journal of Industrial Psychology/SA Tydskrif vir Bedryfsielkunde, 38*(2), Art. #1001, 10 pp. Retrieved from https://doi.org/10.4102/sajip.v38i2.1001.

Groenewald, L. (2016). *The South African business ethics survey 2016* [Research report]. The Ethics Institute of South Africa. Retrieved from http://www.tei.org.za/index.php/resources/research-reports

Hair, J. F., Black, W. C., Babin, B. J., & Anderson, R. E. (2010). *Multivariate data analysis: A global perspective*. Upper Saddle River, NJ: Pearson Education.

Harter, S., Waters, P. L., Whitesell, N. R., & Kastelic, D. (1998). Level of voice among female and male high school students: Relational context, support, and gender orientation. *Developmental Psychology, 34*(5), 892–901.

Hartmann, H. (2010). Capitalism, patriarchy and job segregation by sex. In J. Goodman (Ed.), *Global perspectives on gender and work: Readings and interpretations* (pp. 54–62). Plymouth, UK: Rowman & Littlefield Publishers.

Hofstede, G. (2014). *Countries*. Hofstede Centre. Retrieved from https://geert-hofstede.com/south-africa.html

Ilies, R., Morgeson, F. P., & Nahrgang, J. D. (2005). Authentic leadership and eudaemonic well-being: Understanding leader–follower outcomes. *The Leadership Quarterly, 16*, 373–394.

Joshanloo, M., Wissing, M. P., Khumalo, I. P., & Lamers, S. M. (2013). Measurement invariance of the mental health continuum-short form (MHC-SF) across three cultural groups. *Personality and Individual Differences, 55*(7), 755–759.

Kelley, R. E. (1988). In praise of followers. *Harvard Business Review, 66*(6), 142–148.

Kelley, R. E. (1992). *The power of followership: How to create leaders people want to follow and followers who lead themselves.* New York: Doubleday.

Kelley, R. E. (2008). Rethinking followership. In R. E. Riggio, I. Chaleff, & J. Lipman-Blumen (Eds.), *The art of followership: How great followers create great leaders and organizations* (pp. 5–15). San Francisco: Jossey-Bass.

Kets de Vries, M., & Balazs, K. (2011). The shadow side of leadership. In A. Bryman, D. Collinson, K. Grint, M. Uhl-Bien, & B. Jackson (Eds.), *The SAGE handbook of leadership* (pp. 380–392). London: Sage.

Kotzé, M., & Nel, P. (2015). The influence of trait emotional intelligence on authentic leadership. *SA Journal of Human Resource Management/SA Tydskrif vir Menslikehulpbronbestuur, 13*(1), Art. #716, 9 pp.

Leroy, H., Anseel, F., Gardner, W. L., & Sels, L. (2015). Authentic leadership, authentic followership, basic need satisfaction, and work role performance: A cross-level study. *Journal of Management, 41*(6), 1677–1697.

Little, T. D., Cunningham, W. A., Shahar, G., & Widaman, K. F. (2002). To parcel or not to parcel: Exploring the question, weighing the merits. *Structural Equation Modeling, 9*(2), 151–173.

Luthans, F., & Avolio, B. J. (2003). Authentic leadership: A positive developmental approach. In K. S. Cameron, J. E. Dutton, & R. E. Quinn (Eds.), *Positive organizational scholarship: Foundations of a new discipline* (pp. 241–258). San Francisco: Berrett-Koehler.

Luthans, F., Avolio, B. J., Avey, J. B., & Norman, S. M. (2007). Positive psychological capital: Measurement and relationship with performance and satisfaction. *Personnel Psychology, 60*, 541–572.

Luthans, F., Norman, S. M., Avolio, B. J., & Avey, J. B. (2008). The mediating role of psychological capital in the supportive organizational climate-employee performance relationship. *Journal of Organizational Behavior, 29*(2), 219–238.

Luthans, F., Van Wyk, R., & Walumbwa, F. O. (2004). Recognition and development of hope for South African organizational leaders. *Leadership & Organization Development Journal, 25*(6), 512–527.

Luthans, F., Youssef, C. M., & Avolio, B. J. (2007a). *Psychological capital: Developing the human capital edge.* Oxford, UK: Oxford University Press.

Luthans, F., Youssef, C. M., & Avolio, B. J. (2007b). Psychological capital: Investing and developing positive organizational behavior. In D. L. Nelson & C. L. Cooper (Eds.), *Positive organizational behavior* (pp. 9–24). Thousand Oaks, CA: Sage.

Martin, P., & Barnard, A. (2013). The experience of women in male-dominated occupations: A constructivist grounded theory inquiry. *SA Journal of Industrial Psychology/SA Tydskrif vir Bedryfsielkunde, 39*(2), Art. #1099, 12 pp.

Meade, A. W., & Kroustalis, C. M. (2005). *Problems with item parceling for confirmatory factor analysis tests of measurement invariance of factor loadings.* Proceedings of the 20th annual conference of the Society for Industrial and Organizational Psychology, Los Angeles, CA.

Meindl, J. R., Ehrlich, S. B., & Dukerich, J. M. (1985). The romance of leadership. *Administrative Science Quarterly, 30*, 78–102.

Muchiri, M. K. (2011). Leadership in context: A review and research agenda for sub-Saharan Africa. *Journal of Occupation and Organizational Psychology, 84*, 440–452.

Munyaka, S. A. (2012). *The relationship between authentic leadership, psychological capital, psychological climate, team commitment and intention to quit in a manufacturing organisation.* Unpublished doctoral dissertation, Nelson Mandela Metropolitan University, Port Elizabeth, South Africa.

Northouse, P. G. (2004). *Leadership: Theory and practice* (3rd ed.). Thousand Oaks, CA: Sage.

Owusu-Bempah, J. (2012). Bestowing authentic leadership: A comparative study of two organisations in Ghana. *International Journal of Business and Management, 7*(19), 31–44.

Pillai, R., & Meindl, J. R. (1998). Context and charisma: A 'meso' level examination of the relationship of organic structure, collectivism, and crisis to charismatic leadership. *Journal of Management, 24*, 643–671.

Podsakoff, P. M., MacKenzie, S. B., Lee, J. Y., & Podsakoff, N. P. (2003). Common method biases in behavioural research: A critical review of the literature and recommended remedies. *Journal of Applied Psychology, 88*, 879–903.

Potter, E. H., III, & Rosenbach, W. E. (2006). Followers as partners: The spirit of leadership. In W. E. Rosenbach & R. L. Taylor (Eds.), *Contemporary issues in leadership* (6th ed., pp. 143–158). Boulder, CO: WestView Press.

Rego, A., Sousa, F., Marques, C., & Pina e Cunha, M. (2012). Authentic leadership promoting employees' psychological capital and creativity. *Journal of Business Research, 65*(3), 429–437.

Roux, S. (2010). *The relationship between authentic leadership, optimism, self-efficacy and work engagement: An exploratory study.* Unpublished Master's thesis, University of Stellenbosch, Stellenbosch, South Africa.

Schein, E. H. (2015). Organizational psychology then and now: Some observations. *Annual Review of Organizational Psychology and Organizational Behavior, 2*(1), 1–19.

Schoeman, C. (2012). *How ethical is South Africa? Ethical living.* Retrieved from http://www.ethicsmonitor.co.za/Articles/064-065.pdf

Sergiovanni, T. (1992). *Moral leadership.* San Francisco: Jossey-Bass.

Shamir, B. (2007). From passive recipients to active coproducers: Followers' roles in the leadership process. In B. Shamir, R. Pillai, & M. Uhl-Bien (Eds.), *Follower-centered perspectives on leadership: A tribute to the memory of James R. Meindl* (pp. ix–xxxix). Greenwich, CT: Inform Age.

Simons, J. C., & Buitendach, J. H. (2013). Psychological capital, work engagement and organisational commitment amongst call centre employees in South Africa. *SA Journal of Industrial Psychology, 39*(2), 12 pp.

Snyder, C. R., Irving, L. M., & Anderson, J. R. (1991). Hope and health: Measuring the will and the ways. In C. R. Snyder & D. R. Forsyth (Eds.), *The handbook of social and clinical psychology: The health perspective* (pp. 285–307). Elmsford, NY: Pergamon Press.

Stander, F. W., De Beer, L. T., & Stander, M. W. (2015). Authentic leadership as a source of optimism, trust in the organisation and work engagement in the public health care sector. *South African Journal of Human Resource Management, 13*(1), 1–12.

Stöber, J. (2001). The social desirability scale-17 (SDS-17): Convergent validity, discriminant validity, and relationship with age. *European Journal of Psychological Assessment, 17*(3), 222–232.

Tanoff, G. F., & Barlow, C. B. (2002). Leadership and followership: Same animal, different spots? *Consulting Psychology Journal: Practice and Research, 54*(3), 157–167.

Treviño, L. K., & Brown, M. E. (2007). Ethical leadership: A developing construct. In C. L. Cooper & D. Nelson (Eds.), *Positive organizational behavior* (pp. 101–116). Thousand Oaks, CA: Sage.

Valchev, V. H., Nel, J. A., Van de Vijver, F. J. R., Meiring, D., De Bruin, G. P., & Rothmann, S. (2012). Similarities and differences in implicit personality concepts across ethnocultural groups in South Africa. *Journal of Cross-Cultural Psychology, 44*(3), 365–388. https://doi.org/10.1177/0022022112443856.

Van der Vaart, L., Stander, M. W., & Rothmann, S. (2015). *The validation of the authentic leadership inventory (ALI).* Unpublished manuscript, Optentia Research Focus Area. North-West University, Vanderbijlpark, South Africa. Retrieved from http://www.ianrothmann.com/download.php?conferenceid=37

VanDoren, E. (1998). *The relationship between leadership/followership in staff nurses and employment setting*. Unpublished Master's thesis, Western Michigan University, Kalamazoo, MI.

Walumbwa, F. O., Avolio, B. J., Gardner, W. L., Wernsing, T. S., & Peterson, S. J. (2008). Authentic leadership: Development and validation of a theory-based measure. *Journal of Management, 34*, 89–126.

Walumbwa, F. O., Peterson, S. J., Avolio, B. J., & Hartnell, C. A. (2010). An investigation of the relationships among leader and follower psychological capital, service climate, and job performance. *Personnel Psychology, 63*(4), 937–963.

Woolley, L., Caza, A., & Levy, L. (2011). Authentic leadership and follower development: Psychological capital, positive work climate, and gender. *Journal of Leadership & Organizational Studies, 18*(4), 438–448.

Zhu, W., Avolio, B. J., & Walumbwa, F. O. (2009). Moderating role of follower characteristics with transformational leadership and follower work engagement. *Group & Organization Management, 34*(5), 590–619.

5

A Model for Positive Leadership in Argentinean Firms

Lucas Monzani

Two hundred years after its birth as a nation, Argentina is still a fascinating enigma for leadership and management scholars worldwide. Argentina has the 10th largest territory in the world, vast fertile lands and large reserves of strategic natural resources. However, for the past hundred years, Argentina has been entrapped in a vicious cycle of economic collapse and recovery, which prevented this nation from sustaining veritable growth. Is Argentina truly 'doomed to succeed', or does such cyclic failure just provide evidence of destructive leadership practices?

In this chapter, I will attempt an answer by applying recent developments in leadership theory to the Argentinean context. It is important to signal from the very start of this chapter one major caveat emptor; quantitative empirical research regarding leadership in Argentinean organisations is almost non-existent. Excluding some noteworthy exceptions (Omar & Salessi, 2016; Perugini, Laura, & Solano, 2013), Argentinean management scholars seem apathetic towards evidence-based management. Gantman and Fernández Rodríguez's (2008) review states that

L. Monzani (✉)
Graduate School of Management, Plymouth University, Plymouth, UK

© The Author(s) 2018
D. Cotter-Lockard (ed.), *Authentic Leadership and Followership*, Palgrave Studies in Leadership and Followership, https://doi.org/10.1007/978-3-319-65307-5_5

management scholars treat leadership as a somewhat trivial matter for organisations, and more appropriate for other social disciplines such as sociology and political science. My own review of the authentic leadership literature in Argentina agrees with Gantman and Fernández Rodríguez's (2008) conclusion. Not surprisingly, the studies that emerged from my literature review rely heavily on Weber's (1924) conceptualisation of charisma to explore, qualitatively, the attributes of both historical and contemporary political leaders such as Juan Manual de Rosas (Operé, 2010), Juan Domingo Peron (Decarli, 2015) and Ricardo Alfonsin (González, 1986). Similarly, Raigoza (2014) recently deconstructed the leadership style of former presidents Nestor and Cristina (Fernandez de) Kirchner. Furthermore, there are virtually no scholarly works aimed at organisational leadership in Argentinean firms. Thus, this chapter seeks to understand organisational leadership in Argentina and also provide Argentinean management scholars with a framework that guides future empirical research.

Given the importance that Argentinean scholars paid to leader charisma, in this chapter I will unpack charismatic leadership in Argentina, using both pseudo- and authentic transformational leadership theories (Barling, Christie, & Turner, 2008; Bass & Steidlmeier, 1999). Moreover, I propose as the main thesis of this chapter that in the past 70 years, Argentinean leadership has been 'intoxicated with power' (Owen & Davidson, 2009). To support this thesis, I will draw from Padilla, Hogan, and Kaiser's (2007) 'toxic triangle' model, which consists of a conductive environment, destructive leaders, and susceptible followers. As antithesis, I will present the model of positive leadership developed by Monzani, Braun, and van Dick (2016) to propose a more positive leadership alternative adjusted to Argentinean context. The main idea behind Monzani et al.'s model is that authentic transformational leadership occurs when three 'spheres of virtue' overlap (i.e., personal, relational and organisational spheres). Thus, by opposing vice with virtue, I hope to give Argentinean leaders new insights on how to break the vicious cycle that keeps Argentina struggling with itself.

In this chapter, I first describe the Argentinean business ecosystem and how it is conductive for corporate Machiavellianism (Marshall, Baden, & Guidi, 2013). Second, I illustrate Argentinean destructive leadership in both public and private organisations. In Argentina, corporate and political life are so entangled that very frequently we find corporate leaders running for office to advance their corporate agenda, or political leaders who rely on frontmen to build conglomerates while in power to retain influence after they leave office (Losada, 2007). I shall adopt a neutral political view to describe the pseudo-transformational behaviours of two former presidents: Carlos Saul Menem and Cristina (Fernandez de) Kirchner and their respective 'frontmen' (Alfredo Yabrán and Lazaro Baez, respectively). Third, I will use insights from 'the romance of leadership' framework (Meindl, Ehrlich, & Dukerich, 1985) and Identity Leadership theory (Haslam, Reicher, & Platow, 2011; Steffens et al., 2014) to theorise further about the susceptibility of the Argentinean population to such destructive leadership. I will conclude by applying Monzani et al.'s model of positive leadership to Argentina's business context.

Argentina: A Conductive Environment for Corporate Machiavellianism

'We are doomed to succeed' – Eduardo Duhalde (2009)

Marshall et al.'s (2013) notion of corporate Machiavellianism explains well the collective behaviour of key economic and political actors in the Argentinean context. In short, I define corporate Machiavellianism as the use of unethical means to attain a priori legitimate outcomes such as increasing corporate profits or protecting worker's rights. Corporate Machiavellianism is not limited to business corporations but includes other corporations as well, such as political parties and trade unions. Some examples of corporate Machiavellianism involve firms bribing governmental officials to become state contractors, fiscal evasion or even abusing a dominant market position to impose leonine fees on its customers. Examples of corporate Machiavellianism in trade unions involve using the threat of national strikes to impose a union's unilateral terms in a collective agreement, or even to encourage union members to engage in counterproductive work behaviours (e.g. sabotage, voluntary absenteeism, workplace bullying, or abusive supervision towards non-union members).

Unlike the United States, where the private sector operates with relative independence from the federal government, in several occasions throughout its history, the Argentinean federal government assumed a de facto role in the corporate governance of private firms. Such state interventionism occurred regardless of the government's political orientation, or even whether the government was democratically elected, or rose to power through a *coup d'état*. The latest episode of state interventionism occurred in 2008, as a result of a forced nationalisation of Argentine's private pension funds. Such funds held a significant volume of stock options in Argentina's largest firms as part of their investment portfolio. By seizing control of the pension funds, Cristina Kirchner exploited a legal loophole that enabled her administration to place 'representatives' on these companies' boards. Although per official discourse such representatives were there to hold 'corporate greed' in check, the opposing political factions referred to such representatives as glorified political commissaries with no real leadership expertise. Macroeconomic data for the period 2007–2015 show that this policy of state intromission in Argentinean firms profoundly harmed Argentina's industry and dynamited its business climate. Industrial production rates fell drastically and so did the volume of exported goods (Carmo, 2012). In turn, such reduction in exported goods decreased Argentina's central bank's strategic reserves (USD), unleashing a rampant inflationary spiral that devaluated Argentina's currency, which is still uncontrolled. It is to be noted, however, that Argentina's prior experiments with 'free market' policies (Friedman, 1962) did not result in sustainable growth, nor a spillover of wealth. Whenever unchecked, Argentina's largest firms turn to corporate Machiavellianism to increase their profit margins, at the expense of workers, and even its customers.

Another key difference from the United States, in which worker's unions are relatively independent of each other, is that Argentina's worker representation is centralised in the 'Confederación General del Trabajo' (or *CGT*). The CGT, in theory, exists to coordinate workers' demands across sectors and increase workers' collective bargaining power against management. Although its mandate resembles other national trade unions worldwide, the CGT is a powerful actor in Argentina's political ecosystem, with an agenda that exceeds labour relations and spills over into the political arena (Natalucci, 2015). The CGT's narrative sees this corporation as 'the backbone' of the Peronist party (i.e. a party originally committed to protecting workers' rights). Ironically, during the past 30 years, the CGT's collective leadership behaviours can be truthfully described as 'lacking a backbone', as CGT's leadership compromised with whomever necessary to protect their selfish interests. For example, in the early 1990s, CGT's leadership forged an alliance with Carlos Menem (1989–1999), a neoliberalist president (Smith, 1991). The CGT remained idle throughout Menem's presidency, taking no collective action against a systematic erosion of workers' quality of work life (Fair, 2008). Similarly, CGT's leadership remained inactive during the positive economic cycle of Nestor Kirchner's term, but became increasingly active during Cristina Kirchner's presidency, when an impoverished administration was unable to appease its demands (Natalucci, 2015).

I posit that the unique context in which Argentinean firms operate, such as the frequent state interventions in private firms and the CGT's political manoeuvring, fosters a transaction-oriented culture (Burns, 1978; Bass & Avolio, 1994). In theory, under a transaction-oriented culture, economic actors (e.g., firm owners) seek to establish rational negotiations with other actors (e.g. workers, trade unions, the federal government) to negotiate the contributions of each actor to a common goal and a fair share of the rewards (Bass, 1985). Although a transactional culture in not a negative thing per se, whenever actors rely on corporate Machiavellianism to maximise their benefits by any means necessary, a climate of mutual mistrust will emerge. Thus, in such a climate of mistrust, organisational leaders (e.g., firm owners) are likely to assume that their followers are lazy, only motivated by rewards, and in need of constant vigilance. Similarly, in this climate of mistrust, workers are likely to assume that management only cares for selfishly seizing 'the surplus value' of their work. Whereas workers need to rely on collective action to protect their interests, if collective action is orchestrated by agencies that rely on corporate Machiavellianism to impose their political agenda, such as the CGT, everybody loses. Workers become a 'means to an end' and organisational leaders must bear unsustainable labour costs, increasing the mistrust between parties. Moreover, throughout Argentinean history, this climate of mistrust between organisational leaders and their followers enabled political leaders to use charisma to polarise such factions (the 'us vs. them' effect). Because such abuse of charisma can result in many different outcomes for their followers and society at large (Howell & Shamir, 2005), in recent years, leadership scholars raised concerns about the importance of distinguishing between positive forms of charismatic leadership (socialised charismatic, authentic transformational) and destructive charismatic leadership (personalised charismatic, pseudo-transformational; Barling et al., 2008; Bass & Steidlmeier, 1999). Although positive leaders utilise charisma to align their interests and their followers, destructive leaders use their charisma to exploit their followers' fears, highlighting ideological differences between actors, increasing their mutual mistrust.

Destructive Leadership in Argentina

Pseudo-transformational leaders use their charisma to impose their will on the followers and advance their self-serving agendas. More precisely, instead of embodying virtuous, pro-social values in their leadership behaviours, most pseudo-transformational leaders share the primary aspiration to become personal idols. Although pseudo-transformational leaders can be extremely inspiring to some of their supporters, such leadership inevitably has destructive consequences for the organisations (or countries) they lead. Thus, by the use of deceit and emotional manipulation, and also fear and intimidation, these pseudo-transformational leaders pursue the satisfaction of selfish needs instead of caring for the needs of the followers, or serving the common good (Barling et al., 2008).

Carlos Saul Menem's presidency (1989–1999) exemplifies well a neoliberal pseudo-transformational leadership. Menem's campaign slogan contained several promises that portrayed him as a messianic leader (Lasso, 2008). Menem invited voters 'to follow him as he would not disappoint' in leading them toward 'a revolution of productivity that significantly increases workers' wages' (Fair, 2008, p. 2). Once Menem rose to power, his administration quickly abandoned such promises and adopted Friedman's (1962) ideas by privatising virtually all state-owned companies, most of which, although extremely inefficient, provided affordable public services to society's marginal sectors (e.g., water, electricity, railroads, telecommunication). Furthermore, Menem's administration invited large multinational corporations to invest in Argentina, promising a de-regularised market with little or no state oversight (Treisman, 2003). During Menem's presidency, corporate Machiavellianism (as defined above) was commonplace in Argentinean private firms. Either by choice or calculated inaction, Menem's leadership allowed both local and multinational organisations to take advantage of Argentina's dire economic context and use it to severely erode workers' labour conditions (e.g., reduction in salaries, undocumented labour contracts, unpaid extra-time). Similarly, instead of using Argentina's strategic reserves to reinforce the local industry and protect it against the rising Asian giants, Menem's foreign trade policies enabled industrial dumping. In short, Menem's presidency was destructive as his calculated inaction led to an economic, political and even social meltdown that reached critical mass in 2001, once Menem had already left office (Carranza, 2005).

Although several Argentinean businessmen illegally benefitted from a 'friendship' with Carlos Saul Menem, Alfredo Yabrán was his biggest ally in Argentina's corporate environment. Yabrán was an obscure businessman whose fortune skyrocketed during Menem's administration. Operating within the shadows, Yabrán acquired many of the publicly owned firms that Menem privatised, such as the national mail system, which earned him the name of 'the postman' among Argentinean businessmen. Anecdotal accounts affirm that he exerted a highly personalised leadership, ruling his holdings through fear and intimidation. For example, the journalist who first exposed Yabrán's image, in an investigative article that denounced his illegal dealings with the state, was found dead shortly after the article was published. Ironically, a few months after Yabrán was declared as the main suspect in the journalist's murder case, Yabrán's body was found dead in very dubious circumstances.

The pseudo-transformational leadership of Cristina (Fernandez de) Kirchner (2007–2011; 2011–2015) is a paradigmatic case of neo-populism (Piva, 2013). Her husband, Nestor Kirchner, rose to power following Argentina's 2001 meltdown and ruled from 2003 to 2007. After his death, Cristina Kirchner followed him in office for the next two terms. Her administration continued and extended her late husband's policies. Both Nestor and Cristina Kirchner's campaign slogan gravitated around 'developing a productive matrix that fosters social inclusion and redistribution of wealth' (Messina, 2012, p. 77). However, the macroeconomic indicators for 2012 (one year after her first term concluded) showed that by the end of Cristina Kirchner's first term (2007–2011), Argentina had a steady increase in inflation and showed clear indicators of declining industrial activity (Trombetta, 2012). In other words, similarly to Carlos Menem, Nestor and Cristina Kirchner did the exact opposite of what they promised voters during their presidential campaign. Instead of fostering an 'inclusive, productive matrix', her administration centralised Argentina's economic activity, illegally benefitting a close group of businessmen, in what was termed by the opposition as 'friend-oriented capitalism'. However, unlike Carlos Menem's manipulative destructive style which minimised open conflict with other actors, Cristina Kirchner's government fostered a narrative of open aggression and hatred against anyone who opposed her world views. Such ideological persecution was executed by both the mainstream media (owned by her close colluders) and state agencies, using the 'us vs. them' effect to polarise the Argentinean society.

As Carlos Menem had, Nestor and Cristina Kirchner had a number of 'aligned' businessmen, but their closest corporate counterpart was Lazaro Baez. As it occurred with Yabrán, Baez's fortune grew exponentially during the different Kirchner administrations, making him one of Argentina's richest men to date. Baez benefitted from numerous construction contracts funded by taxpayers' money, on many of which he never delivered. Again, witness accounts of an on-going investigation state that Baez's destructive style involves using intimidation, threats and coercion towards their competitors, to the extent of forcing them out of business, or even to sell them their firms to him at a vile price per share.

To summarise, although the charisma of both Carlos Menem and Cristina Kirchner were undeniable, so was their destructive effect on the Argentinean society. Instead of using their charm and high levels of popular support to elevate the Argentinean society, both leaders chose to advance their personal agenda. Furthermore, instead of generating a sense of national identity that reconciled two opposing factions as Nelson Mandela did in South Africa (Crossan, Mazutis, Seijts, & Gandz, 2013; Haslam et al., 2011), Cristina Kirchner's legacy is an even more divided, polarised and violent society. Such destructive leadership deeply affected Argentinean organisational life. The disregard for the law of both Menem and Kirchner and their colluders placed firm owners and organisational leaders between a 'rock and a hard place'; to survive in such a toxic business ecosystem, large numbers of otherwise honest firm owners had to either choose to 'play ball' or choose to go out of business.

Argentineans as Susceptible Followers

Padilla et al. (2007) distinguish two types of susceptible followers, *conformers* and *colluders*. Conformers comply with destructive leaders out of fear or necessity, whereas the colluders actively participate in their leaders' destructive agenda. These two categories describe well the behavioural style of a vast number of the Argentinean population whenever a destructive leader was in power.

The three elements that characterise *conformers* are unmet basic needs, negative self-evaluations and psychological immaturity (Padilla et al., 2007). Unfortunately, before, during and after both Menem's and Kirchner's administration, a large majority of the Argentinean population remained under the poverty line, which means living with unmet basic needs on a permanent basis (i.e., high situational constraints, Becker, 1960). Living and growing in such a context of poverty will most likely result in negative core self-evaluations (Judge, Locke, Durham, & Kluger, 1998). Thus, instead of demanding veritable work opportunities, many Argentinean citizens settled with receiving material rewards (e.g., unemployment benefit plans) in exchange for their vote (an illegal form of vote buying, or clientelism; Brusco, Nazareno, & Stokes, 2004). For example, because the 1989 hyperinflation crisis devastated Argentina's poor and middle-class wealth, these sectors were thrilled to turn a blind eye to Menem's corrupt administration, as long as they enjoyed the spoils of an artificial, unsustainable exchange rate. Ten years later, a favourable global context for commodities allowed Kirchner's administration to implement welfare policies aimed at the most vulnerable sectors of Argentinean society (Pérez & Natalucci, 2010). Argentinean conformers showed their low maturity by entering a spending spree, drawing heavily on credit to live above their means, without considering the severe deprivation that the Argentinean society suffered as a result of both 1989 hyperinflation and the 2001 meltdowns. Although the government maintained an artificially low US dollar, or provided unsustainable and dubious welfare benefits, conformers disengaged from the undeniably unethical behaviours of their pseudo-transformational leaders, providing enough leeway for corporate Machiavellianism to emerge.

Padilla et al. (2007) describe the *colluders* as selfish, ambitious, and also committed to the values and world views of their destructive leaders. As followers, the colluders are much more destructive than conformers, because whereas conformers only passively suffer their destructive leaders, the colluders take action to advance their leaders' agenda. Regarding ambition, during their time in power, Carlos Menem and Cristina Kirchner were surrounded by several colluders who profited significantly from the widespread corruption that characterised these two leaders' administrations. Some examples of Menem's colluders involve former ministers Jose Luis Manzano (Economy), Carlos Vladimiro Corach (Chief of staff) and Alfredo Yabrán as the main laundering agent. Similarly, examples of Kirchner's colluders involve former ministers Alex Kiciloff (Economy), Anibal Fernandez (Chief of staff), and Lazaro Baez as the main laundering agent. A distinctive trait of Kirchner's colluders was the elevated degree of aggression towards opposing factions, best embodied individually by her minister of Commerce, Guillermo Moreno, and socially by some of the social movements aligned with her administration. Not surprisingly, the colluders tend to derail alongside their destructive leaders. For example, when Menem lost power, his control over Argentine's supreme court weakened (Carrio, 2001). As a result, several previously blocked investigations could move forward, eventually finding several of Menem's colluders guilty of abusing taxpayers' money, awarding public contracts to 'friendly' organisations and illegally selling weapons to Ecuador, in a clear violation of a United Nations (UN) resolution. A decade later, Argentina's Federal Justice is investigating Cristina Kirchner and all the colluders mentioned above for almost the same charges for which Menem and his functionaries were sentenced (excluding the arms deals with Ecuador).

Despite the above accounts, the 'toxic triangle model' seems insufficient to explain why Menem's and Cristina Kirchner's conformers remained so loyal and obedient. I believe that such blind obedience could majorly result from what Meindl et al. (1985) termed as 'the romance of leadership'. In short, the 'romance of leadership' is a strong and irrational follower fascination with their charismatic leader, which in many aspects resembles the infatuation stage at the beginning of a romantic relationship. When this phenomenon occurs, the followers tend to idealise their leaders and ignore their shortcomings, even when presented with clear evidence to the contrary (Monzani, Ripoll & Peiro, 2012). Similarly, empirical studies regarding the social identity model of leadership (SIMOL; Hogg, 2001) showed that when a leader is seen by the group that he or she leads as representing, embodying and advancing the shared unique characteristics of such group, the group members will empower their leaders giving them a certain amount of leeway. Some examples of such leeway include being more tolerant when a leader fails to deliver on their promises (Giessner & van Knippenberg, 2008) or acute breaches of procedural justice (Ullrich, Christ, & van Dick, 2009). I propose that leaders with dubious moral standards, such as pseudo-transformational leaders, will abuse such empowerment and use them to advance their selfish agendas, which most likely will result in hubristic leadership behaviours (Owen & Davidson, 2009) and their downfall. Thus, I posit that when theorising about what leadership looks like in the Argentinean context, the effect of leaders' 'identity work' in their followers (Haslam et al., 2011) should be taken into consideration alongside leaders' authenticity.

Rethinking Authentic Transformational Leadership for the Argentinean Context

> If there is a victory in overcoming the enemy, there is a greater victory when a man overcomes himself. Jose de San Martin (1778–1850)

As Hofstede (1980) noted, when the context in which theory is applied differs drastically from where it was formulated, some adjustment is due. Thus, to 'calibrate' current leadership theories to the Argentinean context, I introduce Monzani et al.'s (2016) model of positive leadership (see Fig. 5.1). This model integrates authentic leadership with other leadership approaches such as leader–member exchange (LMX) and SIMOL (Graen & Uhl-Bien, 1995; Hogg, 2001), giving more importance to the followers and context (Haslam et al., 2011).

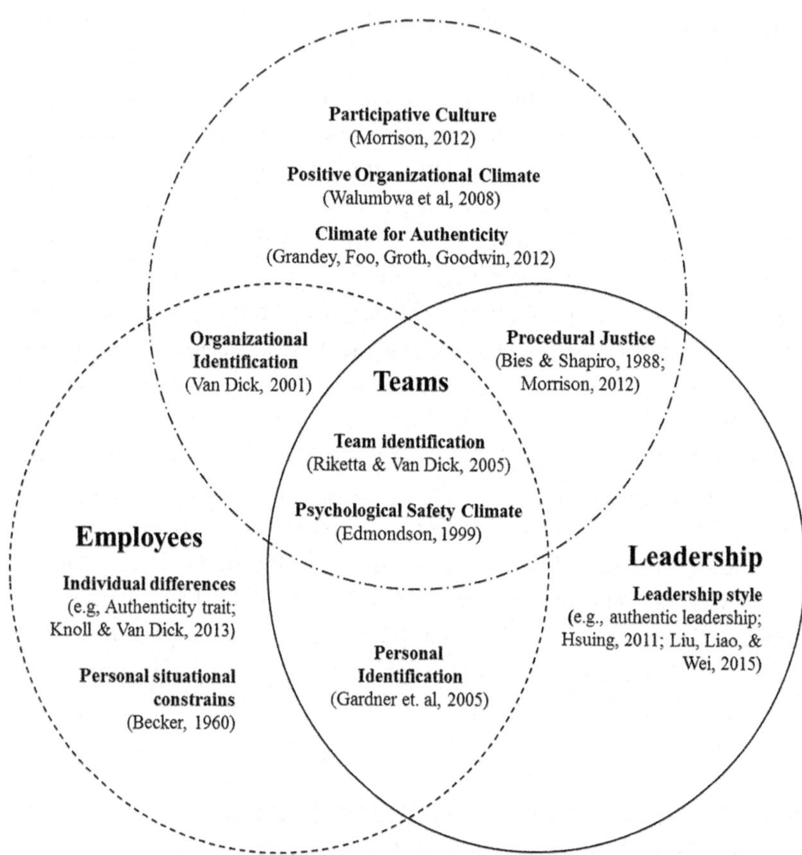

Fig. 5.1 Monzani et al. (2016) model of positive leadership

The first concern of authentic transformational leaders should be to reshape three connected *spheres of virtue* (Monzani et al., 2016). These three spheres are the counterpoint to Padilla et al.'s (2007) toxic triangle, mainly authentic leaders, eudaemonic organisations, and self-determined followers. The main outcome of such positive leadership should be a more virtuous corporate governance (Monzani, Cameron, Crossan, & Wright, 2015). It is to be noted that this model seeks to explain positive organisational leadership and was not designed for political leadership. However, future scholars could extend Monzani et al.'s (2016) positive leadership model to the societal level.

The first sphere of virtue refers to leaders, and it contains (but is not limited to) leader's virtuous characteristics. For example, unlike pseudo-transformational leaders, *authentic* transformational leaders are selfless and therefore use their idealised influence to mobilise followers towards pro-social goals aimed at ensuring the common good of the multiple stakeholders that compose an organisation (e.g. shareholders, employees, customers and society; Davis et al., 1997). Instead of trying to become idols in their followers' eyes, authentic transformational leaders focus on developing their close collaborators to bring the best out of them and prepare them to become leaders in the future (Gardner, Avolio, Luthans, May, & Walumbwa, 2005). As suggested by LMX theory (Graen & Uhl-Bien, 1995), such growth-enhancing relations should not only impact the followers positively but also the leaders (Ilies, Morgeson, & Nahrgang, 2005). For example, some evidence suggests that authentic transformational leadership leads to reduced leaders' work stress and higher satisfaction in the action of leading others (Lopez & Ramos, 2015). Finally, as suggested by Sosik (2006), adopting an authentic transformational leadership style may be a pathway to the development of leader character (Crossan, Gandz, & Seijts, 2012) and its associated organisational performance outcomes (Seijts, Gandz, Crossan, & Reno, 2015).

The second sphere of virtue contains (but is not limited to) those employee's individual characteristics that foster employees' constructive work outcomes (e.g., attitudes and behaviours). For example, trait authenticity (i.e., a psychological state expressing ownership of one's actions and thoughts; Kernis, 2003) positively relates to employee's self-determined behaviours (Ryan & Deci, 2001), such as employee voice (Knoll & Van Dick, 2013). Because authenticity evidences optimal levels of self-esteem, unlike the conformers, the authentic followers do not depend on their leaders to feel good about themselves or satisfy their needs. The authentic followers voluntarily trust and comply with their authentic transformational leaders, because they agree with the leaders' values, respect their ability, and acknowledge their benevolence (Burke, Sims, Lazzara, & Salas, 2007). Hence, whenever the leader no longer represents, nor acts in coherence with the values of the authentic followers, the followers can consciously choose not to comply. In this way, power flows first from the followers to the leader (and not vice versa) and returns to them if the leader no longer represents their collective interests. Furthermore, cultivating authenticity through self-awareness and reflection prevents the followers from becoming susceptible to destructive leaders. Authentic followership is then an essential element of the checks and balances that should exist in any organisation, even when allegedly authentic transformational leaders are in charge. As Lord Acton stated, the exercise of power corrupts (Sturm & Antonakis, 2015), and not all leaders may possess the necessary strength of character to resist such temptation (Sturm & Monzani, in press). If the leaders succumb, it is up to the authentic followers to courageously 'speak truth to power' (Hsiung, 2011; Liu, Liao, & Wei, 2015) and refuse to conform to their pseudo-transformational leaders' agenda.

The third sphere of virtue 'Organisation' comprises organisational-level constructs, both human and non-human. Among the human elements, I include a participative organisational culture (Morrison, 2012) and an overall positive work climate (Walumbwa, Avolio, Gardner, Wernsing, & Peterson, 2007) at different levels of the organisational hierarchy. Instead, I delimit as non-human factors those structural elements that ensure an adequate corporate governance, such as just policies and fair practices. As the non-human element of this model, a comprehensive body of fair policies and practices are essential to ensure that the organisation has mechanisms to prevent the rise of pseudo-transformational leaders, or that good leaders 'break bad' as result of their followers' conformity. Similarly, a just and fair system may prevent the followers from unethically advancing a pseudo-transformational agenda.

Our model also suggests that intersecting spaces connect these three spheres. For example, the organisational sphere of virtue connects with the employee and leader spheres of virtue through its culture and the values (and rewards) that an organisation holds as important. In most organisations, values permeate day-to-day operations so that managers and employees at all levels of the organisation can easily connect and identify with them. The leader sphere of virtue also connects with both the employee and the organisation spheres of virtue, because authentic transformational leaders can not only reshape organisational culture and values but also trigger the followers' authenticity through exemplary role modelling (Leroy, Anseel, Gardner, & Sels, 2015). Finally, the center space overlapping of all three spheres of virtue contains group-specific phenomena that foster excellent team performance (Cameron & Levine, 2006). Some examples are team identification (Riketta & Van Dick,

2005), psychological safety climate (Edmondson, 1999) and a climate for authenticity (Grandey, Foo, Groth, & Goodwin, 2012) understood as a work atmosphere that enables employees to self-express by 'speaking truth to power.' In short, a climate for authenticity allows the followers to raise concerns safely to their supervisors without the fear of a backlash, or negative personal or professional consequences.

Emerging empirical evidence partially supports the proposed positive leadership model. On one hand, laboratory data show that the authentic leaders can self-regulate their behaviour to complement shortcomings in their followers' individual differences and help them attain a more authentic way of functioning by activating their autotelic traits (Nakamura & Csikszentmihalyi, 2002). A laboratory experiment showed that if leaders adopt an authentic feedback style instead of a transactional style, they can significantly increase their followers' performance and satisfaction, especially for those low in conscientiousness or emotional stability (Monzani, Ripoll, & Peiro, 2014b). Regarding attitudes, two complementary studies to the above reported that positive leader practices can elicit positive follower attitudes. For example, authentic leadership elicits a higher loyalty in the followers than transactional leadership, especially if the followers are less agreeable and extroverted (Monzani, Ripoll, & Peiro, 2014a). Similarly, if leaders adjust their goal setting type (directive vs. participative), they can increase their followers' trust in leadership (Monzani, Ripoll, & Peiro, 2015). Although these studies were conducted in Spain (and not in Argentina), both countries share profound cultural similarities, as Argentina was a former Spanish colony.

On the other hand, in a series of field experiments, authentic leadership influenced both the leaders' self-reported attitudes (organisational identification; Monzani, Hernandez Bark, van Dick, & Peiró, 2015) and the followers' behaviours toward the collective in which they belong (e.g., exit, neglect, loyalty; Farrell, 1983; Hirschman, 1970). Such findings are important for this work, because when individuals identify strongly with their organisations, their sense of organisational membership becomes a valued aspect of their self-concept (Van Dick, 2001). For example, when authentic leadership was combined with the follower's organisational identification, it negatively predicted withdrawal behaviours (see Monzani et al., 2016 for a detailed discussion of these findings). Unlike the prior studies, these field experiment studies were conducted in Germany, so it is unclear whether the results will generalise to the Argentinean context.

Undoubtedly, more future empirical research is needed to replicate and extend these findings within an Argentinean organisational setting.

Extending Monzani's et al. (2016) Model into the Political Arena

Finding political leaders who can evidence strength of character and virtuous behaviours within the Argentinean context is extremely difficult, but not impossible. For example, many historians (national and foreign) agree that José de San Martín, one of Argentina's founding fathers, was an authentic transformational leader. His positive influence not only gave Argentina its freedom but also spread throughout Latin America, to earn him the name of 'The liberator of America' (Lynch, 2009). San Martin evidenced character strengths such as transcendence, courage, and drive, and also temperance, humanity and humility throughout, and after the Argentinean independence war (Lynch, 2009). More important for this work is that the integrity of San Martin has stood the test of time, as he managed to deal with the political intrigues of his time and overcome multiple situational pressures, either inside the field of battle or outside it. Hopefully, the rediscovery of Argentina's exemplar leader might inspire future political leaders to put the common good of the nation first, and remember they are only stewards of the *res publica* (the public goods of a nation). In the Argentinean political ecosystem, we would expect to find courageous followers in Argentina's legislative bodies (the Congress and the Senate), as the Congress is seen by politicians at best as a platform to jump into the executive branch. Therefore, to act with virtue, the legislators of a given party should show courage and integrity, 'speaking truth to power', providing advice or eventually halting the selfish agenda of a destructive leader in the executive office. Within a true democratic and republican nation, as Argentina claims to be, such legislative representatives should have some protection to do so. Similarly, an independent judicial system is paramount to ensure that the legislative branch does not collude with the executive branch. Finally, the Argentinean population needs to embrace a culture of democratic participation, where divergent thought is tolerated, analysed, and respectfully discussed.

Conclusion

In this chapter, I explored the vicious cycle that has entrapped Argentina for 200 years. I applied Padilla et al.'s (2007) toxic triangle model to illustrate how an environment tainted by corporate Machiavellianism, pseudo-transformational leadership, and both conforming and colluding followers kept Argentina from reaching its full potential as a nation. Although my theorising was targeted at the Argentinean context, I believe that Argentina is a paradigmatic case which may very well generalise into many other countries in which destructive leadership, under the mask of populism, is on the rise. In the second part, I presented a theoretical framework based on Monzani et al.'s (2016) model of positive leadership and extended it to the political arena. The positive leadership model results from connecting three spheres of virtue (authentic leaders, self-determined followers and ethical corporate governance). I concluded the chapter by presenting empirical evidence that partially supports the model. However, more research is needed to test the model in an Argentinean context. Hopefully, this model will contribute to the structuring of empirical research so that it meaningfully advances the conversation about Argentinean leadership; a discussion that Argentineans owe to themselves to flourish as a modern society.

References

Barling, J., Christie, A., & Turner, N. (2008). Pseudo-transformational leadership: Towards the development and test of a model. *Journal of Business Ethics, 81*, 851–861. https://doi.org/10.1007/s10551-007-9552-8.

Bass, B. M. (1985). *Leadership and performance beyond expectations*. New York: Free Press.

Bass, B. M., & Avolio, B. J. (1994). *Improving organizational effectiveness through transformational leadership*. Thousand Oaks, CA: Sage.

Bass, B. M., & Steidlmeier, P. (1999). Ethics, character, and authentic transformational leadership behavior. *The Leadership Quarterly, 10*, 181–217. https://doi.org/10.1016/S1048-9843(99)00016-8.

Becker, H. S. (1960). Notes on the concept of commitment. *American Journal of Sociology, 66*, 32–40. https://doi.org/10.2307/2773219.

Brusco, V., Nazareno, M., & Stokes, S. C. (2004). Vote buying in Argentina. *Latin American Research Review, 39*, 66–88. https://doi.org/10.1353/lar.2004.0022.

Burke, C. S., Sims, D. E., Lazzara, E. H., & Salas, E. (2007). Trust in leadership: A multi-level review and integration. *The Leadership Quarterly, 18*(6), 606–632. https://doi.org/10.1016/j.leaqua.2007.09.006.

Burns, J. M. (1978). *Leadership*. New York: Harper & Row.

Cameron, K. S., & Levine, M. (2006). *Making the impossible possible: Leading extraordinary performance – The rocky flats story*. San Francisco: Berrett-Koehler.

Carmo, M. (2012, February). Argentina raises new barriers to Brazilian imports. *The Brazilian Economy*, 22–27.

Carranza, M. E. (2005). Poster child or victim of imperialist globalization? Explaining Argentina's December 2001 political crisis and economic collapse. *Latin American Perspectives, 32*, 65–89. Retrieved from http://www.jstor.org/stable/30040267.

Carrio, A. (2001). Argentine Supreme Court ruled "there are no crimes" and former President Menem walked away: That's what friends are for. *Southwestern Journal of Law and Trade in the Americas, 8*, 271–281.

Crossan, M., Gandz, J., & Seijts, G. H. (2012, February). Developing leadership character. *Ivey Business Journal*, 1–7.

Crossan, M. M., Mazutis, D., Seijts, G., & Gandz, J. (2013). Developing character in business programs. *Academy of Management Learning and Education, 12*, 285–305. https://doi.org/10.5465/amle.2011.0024A.

Davis, J. H., Schoorman, F. D., & Donaldson, L. (1997). Toward a stewardship theory of management. *Academy of Management Review, 22*, 20–47. https://doi.org/10.5465/AMR.1997.9707180258.

Decarli, L. D. (2015). Poder y liderazgo peronista: La construcción a partir del 17 de octubre. *Revista Latino-Americana de Historia, 4*(14), 229.

Edmondson, A. (1999). Psychological safety and learning behavior in work teams. *Administrative Science Quarterly, 44*, 350–383. https://doi.org/10.2307/2666999.

Fair, H. (2008). El plan de Convertibilidad y el sindicalismo durante la primera presidencia de Menen. *Trabajo y Sociedad, 9*, 1–17.

Farrell, D. (1983). Exit, voice, loyalty, and neglect as responses to job dissatisfaction: A multidimensional scaling study. *The Academy of Management Journal, 26*, 596–607. Retrieved from http://www.jstor.org/stable/255909.

Friedman, M. (1962). *Capitalism and freedom*. Chicago: The University of Chicago Press.

Gantman, E. R., & Fernández Rodríguez, C. J. (2008). Notas sobre la evolución del conocimiento administrativo en la República Argentina y su comparación con el caso español (1913–2007). *Cadernos EBAPE.BR, 6*, 01–22. https://doi.org/10.1590/S1679-39512008000400002.

Gardner, W. L., Avolio, B. J., Luthans, F., May, D. R., & Walumbwa, F. O. (2005). 'Can you see the real me?' A self-based model of authentic leader and follower development. *Leadership Quarterly, 16*, 343–372. https://doi.org/10.1016/j.leaqua.2005.03.003.

Giessner, S. R., & van Knippenberg, D. (2008). 'License to fail': Goal definition, leader group prototypicality, and perceptions of leadership effectiveness after leader failure. *Organizational Behavior and Human Decision Processes, 105*, 14–35. https://doi.org/10.1016/j.obhdp.2007.04.002.

González, O. R. (1986). Argentina: La transición alfonsinista. *Nueva Sociedad, 82*, 22–27.

Graen, G. B., & Uhl-Bien, M. (1995). Relationship-based approach to leadership: Development of leader-member exchange (LMX) theory of leadership over 25 years: Applying a multi-level multi-domain perspective. *Leadership Quarterly, 6*, 219–247. https://doi.org/10.1016/1048-9843(95)90036-5.

Grandey, A., Foo, S. C., Groth, M., & Goodwin, R. E. (2012). Free to be you and me: A climate of authenticity alleviates burnout from emotional labor. *Journal of Occupational Health Psychology, 17*, 1–14. https://doi.org/10.1037/a0025102.

Haslam, S. A., Reicher, S. D., & Platow, M. J. (2011). *The new psychology of leadership: Identity, influence and power*. London/New York: Psychology Press.

Hirschman, A. O. (1970). *Exit, voice, and loyalty: Responses to decline in firms, organizations, and states*. Boston: Harvard University Press.

Hofstede, G. (1980). Motivation, leadership, and organization: Do American theories apply abroad. *Organizational Dynamics, 9*, 42–63. https://doi.org/10.1016/0090-2616(80)90013-3.

Hogg, M. A. (2001). A social identity theory of leadership. *Personality and Social Psychology Review, 5*, 184–200. https://doi.org/10.1207/S15327957PSPR0503_1.

Howell, J. M., & Shamir, B. (2005). The role of followers in the charismatic leadership process: Relationships and their consequences. *Academy of Management Review, 30*, 96–112. Retrieved from http://www.jstor.org/stable/20159097.

Hsiung, H.-H. (2011). Authentic leadership and employee voice behavior: A multi-level psychological process. *Journal of Business Ethics, 107*, 349–361. https://doi.org/10.1007/s10551-011-1043-2.

Ilies, R., Morgeson, F. P., & Nahrgang, J. D. (2005). Authentic leadership and eudaemonic well-being: Understanding leader-follower outcomes. *The Leadership Quarterly, 16*, 373–394. https://doi.org/10.1016/j.leaqua.2005.03.002.

Judge, T. A., Locke, E. A., Durham, C. C., & Kluger, A. N. (1998). Dispositional effects on job and life satisfaction: The role of core evaluations. *Journal of Applied Psychology, 83*, 17–34. https://doi.org/10.1037/0021-9010.83.1.17.

Kernis, M. H. (2003). Toward a conceptualization of optimal self-esteem. *Psychological Inquiry, 14*, 37–41. https://doi.org/10.1207/S15327965PLI1401_01.

Knoll, M., & Van Dick, R. (2013). Authenticity, employee silence, prohibitive voice, and the moderating effect of organizational identification. *Journal of Positive Psychology, 8*, 346–360. https://doi.org/10.1080/17439760.2013.804113.

Lasso, R. F. (2008). Construcción de liderazgo y actitud mítica en presidentes constitucionales argentinos reelegidos. In *XV Jornadas de Investigación y Cuarto Encuentro de Investigadores en Psicología del Mercosur* (pp. 1–4). UBA-Facultad de Psicología, Buenos Aires, Argentina.

Leroy, H., Anseel, F., Gardner, W. L., & Sels, L. (2015). Authentic leadership, authentic followership, basic need satisfaction, and work role performance: A cross-level study. *Journal of Management, 41*, 1677–1697. https://doi.org/10.1177/0149206312457822.

Liu, S., Liao, J., & Wei, H. (2015). Authentic leadership and whistleblowing: Mediating roles of psychological safety and personal identification. *Journal of Business Ethics, 131*(1) 1–13. https://doi.org/10.1007/s10551-014-2271-z.

Lopez, F. G., & Ramos, K. (2015, November). Predicting well-being in managers: Test of a positive psychology model. *The Journal of Positive Psychology, 97*, 1–10. https://doi.org/10.1080/17439760.2015.1092571.

Losada, L. (2007). ¿Oligarquía o elites? Estructura y composición de las clases altas de la ciudad de Buenos Aires entre 1880 y 1930. *Hispanic American Historical Review, 87*, 43–75. https://doi.org/10.1215/00182168-2006-087.

Lynch, J. (2009). *San Martín: Argentine soldier, American hero*. New Haven, CT: Yale University Press.

Marshall, A., Baden, D., & Guidi, M. (2013). Can an ethical revival of prudence within prudential regulation tackle corporate psychopathy? *Journal of Business Ethics, 117*, 559–568. https://doi.org/10.1007/s10551-012-1547-4.

Meindl, J. R., Ehrlich, S. B., & Dukerich, J. M. (1985). The romance of leadership. *Administrative Science Quarterly, 30*, 78–102. https://doi.org/10.2307/2392813.

Messina, G. M. (2012). Una evaluación de los gobiernos Kirchner: El impacto sobre la exclusión social de los cambios en las políticas sociales argentinas. *Visioni LatinoAmericane, 7*, 72–91. Retrieved from http://hdl.handle.net/10077/7292.

Monzani, L., Braun, S., & van Dick, R. (2016). It takes two to tango: The interactive effect of authentic leadership and organizational identification on employee silence intentions. *German Journal of Human Resource Management: Zeitschrift fur Personalforschung, 30*, 246–266. https://doi.org/10.1177/2397002216649896.

Monzani, L., Cameron, K., Crossan, M. M., & Wright, T. A. (2015). Leader character: Reimagining governance. *Academy of Management Proceedings*, 13698–13698. https://doi.org/10.5465/AMBPP.2015.13698symposium.

Monzani, L., Hernandez Bark, A. S., van Dick, R., & Peiró, J. M. (2015). The synergistic effect of prototypicality and authenticity in the relation between leaders' biological gender and their organizational identification. *Journal of Business Ethics, 132*(4), 737–752. https://doi.org/10.1007/s10551-014-2335-0.

Monzani, L., Ripoll, P., & Peiro, J. M. (2012). Un nou enfocament en el lideratge del segle xxi [A new approach to leadership for the xxi century]. *Anuari de Psicologia de La Societat Valenciana de Psicologia, 14*, 31–41.

Monzani, L., Ripoll, P., & Peiro, J. M. (2014a). Followers' agreeableness and extraversion and their loyalty towards authentic leadership. *Psicothema, 26*, 69–75. https://doi.org/10.7334/psicothema2013.67.

Monzani, L., Ripoll, P., & Peiro, J. M. (2014b). The moderator role of followers' personality traits in the relations between leadership styles, two types of task performance and work result satisfaction. *European Journal of Work and Organizational Psychology, 24*. https://doi.org/10.1080/1359432X.2014.911173.

Monzani, L., Ripoll, P., & Peiró, J. M. (2015). Winning the hearts and minds of followers: The interactive effects of follower's emotional competencies and goal setting types on trust in leadership. *Revista Latinoamericana de Psicología, 47*(1), 1–15. https://doi.org/10.1016/S0120-0534(15)30001-7.

Morrison, E. W. (2012). Employee voice behavior: Integration and directions for future research. *Academy of Management Annals, 5*, 373–412. https://doi.org/10.1080/19416520.2011.574506.

Nakamura, J., & Csikszentmihalyi, M. (2002). The concept of flow. In C. R. Snyder & S. J. Lopez (Eds.), *Handbook of positive psychology* (pp. 89–105). Oxford, UK: Oxford University Press.

Natalucci, A. (2015). Corporatism and politics: Labor movement dilemmas during Kirchnerism. *Población Y Sociedad, 22*(2), 5–25. Retrieved from http://www.poblacionysociedad.org.ar/archivos/22/P&S-V22-N2-Natalucci.pdf

Omar, A., & Salessi, S. (2016). Leadership, trust, and labor flexibility as predictors of organizational identification: A study with Argentinean workers. *Pensamiento Psicológico, 14*, 33–47. 10.11144/Javerianacali.PPSI14-2.lcfl.

Operé, F. (2010). *La Argentina de Rosas*. In: Biblioteca Virtual Universal. Retrieved from www.biblioteca.org.ar

Owen, D., & Davidson, J. (2009). Hubris syndrome: An acquired personality disorder? A study of US Presidents and UK Prime Ministers over the last 100 years. *Brain: A Journal of Neurology, 132*, 1396–1406. https://doi.org/10.1093/brain/awp008.

Padilla, A., Hogan, R., & Kaiser, R. B. (2007). The toxic triangle: Destructive leaders, susceptible followers, and conducive environments. *Leadership Quarterly, 18*, 176–194. https://doi.org/10.1016/j.leaqua.2007.03.001.

Pérez, G. J., & Natalucci, A. (2010). The movement matrix of collective action in Argentina: The experience of the kirchnerista militant space. *América Latina Hoy, 54*, 97–112.

Perugini, L., Laura, M., & Solano, C. (2013). Gender stereotypes and gender of the leader and of the follower: Their influence in attitudes towards women leaders. A study with Argentinian population. *Revista de Psicologia, 9*, 1–17.

Piva, A. (2013). ¿Cuánto hay de nuevo y cuánto de populismo en el neopopulismo? Kirchnerismo y peronismo en la Argentina post 2001. *Trabajo Y Sociedad, 21*, 135–157.

Raigoza, C. (2014). *Explorando el liderazgo femenino en América Latina: Lo que podemos aprender de Michelle Bachelet, Cristina Fernández de Kirchner y Dilma Rousseff*. Bacherlor's thesis, Claremont McKenna College, Claremont, CA.

Riketta, M., & Van Dick, R. (2005). Foci of attachment in organizations: A meta-analytic comparison of the strength and correlates of workgroup versus organizational identification and commitment. *Journal of Vocational Behavior, 67*, 490–510. https://doi.org/10.1016/j.jvb.2004.06.001.

Ryan, R. M., & Deci, E. L. (2001). On happiness and human potentials: A review of research on hedonic and eudaemonic well-being. *Annual Review of Psychology, 52*, 141–166. Retrieved from http://www.annualreviews.org/doi/abs/10.1146/annurev.psych.52.1.141

Seijts, G. H., Gandz, J., Crossan, M., & Reno, M. (2015). Character matters: Character dimensions' impact on leader performance and outcomes. *Organizational Dynamics, 44*, 65–74. https://doi.org/10.1016/j.orgdyn.2014.11.008.

Smith, W. C. (1991). State, market, and neoliberalism in post-transition Argentina: The Menem experiment. *Journal of Interamerican Studies and World Affairs, 33*, 45–82. https://doi.org/10.2307/165879.

Sosik, J. J. (2006). *Leading with character*. Greenwich, CT: Information Age Publishing.

Steffens, N. K., Haslam, S. A., Reicher, S. D., Platow, M. J., Fransen, K., Yang, J., … Boen, F. (2014). Leadership as social identity management: Introducing the identity leadership inventory (ILI) to assess and validate a four-dimensional model. *Leadership Quarterly, 25*, 1001–1024. https://doi.org/10.1016/j.leaqua.2014.05.002.

Sturm, R. E., & Antonakis, J. (2015). Interpersonal power: A review, critique, and research agenda. *Journal of Management, 41*, 136–163. https://doi.org/10.1177/0149206314555769.

Sturm, R. E., & Monzani, L. (in press). Leadership and power. In *The nature of leadership*. New York: Sage.

Treisman, D. (2003). Cardoso, Menem, and Machiavelli: Political tactics and privatization in Latin America. *Studies in Comparative International Development, 38*, 93–109.

Trombetta, M. (2012). Inflación en Argentina y limitaciones del 'modelo' kirchnerista. In *Hic Rhodus. Crisis capitalista, polémica y controversias*. Buenos aires, Argentina: Instituto de Investigaciones Gino Germani.

Ullrich, J., Christ, O., & van Dick, R. (2009). Substitutes for procedural fairness: Prototypical leaders are endorsed whether they are fair or not. *Journal of Applied Psychology, 94*, 235–244. https://doi.org/10.1037/a0012936.

Van Dick, R. (2001). Identification in organizational contexts: Linking theory and research from social and organizational psychology. *International Journal of Management Reviews, 3*(4) 265–283. https://doi.org/10.1111/1468-2370.00068.

Walumbwa, F. O., Avolio, B. J., Gardner, W. L., Wernsing, T. S., & Peterson, S. J. (2007). Authentic leadership: Development and validation of a theory-based measure. *Journal of Management, 34*, 89–126. https://doi.org/10.1177/0149206307308913.

Weber, M. (1924). *The theory of social and economic organizations*. New York: Free Press.

6

The Role of Sociocultural Context in the Leader–Follower Relationship: An Analysis of Lee Kuan Yew's Authentic Transformational Leadership

Deborah Pembleton, John Friend, and Zhiyuan He

With globalisation and cultural diffusion, the study of cross-cultural leadership has become increasingly more important, as multi-cultural environments demand tailored communication and sensitivity to the values, beliefs, and preferences of followers. In this sense, as Bligh and Kohles (2014) note, leadership can be best understood as a "socially constructed interactional phenomenon through which certain individuals attempt to frame, define, or otherwise influence the reality of other individuals

D. Pembleton (✉)
Global Business Leadership Department, College of Saint Benedict and Saint John's University, Collegeville, MN, USA

J. Friend
Department of Political Science, College of Saint Benedict and Saint John's University, Collegeville, MN, USA

Z. He
Department of Political Science and Department of Global Business Leadership, College of Saint Benedict and Saint John's University, Collegeville, MN, USA

© The Author(s) 2018
D. Cotter-Lockard (ed.), *Authentic Leadership and Followership*, Palgrave Studies in Leadership and Followership, https://doi.org/10.1007/978-3-319-65307-5_6

across different contexts" (pp. 143–144). Such an understanding of leadership suggests that cultural values, self-concepts, and situational factors can, and often do, affect leader–follower communication and the leader's ability to shape the attitudes, motives, and behaviours of individuals. Thus, within culturally diverse groups, research shows that effective leadership requires adaptive communication styles that match each member's cultural expectations (Hanges, Aiken, Park, & Su, 2016).

Although many leadership theories address the ways in which leaders communicate and motivate followers (Avolio & Gardner, 2005), recent research on authentic transformational leadership provides new insight into how cultural contexts moderate the leader–follower relationship. Through the formation of a strong vision and collective goals, transformational leaders inspire followers to transcend their own needs and self-interests for the good of the group. Researchers have identified four key dimensions of transformational leadership: idealised influence, inspirational motivation, intellectual stimulation, and individualised consideration (Avolio, Waldman, & Yammarino, 1991; Bass, 1991). More recently, however, some have suggested that authenticity is another important dimension and have explored the ways leaders harness character strengths and moral perspectives to produce outcomes associated with both authentic and transformational leadership styles (Price, 2003; Sosik & Cameron, 2010; Zhu, Avolio, Riggio, & Sosik, 2011). In other words, these two forms of leadership, although traditionally viewed as distinctly different, can be seen as closely related (Banks, McCauley, Gardner, & Guler, 2016), as attributes and traits associated with authentic leadership development such as establishing trust and relational authenticity with followers through shared values are also important in transformational leadership (Avolio & Gardner, 2005; Illies, Morgeson, & Nahrgang, 2005).

Although the characteristics underlying 'authentic transformational leadership' have received a great deal of attention (Li, Chiaburu, Kirkman, & Xie, 2013), less emphasis has been placed on *how and under what conditions* transformational leadership achieves authenticity within the leader–follower relationship. For example, to successfully motivate and gain trust, the leader's message and values should be congruent with the cultural mindset of the group, which often vary greatly across societies (Dorfman, Javidan, Hanges, Dastmalchian, & House, 2012). Incongruent values, on the other hand, can make the message appear less authentic and, thus, hinder the leader's ability to enhance a collective identity and promote a new and inspiring vision (Brown & Treviño, 2009; Krishnan, 2002). Therefore, to better understand the ways in which authentic transformational leadership can be culture-specific, attention should be given to how sociocultural contexts moderate the leader–follower relationship (Hunter, Bedell-Avers, & Mumford, 2007).

Through a case study analysis, this chapter examines the leadership style of Lee Kuan Yew, the first Prime Minister of Singapore, with special attention given to the ways in which he employed cultural values and ideologies to develop a compelling political vision in Singapore. Lee Kuan Yew's leadership style serves as an interesting case for exploring the influences of culture and contextual constraints in leader–follower interactions, as his 'Asian Values' model, despite being well received in Singapore, failed to inspire and motivate a larger East Asian audience (Zakaria, 1994). By addressing the sociocultural contexts in which authentic transformational leadership occurs, this chapter argues that Lee's strategy was unsuccessful at the global level because his message was incongruent with the ontologies and values of other societies in Asia, thus making his message appear less authentic and trustworthy. With this case study, we seek to further develop the authentic transformational leadership construct, as only a few studies have addressed this form of leadership and, as a result, the conditions needed to achieve 'authenticity' in the leader–follower relationship have not been adequately explored.

With this in mind, we address the following central question: how do culture, context, and individual differences affect authentic transformational leadership? To answer this question, we first provide a brief overview of authentic transformational leadership, with a particular focus on the importance of 'authenticity' in value-based leadership. Here, we concentrate our attention on how authenticity, established through self-awareness and values congruency, can build trust to motivate and inspire followers. Second, we discuss how sociocultural context moderates the leader–follower relationship. This section addresses the ways in which cultural values and beliefs shape leadership expectations and influence leader–follower communication. Third, we discuss the importance of the follower's self-concept (i.e., individual differences) within the leader–follower relationship, as globalisation has caused variation within cultural groups. For example, societies that have traditionally valued collectivism may have members who embrace individualism and/or fluctuate between independent and interdependent mindsets depending on situational factors. Finally, following an analysis of Lee Kuan Yew's leadership style and the social constructions of followership in Asia, this chapter offers recommendations for making authentic transformational leadership more functional across different cultural contexts.

Overview of Authentic Transformational Leadership

The construct of authentic transformational leadership refers to leading with the general well-being of humanity in mind. As Avolio, Gardner, Walumbwa, Luthans, and May (2004) note, authentic leaders contribute to the greater good of society in addition to having a focus on profitability. These leaders are defined as,

> ...those individuals who are deeply aware of how they think and behave and are perceived by others as being aware of their own and others' values/moral perspective, knowledge, and strengths; aware of the context in which they operate; and who are confident, hopeful, optimistic, resilient, and high on moral character. (p. 4)

Thus, by incorporating aspects of hope, trust, and positive emotions into the work attitudes of followers, the authentic leader encourages and motivates followers to perform at a far higher level that they thought was possible and attainable (Avolio et al., 2004).

Furthermore, by aligning their identity with that of the followers, authentic leaders assist followers in recognising their individual purpose, which, in turn, stimulates followers to become more purpose-driven (Lord & Brown, 2004) and committed (Avolio et al., 2004). In fact, Luthans and Avolio (2003) point out that a leader who does 'what is right and fair' can identify with a follower more on a personal level. In this sense, as leaders strengthen social identification through an emphasis on strong moral values, honesty, and integrity, followers become more engaged with the group (Hogg, 2001; Tajfel, 1972).

Finally, hope and optimism have also been identified as essential elements of having a strong authentic leader and follower relationship (Avolio et al., 2004). Through the promotion of positive emotions, leaders can build trusting relationships (Robins & Boldero, 2003) and encourage their followers to be hopeful about future goals.

The literature on authentic transformational leadership reveals the importance of value congruency in the leader–follower relationship, as failure to build trust and promote social solidarity can make it more difficult, if not impossible, to motivate and inspire followers. Furthermore, it highlights the role of situational factors and suggests that these factors may moderate the effectiveness of the leader's message. Less attention, however, has been given to the effects of cultural values on perceptions of authenticity in leader–follower interactions and how these cultural effects tend to be context dependent. To further explore such relationships, the following section discusses the importance of cross-cultural perspectives for advancing the study of authentic transformational leadership.

The Effects of Culture and Context on the Leader–Follower Relationship

Previous research suggests that every cultural group has core ideas and values that organise their own socio-psychological processes and socialise members to "think, act, and feel in a more or less adaptive fashion" (Markus & Kitayama, 1994, p. 343). Culture, in this sense, can be understood as shared knowledge about the world, such as values and attitudes, which help individuals interact with others and navigate their surrounding environment (Hong, Morris, Chiu, & Benet-Martinez, 2000). Values guide the way social actors, such as leaders, policymakers, and followers, "select actions, evaluate people and events, and explain their actions and evaluations" (Schwartz, 1999, p. 25).

With the identification of cultural variation in the leader–follower relationship, cross-cultural leadership research has shown that many business practices around the world are, indeed, distinctly different from Western practice (Dickson, Den Hartog, & Mitchelson, 2003), in turn highlighting the importance of cultural competency for today's business leaders (House, Hanges, Javidan, Dorfman, & Gupta, 2004; Javidan, Dorfman, Luque, & House, 2006). Notable studies by Hofstede (2001), Schwartz (1992), and others have highlighted key cultural value dimensions that make up national cultures (e.g., power distance and individualism/collectivism) and social cultures (e.g., embeddedness vs. autonomy and hierarchy vs. egalitarianism).

Furthermore, the leadership literature shows that cultural beliefs and values greatly influence an individual's attitudes, behaviours, and decisions, in turn, reiterating the importance of values congruence within the leader–follower relationship (Brown & Treviño, 2009). For example, prior research has found that Chinese business leadership, in many instances, does not follow the rationalistic and participatory styles found in the West (Cheung & Chan, 2005). In fact, studies by McDonald (2012), Chen and Kao (2009) and Lin (2008) show that Confucianism, paternalism, harmony, and collectivism greatly influence Chinese business leaders; these values are not commonly found in Western business practice. Thus, the findings from these and similar studies suggest that achieving value congruence within the leader–follower relationship requires sensitivity to the sociocultural milieu of the society.

As noted earlier, authenticity is a defining feature of transformational leadership. According to Zhu et al. (2011), authenticity is, in part, achieved when followers are able to embrace the values embedded within the vision and initiatives of the leader. To motivate and inspire followers, value-based leaders either tap into the existing values or offer value-laden visions and goals that are appealing to the group (Lord & Brown, 2001). On this point, the work by Sosik (2005, p. 224) shows that by displaying and transmitting behaviours that reflect the "cherished values of the followers," leaders are able to tap into the perceptions of followers while simultaneously conveying a message of solidarity (collective social identity) and value congruence, notably shared key attributes unique to group members (Lord, Brown, & Freiberg, 1999).

In this sense, effective leaders display authenticity and promote vision attainment by articulating the needs, desires, and hopes of followers (Sosik, 2005). Through this process, authentic transformational leaders are able to appear prototypical, convey that they are 'one of us' and, as a result, "are not only seen as better leaders but are also more effective in getting us to do things and in making us feel good about those things" (Haslam, Reicher, & Platow, 2011, p. 90). Simply put, by meeting followers' cultural expectations and perceptions, leaders are able to better communicate and build trust across cultures (Thomas & Ravlin, 1995).

Recognising the influence of values and beliefs in the leader–follower relationship, an increasing number of studies have begun to focus on the barriers and facilitators of cross-cultural leadership. In particular, the Global Leadership and Organisational Behaviour Effectiveness (GLOBE) Study found that 'societal culture' can have a direct effect on preferred leadership style, and that certain cultural dimensions such as performance orientation are predictors of leadership expectations (Dorfman et al., 2012). Furthermore, GLOBE researchers have shown that societies can be culturally clustered (e.g., Anglo, Confucian Asia, Middle East), as they share specific culture dimensions and desired leadership traits (Gupta & Hanges, 2004). These findings reveal that the leader's value-laden vision must match the cultural mindset of the followers, that is to say, the schemas and scripts that influence the way individuals interpret, behave, and interact within a situation (Hanges et al., 2016).

Despite noticeable similarities across societies, the findings from the GLOBE Study also suggest that some leadership attributes are culturally contingent, such that qualities such as 'face saving' and 'risk taking' are desirable in some cultures, but undesirable in others (Dorfman et al., 2012; Javidan, Dorfman, Howell, & Hanges, 2010). As Lord et al. (1999) report, leadership is a "highly contextual sensitive phenomenon", such that constraints from culture, the organisation, and the needs and identities of followers influence how leadership is defined. Therefore, while culture matters, context cannot be ignored, as it plays a moderating role in the leader–follower relationship. For example, a study by Vroom and Jago (2007) identified three roles that situational variables play in the leadership process: organisational effectiveness, leader's behaviour, and the consequences of the leader's behaviour. With the third variable, Vroom and Jago (2007) argue that leadership behaviour must be tailored to fit the demands and dominant sociocultural values of each situation (also see Elenkov & Manev, 2005).

Consistent with these findings is research in social psychology that has shown message persuasiveness increases when it is framed in culturally relevant terms (Cesario, Grant, & Higgins, 2004; Uskul & Oyserman, 2010). The *culture as situated cognition* model, in particular, provides insight into how cultural values are context-specific. According to Oyserman (2011), situated cognition refers to the non-conscious impact of social context on thinking and action, suggesting that context primes an individual's cultural mindset in a way that makes individualist or collectivist thinking more accessible. In this sense, cultural values are malleable, context-dependent, and socially sensitive.

In other words, effective authentic transformational leadership requires the leader's vision to match the follower's cultural expectations; failure to do so will only make inspirational motivation less likely. Furthermore, followers' interpretation of information depends, in part, on their active cultural mindset (e.g., concepts and schemas), such that "the same action can be interpreted as dishonest or kind, assertive or aggressive" depending on the concepts accessible at the time of judgment or information retrieval (Oyserman, Sorensen, Reber, & Chan, 2009, p. 219). Thus, when trying to articulate a shared vision, Hanges et al. (2016) argue that leaders must pay attention to the ways in which expectations regarding leadership vary within and between culturally diverse groups; this often requires changing leadership styles to 'match each member's cultural expectations' (p. 66).

Individual Differences and Follower's Self-concept

Globalisation and cultural diffusion have made the need for adapting to cultural expectations even more pressing and, in some instances, extremely difficult, as values and beliefs often change when cultures interact (Naylor, 1996). For instance, although Chinese business leadership is distinctive relative to Western practices, Faure and Fang (2008) note that modernisation has caused significant sociocultural changes within China, but not a complete transformation of traditional value orientations. Rather, as the authors point out, Chinese business practices consist of 'paradoxical values' that are context-dependent, such as *guanxi* (trading personal favours to accomplish business objectives) versus professionalism, or group orientation versus individuation.

These findings are supported by recent work on global leadership that has identified ways in which globalisation and acculturation create communication challenges for leaders (e.g., Clapp-Smith & Vogelgesang Lester, 2014). Global leadership is defined here as "the process of influencing others to adopt a shared vision through structures and methods that facilitate positive change while fostering individual and collective growth in the context characterised by significant levels of complexity, flow and presence" (Mendenhall, Reiche, Bird, & Osland, 2012, p. 500). Within this perspective, a global mindset is not a static construct, but rather one that adapts to changing environments (domestic vs global) through a process that Clapp-Smith and Vogelgesang Lester (2014) refer to as 'mindset switching.' Therefore, the authors suggest that in some situations, leaders are required to articulate their "vision in global terms that integrate several cultural, economic, and political perspectives in a generalised fashion" (p. 220).

Mindset switching is important for authentic transformational leaders since not every follower will identify with the dominant national and/or social culture of the group. On this point, Sharma (2010) notes that Hofstede's national cultural dimensions do not accurately predict cross-cultural differences in followers' attitudes and behaviours, as "they may not fully represent the diversity in the cultural orientations of the citizens of a country since they may not possess the same level of their national cultural characteristics" (p. 788). For example, although the United States ranks high on individualism compared to other countries (Hofstede, 2001), not every American will be more individualistic and less collectivistic. To this point, a study by Osyerman, Coon, and Kemmelmeier (2002) found that European American participants were not more individualistic than African Americans or Latinos, and not less collectivistic than Japanese or Koreans.

Case Study: The Successes and Failures of Lee Kuan Yew's Authentic Transformational Leadership

With scant research completed on the authentic transformational leadership construct, a deeper analysis of the effects of culture, context, and individual differences on 'authenticity' is warranted. Many have pointed out the value of the case study for construct and theory development (Dooley, 2002; McCutcheon & Meredith, 1993), noting that "case studies allow a researcher to achieve higher levels of conceptual validity, or to identify and measure the indicators that best represent the theoretical concepts the research intends to measure" (George & Bennett, 2005, p. 21). This is an instrumental case study, which is the study of a person, specific group, occupation, department, or organisation to provide insight into a particular issue. In instrumental case research, "the case facilitates understanding of something else" (Mills, Durepos, & Wiebe, 2010, p. 473). The purpose of this case is to facilitate a deeper understanding of Asian cultural values. We closely follow the definition of case study research, in that we explore a program, event, activity, process, or one or more individuals, and in this instance, Lee Kuan Yew (Stake, 1995; Yin, 2003).

Through an in-depth examination of Lew Kuan Yew's leadership style and the critical response of some East Asian leaders to Lee's political vision (i.e., the Asian Values model), this section seeks to refine the authentic transformational leadership construct by addressing the importance of cultural value congruency and mindset switching in the leader–follower relationship.

Lee Kuan Yew was the first Prime Minister of Singapore (1959–1990) and, according to former U.S. President Richard Nixon, "a world statesman of the first rank" (Josey, 2013, p. 152). In fact, because of his "never-ending struggle to overcome the nation's lack of natural resources, a potentially hostile international environment and a volatile ethnic mix of Chinese, Malays and Indians" (Mydans, 2015), Lee Kuan Yew is considered by many to be the 'patriarch' of Singapore and one of the most influential Asian leaders in the twentieth century (Leong, 2000, p. 99).

His notoriety is, in part, because of his influential role in the transformation of Singapore following independence from British Rule in 1959 and during the country's separation from Malaysia in 1965.

Since Lee was able to transform Singapore into a wealthy and influential nation (with a gross domestic product currently ranked 37th by the World Bank), his leadership and policymaking style has received a great deal of attention, as many attribute Singapore's economic development to Lee's political vision, charisma, and strong principles. Lee's leadership style has been characterised as paternalistic and pragmatic (Josey, 1974; Leong, 2000), as well as consistent with Confucian values that "place great emphasis on forms of conduct within relationships, personal virtue, obedience to authority, family loyalty, and education" (Barr, 2000, p. 311; also see Tan & Wee, 2002).

Lee called for an authoritarian state and voiced strong opposition to the Western liberal democratic model, which he viewed a hedonistic and hyper-individualistic. In Lee's mind, Asia, and 'Asian Values', conflicted with Western values and forms of governance since "Eastern societies believe that the individual exists in the context of his family. He is not pristine and separate" (as cited in Zakaria, 1994, p. 113). Thus, Lee's view of effective leadership required the reinforcement of communitarian values so that the needs and interests of the society or organisation take precedence over the individual. As Roy (1994) points out, this argument assumes that followers in Confucian East Asia "are more inclined than liberal Westerners to accept constraints on individual rights in exchange for stability and economic growth in society as a whole" (p. 234).

Lee Kuan Yew took this argument one step further by asserting that 'culture is destiny' and Confucian values, specifically respect for authority and family, were the driving force behind East Asian economic development. According to Lee, Singapore's economic and social development had deep-seated Asian roots and to deviate from these authentic cultural values would only hinder the country's performance ('Chinese Culture Outside', 1991). Embracing Lee's vision, Goh Chok Tong (1988), Singapore's second Prime Minister (1990–2004), proclaimed that the ideal political leader is a "Confucian gentleman, a *junzi*, someone who is upright, morally beyond reproach, someone people can trust." In this view, the legitimacy and authenticity of the leader are derived from personal qualities, and the belief that individuals are expected to follow certain hierarchical structures is consistent with long-standing customs and traditions (Leong, 2000).

As Singaporean society experienced rapid modernisation and industrialisation, Lee Kuan Yew pushed for the retention of traditional Confucian values in order to prevent Singapore from becoming another poor imitation of the West, "with all the fads and fetishes, the disorders and aberrations of contemporary Western societies" (as cited in Chen, 1977, p. 22). In other words, according to Lee (2013), "the exuberance of democracy leads to undisciplined and disorderly conditions which are inimical to development" in Asia (p. 27).

In this sense, according to Lee, authority and hierarchy are important dimensions of the leader–follower relationship, such that the paternal relationship between the leader and follower was akin to that of the father and son. As Barr (2000) notes, Lee's vision of society reflected a 'social pyramid' that consisted of 'top leaders' at the top, 'good executives' in the middle, and a 'highly civic-conscious broad mass' at the base (p. 322). Thus, to transform society, it is the duty of a determined leader to discipline and educate followers since, according to Lee (1959–1990), 'if you don't get social discipline, everybody does what he likes to do, or will not bustle about what he is told to do'. He further adds that even with a strong leader, followers need a 'rugged national culture', one that has the capacity, stamina, and sufficient social cohesiveness needed to promote the good of the national community (Yao, 2007, p. 58). This understanding of social transformation led Lee to warn business leaders in the Philippines of the need for 'discipline more than democracy' ('Mr. Lee Goes to Manila', 1992).

Lee often spoke of the need to inspire and motivate followers, as failure to do so would lead to a dispirited and directionless society. In particular, a political leader "must paint his vision of the future to his people, then translate that vision into policies which must convince the people are worth supporting, and finally galvanise them to help him in their implementation" (Lee, 2013, p. 114). To achieve this, Lee (2013) argued for 'leading by example' to promote authenticity in the leader–follower relationship. Moral character is critical in this regard, as "there is no better way than personal example of managers and grassroots leaders to bring about this change of attitudes and values" (p. 90).

Lee Kuan Yew's promotion of Confucian ethics was well received in Singapore and, as a result, has shaped management styles in Singaporean firms, which tend to place a great deal of emphasis on efficient political leadership and a disciplined workforce (Lu, 1998; Scarborough, 1998). Within Lee's Confucian heritage cultural model, good relationships between the leader and follower, in which employees are treated like family members, is a defining feature of authentic business practice. On this point, a study by Low (2006) on Singaporean corporate and business leaders found that participants valued hierarchy and 'fatherly' roles to a high degree such that experience, seniority, and filial piety were considered to be the most important dimensions of effective management decision making. Along similar lines, a study of the influence of Confucian values on individual job attitudes in Singapore by Leong, Huang, and Mak (2014) found that participants who endorsed Confucian diligence and Confucian harmony felt more satisfied with their jobs and committed to the success of the organisation. These findings are consistent with research on the Confucian foundations of leadership in other Asian countries, notably China and parts of Southeast Asia, which have revealed the distinctive long-standing ideological and cultural orientations shaping leader–follower relationships (McDonald, 2012).

Having succeeded in uniting Singaporeans under this Asian Values model, Lee Kuan Yew attempted to replicate the model throughout East Asia, as he believed the region faced many of the same problems that once plagued Singapore, particularly the negative effects of westernisation. In this sense, Lee sought to transform the region, which he believed shared a distinct cultural heritage, by leading other Asian leaders in opposition to the individualism and liberal democratic values of the West. Thus, taking a global leadership role, which Beechler and Javidan (2007) note involves crossing a variety of boundaries, Lee attempted to inspire and unite the political elite of East Asia under a positive vision and clear set of 'authentic' Asian values that would support growth and development throughout the region.

However, although Lee's political vision and call for paternal leadership fit well within the sociocultural milieu of Singapore as well as mainland China in the 1980s (Englehart, 2000, p. 549), other East Asian societies rejected his anti-democracy message and its emphasis on intrinsic Asian values. In fact, Thompson (2001) notes that although officials in Singapore championed Asian values, societies throughout East Asia experienced the rise of democracy movements and growing individualism. By acknowledging that leadership is not a value-neutral process, void of context (Haslam et al., 2011), we can see that Lee Kuan Yew failed to accomplish what effective cross-cultural leadership requires to achieve authenticity in the leader–follower relationship: recognition of, and adaptation to, various situational factors (Hanges et al., 2016). In other words, the different histories and experiences of countries throughout East Asia produced cultural mindsets that were incongruent with Lee's worldview.

For many outside of Singapore, liberal democracy was considered to be compatible with the traditions and customs found in Asia (Subramaniam, 2000). According to Ng (1998), democracy was desired in Hong Kong because it would give the people "a say in decisions concerning their lives, and because it was the only instrument that could provide real protection for human rights against an authoritarian government" (p. 6). Moreover, others argued that the growth of democracy in Asia is an "unfinished project" that needs to be "clarified, refined, and developed" (Tatsuo, 1999, p. 29).

Therefore, despite the prevalence of Confucian cultural traditions, some have correctly pointed out the cultural diversity in East Asia and that national conditions and histories have shaped the region in different ways (Friedman, 1994). For example, Indonesians are overwhelmingly Islamic, Filipinos disproportionately Catholic, and communist regimes in China and Vietnam rejected Confucianism, all of which suggest that adherence to Confucian principles and values varies considerably across East Asia (Dalton & Ong, 2005).

A clear rejection of Lee Kuan Yew's vision, along with his failure to inspire and motivate the political elite in the region, can be seen in the critiques of the Asian Values model put forth by Kim Dae-jung, former President of South Korea (1998–2003), and Lee Teng-hui, former President of Taiwan (1988–2000). For Kim Dae-jung, many Asian countries have successfully adopted the Western free-market economy model and have made great strides toward democracy. The paternal leadership and soft authoritarianism rooted in Lee's political vision, according to Kim (1994), was inconsistent with the experiences of South Korea, as "policies that try to protect people from the bad elements of economic and social change will never be effective if imposed without consent" (p. 193). Rather, Kim believed that policies arrived at through an open public debate "will have the strength of Asia's proud and self-reliant people" (p. 193).

A similar stance was taken by former Taiwanese President Lee Teng-hui who argued that culture is not immutable and Confucianism can improve democratic systems in Asia (Chen & Chen, 2015; Mirsky, 1998). Therefore, according to Lee Teng-hui (1999), "this choice does not compel us to give up Confucianism, but rather encourages us to embrace those of its ethical concepts that are not only compatible with democracy, but able to mend democracy's possible shortcomings" (p. 18). Kim Dae-jung and Lee Teng-hui rejected Lee's vision and paternal leadership style because they both strongly believed that Confucian values could be moulded to improve democratic governance in the region (Shin, 2011, p. 58).

Within the cultural context of Singapore, Lee Kuan Yew was an effective authentic transformational leader, as his message, values, and vision were congruent with the cultural mindsets within the country. By articulating the needs, desires, and hopes of Singaporeans, Lee appeared authentic and trustworthy. Furthermore, by emphasising dominant sociocultural values (i.e., Confucian diligence and harmony), Lee was able to tap into the perceptions of his followers and convey an inspiring and motivating message of solidarity.

However, as Hanges et al. (2016) and Mendenhall et al. (2012) suggest, the effective cross-cultural communication needed for global leadership requires adaptation to situational factors and constant adjustments in leadership style. By assuming that 'culture is destiny' and, thus, failing to tailor his Asian Values message to the needs and interests of a larger East Asian audience, Lee Kuan Yew's vision was rejected by many as it appeared inauthentic and untrustworthy. A close examination of the cultural diversity and historical experiences in East Asia shows that Lee's emphasis on Confucian ethics within the leader–follower relationship was incongruent with the expectations and values of many Asian societies. For Kim Dae-jung, Lee Teng-hui, and other democracy advocates in East Asia, Confucianism was not immutable and, therefore, Lee's anti-democracy message and sharp distinction between East and West were incompatible with the personal experiences and self-concepts of his targeted audience. Simply put, Lee was unsuccessful at balancing domestic and global leadership behaviours and, as a result, he appeared inauthentic to many in Asia.

As in case study research, our case study does have limitations. Case studies are not necessarily generalisable on a larger scale and in a straightforward manner. Although Lee Kuan Yew was one individual, his role is not necessarily applicable throughout the diverse populations within Asia. As a result, future research should address the effects of cultural and situational factors on authentic transformation leadership styles in other regions of the world, as these factors may have stronger or weaker influences in societies with different historical, political, and economic experiences. For this, a large-N analysis can be employed to further support theory development in that "generalisation and complex relationships are better supported by large-N comparisons, which provide the degrees of freedom necessary to handle many variables and complex relationships" (Coppedge, 1999, p. 473).

Nonetheless, through an in-depth analysis of Lee Kuan Yew's successes and failures as an authentic transformational leader, we are able to gain a better appreciation for how individual differences, culture, and context influence the leader–follower relationship. Such an understanding provides deeper insight into the underlying dimensions of the authentic transformational leadership construct. Building from the conclusions drawn from our case study, the following section offers recommendations for improving authentic transformation leadership in cross-cultural settings.

Recommendations and Conclusions

What can we learn and apply from Lee Kuan Yew's successes and failures as an authentic transformational leader to cross-cultural organisation settings? Although Lee Kuan Yew's paternalistic and pragmatic style worked for Singapore, an effective leader must understand that one management style does not apply to all cultures, even though those cultures may seem similar. With this mind, a manager should avoid cultural stereotypes and simple assumptions about an employee's career direction; rather, emphasis should be placed on developing a deeper understanding of the employee's goals and ambitions. To show support for their employees, managers should be able to articulate the needs, desires, and hopes of followers so the followers are committed to fulfilling company objectives. Although these examples primarily focus on the human resources functional area of an organisation, similar applications may be applied to the marketing, finance, and manufacturing operations of a business.

With this in mind, we recommend three primary areas for applying the lessons of Lee Kuan Yew to the leader–follower relationship in cross-cultural business environments:

1. The cultural competence of the global leader is vital to the sustainability of a constructive work environment for all employees.
2. Global leaders must acknowledge and appreciate the importance of the followers' culture as a positive contribution to the work environment.
3. Global leaders must recognise the cultural differences among employees and must also acknowledge individual differences among employees, even if the employees may belong to the same or similar cultural groups.

By acknowledging the role of value congruency and situational factors, the authentic transformational leadership model provides us with a deeper understanding of how managers, who must also be global leaders, may motivate culturally diverse employees in the workplace. As an organisation conducts strategic planning efforts, the leadership should be mindful of how their decisions may be interpreted differently by employees of different cultures and, thus, impact the overall effectiveness of the organisation. By adapting to different groups, managers are better able to develop an organisation that is growth-oriented.

When considering how to manage human resources, the manager, as a global leader, must have a comprehensive understanding of the nuances in cultural differences within the workplace. There must be an atmosphere that fosters acceptance of, and appreciation for, cultural differences among workers, no matter how slight the differences may seem.

Managers should hire employees who share an appreciation and acceptance of cultural difference. By doing so, leaders within the organisation are more apt to have an organisation that is committed to the overall success of all members within the organisation.

Company leadership should also take into account the contextual environment when making decisions. Findings from the GLOBE Study have identified important cultural clusters that are more specific to varying cultural dimensions. Again, if we were to consider these different cultural clusters from a human resources perspective, different employees may have distinctly differing needs. For example, when making a decision about management in an organisation, leadership should consider whether employees who are selected for future leadership positions reflect what are considered to be the five primary traits of authentic leaders (George, 2003):

- Understanding their purpose—values and integrity
- Practicing solid values—study introspection, and consultation with others
- Leading with the heart—caring for others
- Establishing connected relationships—deeply rooted relationships
- Demonstrating self-discipline—staying on course, being focused on goals

Furthermore, managers need not be afraid of vulnerability and openness when making mistakes. This will enable workers to be more open-minded risk takers, an essential element for a growing, innovative company. Managers also need to tap into the attitudes, behaviours, and decisions that influence employee behaviour. These influences could come from outside the company, such as economic, social, legal, or political variables that may impact behaviour. The manager needs to understand the overall context under which decisions are made and then must be able to tailor solutions to fit the demands of each situation. Through these approaches to the leader–follower relationship, authentic transformational leadership can be more functional across different cultural environments.

References

Avolio, B. J., & Gardner, W. L. (2005). Authentic leadership: Getting to the root of positive forms of leadership. *The Leadership Quarterly, 16*, 315–338.

Avolio, B. J., Gardner, W. L., Walumbwa, F. O., Luthans, F., & May, D. R. (2004). Unlocking the mask: A look at the process by which authentic leaders impact follower attitudes and behaviors. *The Leadership Quarterly, 15*, 801–823.

Avolio, B. J., Waldman, D. A., & Yammarino, F. J. (1991). Leading in the 1990s: The four I's of transformational leadership. *Journal of European Industrial Training, 15*, 9–16.

Banks, G. C., McCauley, K. D., Gardner, W. L., & Guler, C. E. (2016). A meta-analytic review of authentic and transformational leadership: A test for redundancy. *The Leadership Quarterly, 27*, 634–652.

Barr, M. D. (2000). Lee Kuan Yew and the 'Asian values' debate. *Asian Studies Review, 24*, 309–334.

Bass, B. M. (1991). From transaction to transformational leadership: Learning to share the vision. *Organizational Dynamics, 18*, 19–31.

Beechler, S., & Javidan, M. (2007). Leading with a global mindset. In M. Javidan, R. M. Steers, & M. A. Hitt (Eds.), *The global mindset* (pp. 131–169). Bingley, UK: Emerald Group Publishing Limited.

Bligh, M. C., & Kohles, J. C. (2014). Comparing leaders across contexts, culture, and time: Computerized content analysis of leader–follower communications. *Leadership, 10*, 142–159.

Brown, M. E., & Treviño, L. K. (2009). Leader–follower values congruence: Are socialized charismatic leaders better able to achieve it? *Journal of Applied Psychology, 94*, 478–490.

Cesario, J., Grant, H., & Higgins, T. E. (2004). Regulatory fit and persuasion: Transfer from 'feeling right'. *Journal of Personality and Social Psychology, 86*, 388–404.

Chen, H. P., & Chen, W. H. (2015, March 29). Lee Teng-hui says his politics differed from Lee Kuan Yew. *Taipei Times*, p. 3.

Chen, H. Y., & Kao, H. S. R. (2009). Chinese paternalistic leadership and non-Chinese subordinates' psychological health. *The International Journal of Human Resource Management, 20*, 2533–2546.

Chen, P. S. J. (1977). Asian values and modernization: A sociological perspective. In S. Chee-Meow (Ed.), *Asian values and modernization*. Singapore: Singapore University Press.

Cheung, C., & Chan, A. C. (2005). Philosophical foundations of eminent Hong Kong Chinese CEOs' leadership. *Journal of Business Ethics, 60*, 47–62.
Chinese Culture Outside China Changing with the Generations. (1991, August 11). *Sunday Times*, p. 21.
Clapp-Smith, R., & Vogelgesang Lester, G. (2014). Defining the 'Mindset' in global mindset: Modeling the dualities of global leadership. In J. Osland, M. Li, & Y. Wang (Eds.), *Advances in global leadership* (Vol. 8, pp. 205–228). Bingley, UK: Emerald.
Coppedge, M. (1999). Thickening thin concepts and theories: Combining large N and small in comparative politics. *Comparative Politics, 31*, 465–476.
Dalton, R. L., & Ong, N. T. (2005). Authority orientations and democratic attitudes: A test of the 'Asian values' hypothesis. *Japanese Journal of Political Science, 6*, 1–21.
Dickson, M. W., Den Hartog, D. N., & Mitchelson, J. K. (2003). Research on leadership in a cross-cultural context: Making progress, and raising new questions. *The Leadership Quarterly, 14*, 729–768.
Dooley, L. M. (2002). Case study research and theory building. *Advances in Developing Human Resources, 4*, 335–354.
Dorfman, P., Javidan, M., Hanges, P., Dastmalchian, A., & House, R. (2012). GLOBE: A twenty year journey into the intriguing world of culture and leadership. *Journal of World Business, 47*, 504–518.
Elenkov, D., & Manev, I. M. (2005). Top management leadership and influence on innovation: The role of sociocultural context. *Journal of Management, 31*, 381–402.
Englehart, N. A. (2000). Rights and culture in the Asian values argument: The rise and fall of Confucian ethics in Singapore. *Human Rights Quarterly, 22*, 548–568.
Faure, G. O., & Fang, T. (2008). Changing Chinese values: Keeping up with paradoxes. *International Business Review, 17*, 194–207.
Friedman, E. (Ed.). (1994). *The politics of democratization: Generalizing East Asian experiences*. Boulder, CO: Westview.
George, B. (2003). *Authentic leadership: Rediscovering the secrets to creating lasting values*. San Francisco, CA: Wiley.
George, A. L., & Bennett, A. (2005). *Case studies and theory development in the social sciences*. Cambridge, MA: MIT Press.
Goh, C. T. (1988, June 1). Why we had no choice but to react. *Straits Times*, p. 15.
Gupta, V., & Hanges, P. (2004). Regional and climate clustering of societal cultures. In R. J. House, P. J. Hanges, M. Javidan, P. Dorfman, & V. Gupta

(Eds.), *Leadership, culture and organizations: The GLOBE study of 62 societies* (pp. 178–215). Thousand Oaks, CA: Sage.

Hanges, P. J., Aiken, J. R., Park, J., & Su, J. (2016). Cross-cultural leadership: Leading around the world. *Current Opinion in Psychology, 8*, 64–69.

Haslam, S. A., Reicher, S. D., & Platow, M. (2011). *The new psychology of leadership*. New York: Psychology Press.

Hofstede, G. (2001). *Culture's consequences: Comparing values, behaviors, institutions, and organizations across nations*. Thousand Oaks, CA: Sage.

Hogg, M. A. (2001). A social identity theory of leadership. *Personality and Social Psychology Review, 5*, 184–200.

Hong, Y., Morris, M. W., Chiu, C., & Benet-Martinez, V. (2000). Multicultural minds: A dynamic constructivist approach to culture and cognition. *American Psychologist, 55*, 709–720.

House, R. J., Hanges, P. J., Javidan, M., Dorfman, P. W., & Gupta, V. (2004). *Culture, leadership, and organization: The globe study of 62 societies*. Thousand Oaks, CA: Sage.

Hunter, A., Bedell-Avers, K. E., & Mumford, M. D. (2007). The typical leadership study: Assumptions, implications, and potential remedies. *The Leadership Quarterly, 18*, 435–446.

Illies, R., Morgeson, F. P., & Nahrgang, J. D. (2005). Authentic leadership and eudaemonic well-being: Understanding leader–follower outcomes. *The Leadership Quarterly, 16*, 373–394.

Javidan, M., Dorfman, P. W., Howell, J. P., & Hanges, P. J. (2010). Leadership and cultural context: A theoretical and empirical examination based on project GLOBE. In N. Nohria & R. Khurana (Eds.), *Handbook of leadership theory and practice* (pp. 335–376). Boston: Harvard Business Press.

Javidan, M., Dorfman, P. W., Luque, M. S., & House, R. J. (2006). In the eye of the beholder: Cross cultural lessons in leadership from project globe. *The Academy of Management Perspectives, 20*, 67–90.

Josey, A. (1974). *Lee Kuan Yew: The struggle for Singapore*. Sydney, Australia: Angus and Robertson.

Josey, A. (2013). *Lee Kuan Yew: The critical years: 1971–1978* (Vol. 2). Singapore: Marshall Cavendish.

Kim, D. J. (1994). Is culture destiny? The myth of Asia's anti-democratic values. *Foreign Affairs, 73*, 189–194.

Krishnan, V. R. (2002). Transformational leadership and value system congruence. *International Journal of Value-Based Management, 15*, 19–33.

Lee, K. Y. (1959–1990). *Prime Minister's speeches, press conferences, interviews, statements, etc.* Singapore: Prime Minister's Office.

Lee, K. Y. (2013). The future of national economic growth. In G. Allison, R. D. Blackwell, & A. Wyne (Eds.), *Lee Kuan Yew: The grand master's insights on China, the United States, and the world* (pp. 82–94). Cambridge, MA: MIT Press.

Lee, T. H. (1999). Confucian democracy: Modernization, culture, and the state in East Asia. *Harvard International Review, 21*, 16–18.

Leong, F. T. L., Huang, J. L., & Mak, S. (2014). Protestant work ethic, Confucian values, and work-related attitudes in Singapore. *Journal of Career Assessment, 22*, 304–316.

Leong, H. K. (2000). Prime ministerial leadership and policy-making style in Singapore: Lee Kuan Yew and Goh Chok Tong compared. *Asian Journal of Political Science, 8*, 91–123.

Li, N., Chiaburu, D. S., Kirkman, B. L., & Xie, Z. (2013). Spotlight on the followers: An examination of moderators of relationships between transformational leadership and subordinates' citizenship and taking charge. *Personnel Psychology, 66*, 225–260.

Lin, C. (2008). Demystifying the chameleonic nature of Chinese leadership. *Journal of Leadership and Organizational Studies, 14*, 303–321.

Lord, R. G., & Brown, D. J. (2001). Leadership, values, and subordinate self-concepts. *The Leadership Quarterly, 12*, 133–152.

Lord, R. G., & Brown, D. J. (2004). *Leadership processes and follower self-identity.* Mahwah, NJ: Lawrence Erlbaum.

Lord, R. G., Brown, D. J., & Freiberg, S. J. (1999). Understanding the dynamics of leadership. The role of follower self-concepts in the leader/follower relationship. *Organizational Behavior and Human Decision Processes, 78*, 167–203.

Low, K. C. P. (2006). Father leadership: The Singapore case study. *Management Decision, 44*, 89–104.

Lu, D. (1998). Do values matter in development? Reflections on the role of Confucianism in Singapore's public policies. In H. Lim & R. Singh (Eds.), *Values and development: A multidisciplinary approach with some comparative studies* (pp. 209–222). Singapore: National University of Singapore.

Luthans, F., & Avolio, B. J. (2003). Authentic leadership: A positive developmental approach. In K. S. Cameron, J. E. Dutton, & R. E. Quinn (Eds.), *Positive organizational scholarship* (pp. 241–261). San Francisco: Barrett-Koehler.

Markus, H., & Kitayama, S. (1994). The cultural shaping of emotion: A conceptual framework. In H. Markus & S. Kitayama (Eds.), *Emotion and culture: Empirical studies of mutual influence* (pp. 339–351). Washington, DC: American Psychological Association.

McCutcheon, D. M., & Meredith, J. R. (1993). Conducting case study research in operations management. *Journal of Operations Management, 11*, 239–256.

McDonald, P. (2012). Confucian foundations to leadership: A study of Chinese business leaders across greater China and Southeast Asia. *Asia Pacific Business Review, 18*, 465–487.

Mendenhall, M. E., Reiche, B. S., Bird, A., & Osland, J. S. (2012). Defining the 'global' in global leadership. *Journal of World Business, 47*, 493–503.

Mills, A. J., Durepos, G., & Wiebe, E. (Eds.). (2010). *Encyclopedia of case study research* (1st ed.). Thousand Oaks, CA: Sage.

Mirsky, J. (1998, April 10). What are 'Asian values'? A justification for repression. *The New York Times.* Retrieved from http://www.nytimes.com/1998/04/10/opinion/what-are-asian-valuesa-justification-for-repression.html

Mr. Lee Goes to Manila. (1992, December 10). *Far Eastern Review*, p. 4.

Mydans, Seth (2015, March 22). Lee Kuan Yew, founding father and first premier of Singapore, Dies at 91. *The New York Times.* Retrieved from https://www.nytimes.com/2015/03/23/world/asia/lee-kuan-yew-founding-father-and-first-premier-of-singapore-dies-at-91.html

Naylor, L. L. (1996). *Culture and change: An introduction.* Westport, CT: Bergin & Garvey.

Ng, M. (1998). Why Asia needs democracy: A view from Hong Kong. In L. Diamond & M. F. Plattner (Eds.), *Democracy in East Asia* (pp. 3–16). Baltimore: Johns Hopkins University Press.

Oyserman, D. (2011). Culture as situated cognition: Cultural mindsets, cultural fluency, and meaning making. *European Review of Social Psychology, 22*, 164–214.

Oyserman, D., Coon, H. M., & Kemmelmeier, M. (2002). Rethinking individualism and collectivism: Evaluation of theoretical assumptions and meta-analyses. *Psychological Bulletin, 128*, 3–72.

Oyserman, D., Sorensen, N., Reber, R., & Chan, S. X. (2009). Connecting and separating mind-sets: Culture as situated cognition. *Journal of Personality and Social Psychology, 97*, 217–235.

Price, T. L. (2003). The ethics of authentic transformational leadership. *The Leadership Quarterly, 14*, 67–81.

Robins, G., & Boldero, J. (2003). Relational discrepancy theory: The implications of self-discrepancy theory for dyadic relationships and for the emergence of social structure. *Personality and Social Psychology Review, 7*, 56–74.

Roy, D. (1994). Singapore, China, and the 'soft authoritarian' challenge. *Asian Survey, 34*, 231–242.

Scarborough, J. (1998). Comparing Chinese and Western cultural roots: Why 'East is East and …'. *Business Horizons, 41*, 15–24.

Schwartz, S. H. (1992). Universals in the content and structure of values: Theoretical advances and empirical tests in 20 countries. In M. P. Zanna (Ed.), *Advances in experimental social psychology* (pp. 1–65). San Diego, CA: Academic Press.

Schwartz, S. H. (1999). A theory of cultural values and some implications for work. *Applied Psychology, 48*, 23–47.

Sharma, P. (2010). Measuring personal cultural orientations: Scale development and validation. *Journal of the Academy of Marketing Science, 38*, 787–806.

Shin, D. C. (2011). *Confucianism and democratization in East Asia*. Cambridge, UK: Cambridge University Press.

Sosik, J. J. (2005). The role of personal values in the charismatic leadership of corporate managers: A model and preliminary field study. *The Leadership Quarterly, 16*, 221–244.

Sosik, J. J., & Cameron, J. C. (2010). Character and authentic transformational leadership behavior: Expanding the ascetic self toward others. *Consulting Psychology Journal, 62*, 251–269.

Stake, R. E. (1995). *The art of case study research*. Thousand Oaks, CA: Sage.

Subramaniam, S. (2000). The Asian debate: Implications for the spread of liberal democracy. *Asian Affairs, 27*, 19–35.

Tajfel, H. (1972). Social categorization. English manuscript of 'La Categoristion sociale'. In S. Moscovici (Ed.), *Introduction á la pyschologie sociale* (Vol. 1, pp. 272–302). Paris, France: Larousse.

Tan, H. H., & Wee, G. (2002). The role of rhetoric content in charismatic leadership: A content analysis of a Singaporean leader's speeches. *International Journal of Organization Theory and Behavior, 5*, 317–342.

Tatsuo, I. (1999). Liberal democracy and Asian orientalism. In J. R. Bauer & D. Bell (Eds.), *The East Asian challenge for human rights*. Cambridge, UK: Cambridge University Press.

Thomas, D. C., & Ravlin, E. C. (1995). Response of employees to cultural adaption by a foreign manager. *Journal of Applied Psychology, 80*, 133–146.

Thompson, M. R. (2001). Whatever happened to 'Asian values'? *Journal of Democracy, 12*, 154–165.

Uskul, A. K., & Oyserman, D. (2010). When the message-frame fits salient cultural-frame, messages feel more persuasive. *Psychology and Health, 25*, 321–337.

Vroom, V. H., & Jago, A. G. (2007). The role of the situation in leadership. *American Psychologist, 62*, 17–24.

Yao, S. (2007). *Singapore: The state and the culture of excess*. New York: Routledge.

Yin, R. K. (2003). *Case study research: Design and methods* (3rd ed.). Thousand Oaks, CA: Sage.

Zakaria, F. (1994). Culture is destiny: A conversation with Lee Kuan Yew. *Foreign Affairs, 73*, 109–126.

Zhu, W., Avolio, B. J., Riggio, R. E., & Sosik, J. J. (2011). The effect of authentic transformational leadership on follower and group ethics. *The Leadership Quarterly, 22*, 801–817.

Part II

Conceptual Perspectives

7

The Transformational Influence of Authentic Leadership on Followers in Early Career Relationships

Kim Bradley-Cole

The study outlined in this chapter fits into the body of research that adopts a social-relational approach, which attempts to understand how people perceive varying forms of leadership (Brown & Mitchell, 2010) and contributes to our understanding of how leaders help create effective organisations through their impact on the performance and psychological capital of followers (Dinh, Lord, Gardner, & Meuser, 2014). With regard to authentic leadership theory, Gardner et al. (2005) first acknowledged the role of relational context in the development of both leader and follower authenticity by proposing that an authentic leader helps their follower become "more self-aware and establish an authentic and positive relationship" (p. 359). They also suggested that authentic relationships are developed primarily through the authentic behaviours of the leader, by demonstrating informal behaviours exhibiting transparency, openness, and trust, and also more

K. Bradley-Cole (✉)
University of Winchester, Winchester, UK

© The Author(s) 2018

D. Cotter-Lockard (ed.), *Authentic Leadership and Followership*, Palgrave Studies in Leadership and Followership, https://doi.org/10.1007/978-3-319-65307-5_7

formalised behaviours of guiding followers towards worthy objectives and placing emphasis on their development. However, despite general agreement that authentic behaviour at work increases well-being for both the leaders and followers exposed to it (Ilies, Morgeson, & Nahrgang, 2005), there remains a need to understand in more detail how authentic leadership operates in work relationships and whether the theory adequately captures the perceived meaning and psychological outcomes for followers.

The aim of the broader research project in which this study sits is to better understand how authentic leadership is perceived and understood by followers through their sensemaking of key leader–follower relationships across their career span. The research inductively highlights the pivotal influence that working with an authentic leader at an early career stage has on followers' current leader self-concepts and their own leadership practices, and it is this finding that is the focus of this chapter.

Theoretical Considerations

Two aspects of this research approach support its novel contribution to theory. First, the research adopts an attributional perspective seeking to understand how followers implicitly determine whether their leader is authentic or not. Second, it explores these attributions through the narratives of experienced leaders, derived from their relational perspective as followers rather than leaders. This second aspect acknowledges that the academic practice of dichotomously separating leaders and followers does not reflect the fluid and interconnected reality of organisational life, in which managers are expected to adopt both follower and leader roles across different projects and work contexts. This approach facilitates the exploration of authentic leadership as a perceptual construct and makes it possible to accommodate social context within the sphere of enquiry, thus linking those follower-centred perceptions to leaders' current attitudes and their own enactment of leadership.

Leadership as a Perceptual Attribution

The influence of implicit knowledge structures on attitudes and beliefs is widely accepted in social psychology (Uleman, Adil Saribay, & Gonzalez, 2008). In the leadership field, Implicit Leadership Theory (ILT) was proposed by Eden and Leviatan (1975) as an individual-difference term applied to the idealised characteristics and behaviours attributed to the word "leader" and the enactment of leadership reflective of "an underlying social reality" (p. 740). Researchers have previously demonstrated the influence of ILTs in both peoples' appraisal of leader effectiveness and their willingness to follow (Felfe & Schyns, 2010; Gray & Densten, 2007; Schyns, Felfe, & Blank, 2007).

Hinojosa et al. (2014) acknowledge an accepted proposition that permeates all perspectives of authentic leadership, namely that individuals' personal histories shape their understanding of authenticity, and that these personal histories are influenced by their perceptions of key developmental events and relationships they encounter over time. The purpose of the research output discussed here is to clarify and deepen our understanding of the meaning and influence of authentic leadership for followers derived from their perceptions of these formative leader–follower relationships.

A Relational Context

Eagly (2005) was the first to assert that several theoretical criticisms could be better addressed by deepening our understanding of authentic leadership's relational processes. Lawler and Ashman (2012) also call for a greater focus on relational interactions and argue that the current approach of classifying authentic leaders by a list of normative traits is itself disabling and inauthentic for individuals. They argue that authentic leadership theory must acknowledge both leaders' and followers' behavioural freedom, as well as consider the role of sensemaking (Weick, 1995). Ford and Harding (2011) express similar concerns; they suggest that accepting the theory's normative direction and ideological assumptions means accepting that authentic leaders will have a "deleterious" (p. 464) impact on followers' identities, rendering authentic followership a conceptual impossibility. In a recent meta-analytic review, Banks et al. (2016) identify the unique influence of authentic leadership on group performance and organisational citizenship behaviours, yet also raise the point that without further research into the differential influence of the four dimensions, it is difficult to determine the discriminant and structural validity of authentic leadership as a construct that is distinct from transformational leadership.

Method

A Personal Construct Psychology (PCP) Approach

PCP (Kelly, 1955) offers a unique methodological approach to address the key theoretical criticisms surrounding authentic leadership. PCP explores the ILTs of leaders themselves in a manner that acknowledges the influence of their personal histories and follower roles on the construction of their own leader identities. A personal history perspective is theoretically congruent with the life-story and narrative approaches to authentic leadership theory proposed by Shamir and Eilam (2005) and Sparrowe (2005), as well as by George (2003) and George and Sims (2007), but has not been widely used in empirical research.

The Repertory Grid Method

Lord and Maher (1991) argue that understanding leadership as a perceived phenomenon relies on identifying how perceivers interpret the information they receive across varying situational contexts. Within PCP, repertory grids are the most common method for exploring in depth how people make sense of a given phenomenon and are a recognised investigative tool for unearthing people's implicit perceptions of others that cannot be captured by self-report measures (Uleman et al., 2008). To achieve a breadth of contexts and ensure that the grid in this study represented the phenomenon under investigation (leadership), each participant was asked to select, compare, and rate a range of positive, negative, and average actual leaders (grid elements) with whom they had worked, and then to use their elicited attributes to construct an authentic leader prototype.

Participants

Twenty-five leaders with at least ten years' management experience gained in UK-based organisations of over 500 employees were recruited for the wider project. Of these, 20 participants (8 male and 12 female) were included in this study because they all freely selected an early career leader (ECL) as one of their grid elements, with this ECL being identified as either their first or second close leader relationship in their career chronology. Participants for the ECL study were aged 38–55 years (mean age = 48 years), managing a range of team sizes (from <10 to >100 employees). The sample provided a spread of experiences across a range of organisations (15), industry sectors (10), functions (10) and managerial level (functional managers to board directors).

Procedure

Before each interview, participants were asked to compile a chronological career history, listing all the leaders with whom they had worked (including both direct and indirect reporting lines) over their career span. In the interview, each participant was asked to think about these leaders in the context of how enabling they felt their working relationship had been, and the first six grid elements were chosen to reflect their two most positive leader relationships, their two most negative, and two they would describe as average. Constructs (being the discriminatory, bipolar distinctions that explain people's attributions) were freely elicited using the triadic method for comparing elements (see Denicolo, Long, & Bradley-Cole, 2016, for a review) and laddered as the conversation unfolded to surface core beliefs (Bannister & Fransella, 1986). After all constructs were elicited and scored on a Likert scale of 1–5 (where 1 = the emergent pole and 5 = the contrast pole), participants were asked to score each leader against the provided construct of "Behaves authentically–Behaves far from authentically". Then they were provided with the prototypical element of an "authentic leader" and asked to score this element against their elicited constructs and add any additional constructs they thought may be relevant. Finally, the constructs were cross-verified by asking participants some semi-structured questions relating to authentic behaviour, an authentic leader, and which leader had the most impact on how they feel about themselves today, their ability to do their job and their own leadership style.

Analysis

To identify how the participants make sense of authentic leadership in the context of their own leader relationships, each grid was analysed in RepGrid5, a programme that sorts elements and constructs using "nearest sum of differences" measures appropriate to the data level. Focus plots were produced to determine which constructs clustered most closely with the provided "Behaves authentically" construct and which leaders most closely personified the prototypical idea of an "authentic leader". To ensure that the analysis remained close to each narrative account, the verbatim transcribed interviews were analysed ideographically using Interpretative Phenomenological Analysis, guided by the six-step process advocated by Smith, Flowers, and Larkin (2009). All names were replaced with pseudonyms in the analysis.

From the inductive analysis above, thematic patterns emerged from the data indicating clear distinctions in both the element positions (positive versus negative leader relationships) and narratives relating to leaders that participants scored as behaving authentically compared to those they described as behaving inauthentically. The six non-prototypical elements were then re-analysed on the dimension of leader impact, which surfaced differences in the influential nature of authentic and inauthentic ECLs.

Findings

Evaluation of ECL Elements

Table 7.1 highlights the 9 participants who recalled overall positive relational experiences with their ECL and the associated authentic leader behaviours displayed by them. Seven participants selected their ECL as one of their two most positive leader relationships throughout their career, with 4 selecting them as the leader who has had the most impact on their own leadership identity (marked with a[b]). In contrast, Table 7.3 highlights the 11 participants who recalled overall negative relational experiences with their ECL, with 10 selecting their ECL as one of their two most negative leader relationships throughout their career, and 4 selecting them as the leader who has had the most impact on their identity (marked with a[b]).

The impact response indicates the enduring influence of ECLs on current leadership practice. The average career length for all 20 participants was 27 years and, despite the numerous and varied leader relationships each would have had during this time, 17 participants selected their ECL as one of their most profound managerial relationships, and 8 participants felt that their current sense of leader identity was most impacted by this ECL. Carol explained the impact of working with an authentic leader at an early career stage had on her: "when I worked with Nancy I was 19–20 years old, [and] thought I knew everything and yet had everything to learn ... she knocked me into shape and made me a nicer person".

The Meaning of Authentic Leadership in ECL Relationships

Table 7.1 illustrates that all 9 positive ECLs were rated as behaving authentically, with 5 rated as always authentic (score = 1) and 4 rated as usually authentic (score = 2). Comparison of the two means scores show how closely each ECL meets that participant's prototypical view of an

Table 7.1 Participants with positive ECL relationships and associated authentic leader behaviours

Participant[a]	Kathy	Carol	Phil	Colin	Juliet	Nick	Darren	Katherine	Helen	Total
Early career leader (ECL)	Harry	Nancy	Gordon[b]	Guy	Paxton[b]	Ken	Gareth[b]	Lawrence[b]	Nigel	constructs
Behaves authentically rating[c]	1	1	1	1	1	2	2	2	2	
Number of authentic leader (AL) constructs by theme:										
Inclusive	2	3	3	1	4	[d]	4	5	3	25
Integrity	3	3	1			2	4		5	18
Collaborative	3	7	1	1	1	1	2			16
Transparent	1	1	1	2	2	1	2	1	1	12
Courage			2	1	2	[d]	1			6
Empowering	1	[d]		2						3
Vision					[d]					0
Total constructs elicited for ECL	10	14	8	7	9	4	13	6	9	80
Total constructs elicited for AL prototype	10	18	8	7	10	6	13	6	9	87
Mean score for ECL	1.55	1.96	1.56	1.8	1.93	2.87	1.55	1.41	2.1	
Mean score for AL prototype	1.33	1.13	1.59	1	1	1.43	1.13	1.29	1.3	

[a]All participant names are pseudonyms
[b]This leader had the most (positive) impact on my own leadership identity and practice
[c]Likert scale, 1 (always behaves authentically) to 5 (never behaves authentically)
[d]Behaviours associated with an Authentic Leader, but not associated with this leader

Table 7.2 Behaviours associated with an authentic leader

Master theme	Lower level themes (not weighted)
Inclusive	Personal interest, mutual regard/respect, open for debate, cares, individualised consideration, friendly, understands my role, trusts me, I feel special, emotional warmth, can be me
Integrity	Does right thing, moral, sincere, respected by others, genuine, true to self, higher motive, confident, passionate/creates energy to do the right thing, role model, leads by example, trust, credibility
Collaborative	Supportive, invests time in others, unselfish, fair, equitable, finds solutions, supports me/others, helps, honest feedback, champions the team.
Transparent	Honest, open, what you see is what you get (WYSIWYG), consistent/no surprises, delivers promises, no ego, content/ nothing to prove, clear messages
Courage	Brave, takes risks, challenges status quo, thinks outside the box, instinctive, decisive, engenders fun, stands up for others/team
Empowers	Empowers, delegates, inspires growth and confidence
Vision	Creates a vision, charismatic

authentic leader. Gordon (mean = 1.56) is an almost direct match to Phil's prototypical view (mean = 1.59), whereas Ken (mean = 2.87) exhibits a number of authentic behaviours but is more removed from Nick's prototypical view of an authentic leader (mean = 1.43). Gordon was also identified as the leader who had the most impact on Phil's own leadership style, whereas Nick did not select Ken as one of his most profound managerial relationships.

Five master themes were identified that relate to the behaviours these 9 participants implicitly associate with an authentic leader and explain their categorisation of these ECLs as authentic: (1) inclusion, (2) integrity, (3) collaboration, (4) transparency and (5) courage. Table 7.2 presents the lower level themes for each master theme.

In the discussion that follows, quotations were selected from the detailed transcripts of the repertory grid interviews to illustrate how participants elaborated their meanings, summarised on the grids as bipolar constructs.

Table 7.3 Participants with negative ECL relationships and associated inauthentic leader behaviours

Participant[a]	Peter	Brian	Ann	Jessica	Sarah	Amanda	Emma	Simon	Craig	Melinda	Ava	Total
Early career leader (ECL)	Philip[b]	Gerald	Eddie[b]	Roger[b]	Dianne	Trisha	Gerard	Howard	Len	Aileen [b]	Sajan	constructs
Behaves authentically rating [c]	5	5	5	5	4	3	3	3	3	2	1	
Number of inauthentic leader constructs by theme:												
Self-centred	2	4	3	6	2	4			3	2	2	28
Emotionless	1		4	2		1	2	2	3	3		18
Autocratic	3	3	2			5			1	1	1	16
Critical	1	1	4	1			2		1	1	1	12
Manipulative	2	3	1	2							1	9
Erratic			1		1				2	1		5
Lacks expertise		[d]					1	1	1		1	4
Total constructs elicited for ECL	9	11	15	11	3	10	5	3	11	8	6	92
Total constructs elicited for AL prototype	9	13	15	11	3	10	9	4	11	8	14	107
Mean score for ECL	4.41	4.05	4.26	4.52	4.45	4.76	2.44	3.27	3.42	3.09	2.94	
Mean score for AL prototype	1.3	1.76	1.06	1.64	1.75	1.4	1	1.5	1.14	2.14	1.33	

[a]All participant names are pseudonyms
[b]This leader had the most (negative) impact on my own leadership identity and practice
[c]Likert scale, 1 (always behaves authentically) to 5 (never behaves authentically)
[d]Behaviours associated with an Inauthentic Leader, but not associated with this leader

Inclusion

This theme denotes a quality of the dyadic exchange relationship, in which the leader makes the subordinate feel they care for them. Darren explained that his ECL, Gareth, "took you on board and didn't just leave you out to the side. [He] wanted you to be part of [his] team".

Juliet and Katherine both reported paternalistic work relationships with their ECLs and vividly recalled examples of pivotal events from the 1980s where these leaders made them feel nurtured and valued. Katherine described her relationship with Lawrence as one where she "absolutely [had] always been myself", therefore she has retained an essence of open self-expression and non-conformity as core aspects of her current identity as a leader:

> So, the older I've got and the more confident I have felt in being myself, which is a woman and not a shoulder padded fake man who is working in the City, that is better for me and the people working with me and I recognise that. So, the more like myself I am and the more like myself I become, I think the more effective I am.

Integrity

This theme concerns the leader's perceived moral goodness, which is associated with participant perceptions of them as being genuine and "real". It relates to "doing what's right" and is manifested through behaviours that demonstrate the leader's originality and non-conformity, which also relates to the theme of courage. Katherine described it as "acting on his or her own beliefs and not playing a role, acting, being themselves. I think those are the two most important things".

Darren described Gareth as behaving "true to himself" and Juliet, who referred to Paxton as "a really good guy" because of his integrity, perceived this as an internal moral code, where the leader consistently acts in accordance with "what they believed was right, not necessarily what they thought was political or flavour of the month. They would be consistent in that".

The notion of integrity appears to be intertwined with the belief that this person is trustworthy, as highlighted by Carol, "I would trust Nancy with my keys, with my son, anything". Similarly, Phil explained:

> [Gordon] was a guy you'd follow. You know if he told you something, you'd follow, you just trusted the guy … he had no concept of lying and he was straight talking … Gordon was the best leader.

Collaboration

This theme identifies that what an ECL does to create a supportive and collaborative environment at the team level is seen by participants as an important aspect of perceiving the leader as authentic. Kathy explicitly described Harry as being authentic because of his "supportive" and "developmental" approach to his team and because "he wouldn't really step on you to get where he wanted to go". Collaborative behaviours appear to manifest themselves in the leader's informal, rather than formal, encounters with others, as Helen recalled:

> I learnt so much from [Nigel]. I learnt the basics from him about good management of people, which is quite close involvement with them, understanding them and then giving them what they need.

Phil described how an informal approach to collaboration permeates his leadership style today:

> If people come to me … I can give little tips on how to cope with issues. I do get a lot of that and am quite flattered that people feel able to share their problems with me, if I can help them out I will. I would say I am an authentic manager.

Similarly, Darren said:

> Gareth [was] quite a relaxed person and I see my management style as quite relaxed … my view is give people space and let them grow within that … I like to be seen as someone you can go and talk to, someone who is approachable, that fits more with the Gareth style.

Transparency

This theme reflects an association between authenticity in leadership and social competence behaviours such as openness, honesty, and straight-talking, along with an absence of impression management and self-serving political behaviours. Nick summed it up as being "upfront", "so you absolutely understand where you are in relation to this other person"; Darren talked about Gareth having "his heart on his sleeve". Similarly, Juliet described Paxton as "very much an authentic person I would say. What You See Is What You Get". Katherine illustrated the value of transparency in dealing with organisational change:

> [When you] give people difficult messages, then you … do it honestly and give people … respect for their intellect and their own emotions … you always need to tell people the whole thing.

Courage

This theme is linked to the theme of Integrity, because "doing the right thing" often requires the leader to challenge the status quo and stand up for others. Katherine, when talking about her own leadership style, explained "it is quite a brave thing, I think to be authentic … you have to hold your eye on the horizon".

Courage is a unifying construct across all participants except Ava and Colin and, as a manifestation of authenticity, is commonly perceived as maverick type behaviours enacted in situations where the leader is seen to champion the interests of their group or team above those of the organisation. For example, Juliet recalled several events where Paxton's decisions were biased in favour of his team and apparently driven by a sense of paternalistic responsibility, which required him to stand in opposition to the organisation and, as a result, engendered a sense of mutual trust and an affective connection.

The Meaning of Inauthentic Leadership in ECL Relationships

Constructs are bipolar (where the meaning of the elicited descriptor – the emergent pole – is elaborated through the choice of the contrast pole/descriptor). As such, a person's beliefs can best be understood from the exploration of both poles (Denicolo et al., 2016). Therefore, in order to understand how leaders construe the authentic behaviour of their ECLs, we need to also understand what behaviours they construe as inauthentic in the context of those relationships. Table 7.3 illustrates that, in the 11 negative ECL relationships, 5 ECLs (Philip, Gerald, Eddie, Roger and Dianne) were rated as always or usually behaving inauthentically (score = 5 or 4).

Five master themes were identified that relate to the inauthentic behaviours of these 5 ECLs: (1) self-centred, (2) emotionless, (3) autocratic, (4) critical and (5) manipulative. Table 7.4 presents the lower level themes for each master theme, and all 5 can be grouped together under the superordinate theme of "egocentric orientation". Collectively, these themes explain the importance of adopting a prosocial orientation to be perceived as authentic. For example, Peter described his ECL, Philip, as emotionless because he dealt with people as "a resource to use" rather than as individuals. Ann regarded Eddie as manipulative because he would:

Table 7.4 Behaviours associated with an inauthentic leader

Superordinate theme: 'egocentric orientation'	
Master theme	Lower level themes (not weighted)
Self-centred	Unsupportive, ego-driven, inconsiderate, lacks morals, personal motives, unaware of impact on others, non-reflective, doesn't grow/recognise others
Emotionless	Cold, disconnected from others, lacks empathy, doesn't care, ignores people implications
Autocratic	Directive, aggressive, not one of team, not listening, closed body language, controlling, not hands on, doesn't sort problems, delegates problems, task focused (not people focused)
Critical	Micromanaging, no trust, focusing on deficits, no fun, blames others
Manipulative	Impression management, hidden agenda, divisive, inner circle, unprofessional, game player

> ... say one thing to one person and the polar opposite to someone else, with the result of creating confusion. Undermined people, made them feel they weren't sure about what they were doing, made them feel there was actually something going on that they didn't know about ... could make people feel scared for their jobs.

Egocentric Orientation

This overarching theme suggests that a leader who is perceived to act predominantly in their own interests and who treats others in their group or team without proper regard is categorised as inauthentic. The case of Melinda's ECL, Aileen, demonstrates this (see Table 7.3). Melinda rated Aileen as usually behaving authentically because she exhibited openness and honesty, was not manipulative and was brave in standing up for her beliefs. However, she was not implicitly categorised as an authentic leader because she also lacked emotional warmth and focused her bravery towards satisfying her own motives, rather than those of the team. The strength of the relationship between follower perceptions of authenticity and the leader's prosocial orientation is also illustrated by the ECLs Howard and Dianne, who both exhibited only a few inauthentic behaviours, yet were not categorised as authentic leaders because they were not perceived as championing group interests.

The Impact of Authentic Versus Inauthentic ECLs on Leaders' Identity and Practices

Gordon, Paxton, Gareth, and Lawrence (see Table 7.1) were rated as being authentic leaders and as having a profound and enduring positive impact on participants' own leadership style. The 4 participants who worked for these authentic ECLs speak of a more personal, emotionally connected relational experience, which helped them develop a stable sense of self-confidence. As Juliet explained, her relationship with Paxton "made me feel very confident about myself, my possibilities and my potential". They also made more explicit links between their own authentic behaviours at work and these early relationships, particularly in relation to their personal willingness to stand up for others, be supportive, take risks, and express their own individuality.

Philip, Eddie, and Roger (see Table 7.3) were rated as inauthentic leaders who had a profound and enduring negative impact on participants' self-esteem. Peter described his relationship with Philip as "destructive" and "humiliating," Ann portrayed Eddie as having "a massive ego" that was "off the Richter scale," and Jessica remembered Roger as being "totally unethical". These negative early leader relationships disrupted trust, which lingers in how these leaders continue to approach their current work relationships, as Peter said:

> If I disclosed to someone I couldn't trust the fear is that they would use it against me and try and undermine me in front of others.

This view was shared by Brian:

> If you mistrust someone, you are not going to say what you think because you're going to be worried about, is he going to take it the wrong way, is it going to be used against me ... I'm super protective and that then becomes quite negative.

Helen explained how the leader's authenticity improves the perceived quality of the managerial relationship:

> I think it's just things like trust and confidence and actually it's taking away that worry isn't it? If you know where you stand with somebody and you know what their views are and where they're going, you can focus on the job, so it's one less distraction.

Discussion

In line with the suggestion by Ruiz, Ruiz, and Martinez (2011) that more can be learnt about leadership from understanding the reasons why people are motivated to follow; this study contributes to our understanding of authentic leadership in three ways. First, it challenges the current conceptualisation of authentic leadership and the differential contribution of the four dimensions first proposed by Gardner et al. (2005). Second, it introduces more clearly the role of the leader's prosocial and moral orientation and, third, it identifies a lasting legacy of authentic ECLs on the development of followers own authentic leadership identity and practices. The following discussion explores these contributions in more detail.

A Flexible Construct

A constructivist methodology adopts the position that the experiential reality of authentic leadership can only be understood through people's perceptions and interpretations. Within ECL relationships, authentic leadership appears to be a more flexible construct than is suggested in the mainstream theory and not something that adheres rigidly to the four dimensions of self-awareness, balanced processing, relational transparency and internalised moral perspective (Gardner et al., 2005; Walumbwa & Wernsing, 2013). The following sections consider the key challenges to mainstream theory presented by the findings and alternative perspective offered by this study.

Self-Awareness

Gardner et al. (2005) originally framed this dimension around an identity reflection process in which the leader is presented as knowing and trusting their values, motives, feelings, and self-relevant cognitions. Participants did not make any references to their authentic leaders being particularly self-aware or reflective and made more references to emotional responses, such as being instinctive, decisive, and fun. They also talked more about consideration and behavioural consistency, which suggest the leader has achieved a level of self-direction and self-acceptance that is not adequately captured in this dimension as it is currently framed. The notion of consistency is also referenced by Sparrowe (2005) as a central tenet of authentic leadership, which he presents as one who acts within character across events. Participants also perceptually associated behavioural consistency with caring, raising their self-esteem, and being dependable.

Balanced Processing

Kernis' (2003) original view placed this dimension closer to being an outward expression and consequence of self-awareness. Gardner et al. (2005) similarly presented it and described it in the context of accurate self-assessments and social comparisons. They also referenced high self-esteem and absence of ego-defensive behaviours. Ten years later, Walumbwa and Wernsing's (2013) definition bears little resemblance to its roots and presents it as an overarching decision-making skill that encompasses objective analysis, opinion seeking, critical reflection, and accurate judgement. The ALQ (Walumbwa, Avolio, Gardner, Wernsing, & Peterson, 2008) factor references opinion seeking, listening, and objective judgement. Overall, the findings do not support these later interpretations of balanced processing as a perceptual trigger of authentic leadership. In fact, participants frequently recalled events where their authentic ECLs behaved emotionally rather than objectively. Juliet related Paxton's authenticity to his emotionally open and straight-talking approach. Gardner et al.'s (2005) absence of ego-defensiveness can be related to the lack of impression management that was commonly mentioned and is reflected in phrases such as "transparent", "What You See Is What You Get", and "know where you stand". In isolation, these associations appear to relate more to the relational orientation of the authentic leader than to their cognitive processing style. Therefore, findings suggest that the dimension of balanced processing, in its current form, does not capture the emotional nature of authentic expression in leaders or the affective ties it creates in followers.

Relational Transparency

This refers to the leader's presentation of their authentic-self to others in the context of their close relationships. Terms such as openness, honesty, transparency, and self-disclosure are used throughout this dimension's various iterations, which is congruent with the terminology used by participants in this study. Walumbwa and Wernsing (2013) make three-dimensional additions: they broaden the relationship definition to include accountability; they include the process of introspection for increasing leader self-knowledge, and; they rationalise the leader's behaviour by specifically referencing their efforts to "minimize displays of inappropriate emotions" (p. 396), although the nature of what is deemed inappropriate is not made clear. The authors appear to have moved the dimension towards a more objective, sanitised notion of acceptable leader behaviours, which again fails to acknowledge the leader's outward emotional expression of their inner values that feature strongly in participants' attributions of authentic leadership.

These findings suggest that authentic leadership is an emotionally expressive and prosocial concept, which alters the nature of the relationship experience for followers. Whilst this dimension utilises some similar terminology, it arguably does not go far enough to adequately explain the transformational effects that this deep, emotionally laden connection can have on followers' relational experiences and identity processes. Walumbwa and Wernsing (2013) make no reference to experiences of collaboration, inclusion, caring, warmth, or fairness that dominate participants' narratives. Therefore, it can be argued that this dimension has been narrowly interpreted, is not reflective of the relationally derived emotional connections that are created by the leader's authentic behaviour, and does not do justice to its overall relational value.

Internalised Moral Perspective

This dimension overlaps considerably with the moral person element of ethical leadership proposed by Trevino, Hartman, and Brown (2000). Its inclusion within authentic leadership theory is contested by Shamir and Eilam (2005, 2013), who stay closer to the root idea of authenticity being 'to know thyself'. Kernis (2003) also made no reference to morality in his definition of personal authenticity and spoke more in terms of behaving true to one's self as a self-liberating experience and a method of enabling others to "see the real you, good and bad" (p. 15), a view supported by Ilies et al. (2005). Other authors, however, have linked authenticity to the notion of intrinsic morality. Bass and Steidlmeier (1999) regarded authenticity as the defining moral difference in transformational leadership, and it was part of Luthans and Avolio's (2003) original conceptualisation.

The findings in this study strongly support the inclusion of the moral self as the foundation of authentic leadership. In the latest iteration by Walumbwa and Wernsing (2013) the authors make specific reference to authentic leaders demonstrating increased prosocial and ethical behaviours, which is also substantiated by this study. These findings support the presentation of authentic leadership as the enactment of the moral self, which encompasses both the integration of morality into one's sense of self and its manifestation within cognitive and affective self-regulation processes (Jennings, Mitchell, & Hannah, 2014).

Gardner et al. (2005) also included being a positive role model in this dimension, which has been lost in subsequent elaborations and does not explicitly feature in any of the measures of authentic leadership. However, these findings indicate that the role modelling of high ethical and moral standards is a key discriminant for the attribution of authentic leadership, which participants associated with their own leadership aspirations. The diffusion of positive role modelling to subordinates' enactment of their own leadership role can be explained in social learning terms (Bandura, 1977). As such, this dimension may be better explained as acting as an ethical role model, or, in social identity terms, creating a cohesive team identity and positively promoting group interests (Haslam, Reicher, & Platow, 2011).

Summary

The findings strongly support the dimension of an "internalised moral self-concept" that is consistently enacted across observable behaviours and events, which, in turn, may be better explained in social learning or social identity terms. The relational enactment of authentic leadership has been identified as having a potentially transformative psychological impact on followers that is not adequately captured in the narrow description of "relational transparency". This dimension could be broadened out to a holistic relational orientation level that encompasses the aspects of psychological voice and lack of ego-defensiveness/impression management that are currently encapsulated within the balanced processing dimension. "Self-awareness" could be more usefully expressed as a state of self-acceptance where leaders feel liberated from organisational and role pressures and are able to act in a self-directed, considerate and consistent manner. Finally, findings suggest that the dimension of "balanced processing" does not relate to perceptions of authentic leadership, which appears to be based more on emotional connections and affective ties that are themselves inextricably intertwined with group processes and social understanding.

The Prosocial and Moral Orientation of an Authentic Leader

As discussed above, these findings clarify the key role of perceived moral goodness in attributions of authentic leadership, which is counter to the view presented by Shamir and Eilam (2005). An authentic leader here is perceived as being ethical, with descriptions such as "do the right thing", "integrity", and "honest". There is also the suggestion of them being value driven or non-conformist in "instinctive" and "brave". Participants also use mostly relationally oriented words, rather than competency based, supporting an association between authenticity and prosocial behaviours, with terms such as "cares", "fair", and "emotional warmth". When encountered at an early career stage, authentic leaders create a sense of psychological attachment for followers through the adoption of a nurturing/caring role, collaboration and focusing on building high-quality work relationships that transcend formal boundaries.

Impact of Authentic Leadership in Early Career Stages

Overall, the findings suggest that authentic leadership transforms both the early career experiences of followers and helps shape their ideological view of leadership, which encourages them to aspire to behave in similar ways as they develop their own leadership style. This study addresses a key criticism levelled at the current theory by Ford and Harding (2011), namely that, by dictating the dominant values to be followed, authentic leaders subsume followers' identities and render authentic followership a false ideology because followers are expected to align themselves to the collective. By providing greater insight to the experience of authentic leadership in early career relationships, findings indicate that authentic leaders, within a more flexible definition of authentic leadership, develop other authentic leaders by role modelling and legitimising self-expression and non-conformity at work. Leaders who had an authentic ECL demonstrated greater self-acceptance, inter-personal trust, and less self-doubt in the enactment of their current roles than those participants who had worked for an inauthentic ECL.

References

Bandura, A. (1977). Self-efficacy: Toward a unifying theory of behavioral change. *Psychological Review, 2*, 191–215. https://doi.org/10.1037/0033-295X.84.2.191.

Banks, G. C., McCauley, K. D., Gardner, W. L., & Guler, C. E. (2016). A meta-analytic review of authentic and transformational leadership: A test for redundancy. *Leadership Quarterly, 27*(4), 634–652. https://doi.org/10.1016/j.leaqua.2016.02.006.

Bannister, D., & Fransella, F. (1986). *Inquiring man: The psychology of personal constructs* (3rd ed.). London: Croom Helm.

Bass, B. M., & Steidlmeier, P. (1999). Ethics, character, and authentic transformational leadership behavior. *Leadership Quarterly, 10*(2), 181–217. https://doi.org/10.1016/S1048-9843(99)00016-8.

Brown, M. E., & Mitchell, M. S. (2010). Ethical and unethical leadership: Exploring new avenues for future research. *Business Ethics Quarterly, 20*(4), 583–616. https://doi.org/10.5840/beq201020439.

Denicolo, P., Long, T., & Bradley-Cole, K. (2016). *Constructivist approaches and research methods. A practical guide to exploring personal meanings*. London: Sage.

Dinh, J. E., Lord, R. G., Gardner, W. L., & Meuser, J. D. (2014). Leadership theory and research in the new millennium: Current theoretical trends and changing perspectives. *The Leadership Quarterly, 25*, 36–62. https://doi.org/10.1016/j.leaqua.2013.11.005.

Eagly, A. H. (2005). Achieving relational authenticity in leadership: Does gender matter? *The Leadership Quarterly, 16*(3), 459–474. https://doi.org/10.1016/j.leaqua.2005.03.007.

Eden, D., & Leviatan, U. (1975). Implicit leadership theory as a determinant of the factor structure underlying supervisory behaviour scales. *Journal of Applied Psychology, 60*, 736–741. https://doi.org/10.1037/0021-9010.60.6.736.

Felfe, J., & Schyns, B. (2010). Followers' personality and the perception of transformational leadership: Further evidence for the similarity hypothesis. *British Journal of Management, 21*(2), 393–410. https://doi.org/10.1111/j.1467-8551.2009.00649.

Ford, J., & Harding, N. (2011). The impossibility of the 'true self' of authentic leadership. *Leadership, 7*(4), 463–479. https://doi.org/10.1177/1742715011416894.

Gardner, W. L., Avolio, B. J., Luthans, F. O., May, D. R., & Walumbwa, F. (2005). "Can you see the real me?" A self-based model of authentic leader and follower development. *The Leadership Quarterly, 16*(3), 343–372. https://doi.org/10.1016/j.leaqua.2005.03.003.

George, B. (2003). *Authentic leadership: Rediscovering the secrets of creating lasting value*. San Francisco: Jossey-Bass.

George, W., & Sims, P. (2007). *True north: Discover your authentic leadership*. San Francisco: Jossey-Bass.

Gray, J. H., & Densten, I. L. (2007). How leaders woo followers in the romance of leadership. *Applied Psychology Special Issue: On the Romance of Leadership-in Memory of James R Meindl, 56*(4), 558–581. https://doi.org/10.1111/j.1464-0597.2007.00304.x.

Haslam, S. A., Reicher, S., & Platow, M. (2011). *The new psychology of leadership: Identity, influence, and power*. Hove, UK: Psychology Press.

Hinojosa, A. S., McCauley, K. D., Randolph-Seng, B., & Gardner, W. L. (2014). Leader and follower attachment styles: Implications for authentic leader–follower relationships. *The Leadership Quarterly, 25*(3), 595–610. https://doi.org/10.1016/j.leaqua.2013.12.002.

Ilies, R., Morgeson, F. P., & Nahrgang, J. D. (2005). Authentic leadership and eudaemonic well-being: Understanding leader–follower outcomes. *The Leadership Quarterly, 16*(3), 373–394. https://doi.org/10.1016/j.leaqua.2005.03.002.

Jennings, P. L., Mitchell, M. S., & Hannah, S. T. (2014). The moral self: A review and integration of the literature. *Journal of Organizational Behavior, IRIOP Annual Review*, Retrieved from http://media.terry.uga.edu/socrates/

publications/2015/01/Jennings_Mitchell__Hannah_in_press_The_moral_self_JOB.pdf

Kelly, G. A. (1955). *The psychology of personal constructs. Volume 1: A theory of personality*. New York: W.W. Norton and Company.

Kernis, M. H. (2003). Toward a conceptualization of optimal self-esteem. *Psychological Inquiry, 14*(1), 1–26. https://doi.org/10.1207/S15327965PLI1401_01.

Lawler, J., & Ashman, I. (2012). Theorizing leadership authenticity: A sartrean perspective. *Leadership, 8*(4), 327–344. https://doi.org/10.1177/1742715012444685.

Lord, R. G., & Maher, K. G. (1991). *Leadership and information processing: Linking perceptions and performance*. Boston: Unwin Hyman.

Luthans, F., & Avolio, B. (2003). Authentic leadership: A positive developmental approach. In J. C. Cameron, J. E. Dutton, & R. E. Quinn (Eds.), *Positive organizational scholarship: Foundations of a new discipline* (pp. 241–258). San Francisco: Berrett-Koehler.

Ruiz, P., Ruiz, C., & Martínez, R. (2011). Improving the "leader–follower" relationship: Top manager or supervisor? The ethical leadership trickle-down effect on follower job response. *Journal of Business Ethics, 99*(4), 587–608. https://doi.org/10.1007/s10551-010-0670-3.

Schyns, B., Felfe, J., & Blank, H. (2007). Is charisma hyper-romanticism? Empirical evidence from new data and a meta-analysis. [Special issue: On the romance of leadership-In memory of James R. Meindl]. *Applied Psychology, 56*(4), 505–527. https://doi.org/10.1111/j.1464-0597.2007.00302.x.

Shamir, B., & Eilam, G. (2005). "What's your story?" A life-stories approach to authentic leadership development. *The Leadership Quarterly, 16*(3), 395–417. https://doi.org/10.1016/j.leaqua.2005.03.005.

Shamir, B., & Eilam, G. (2013). Essay: Life stories, personal ambitions and authenticity: Can leaders be authentic without pursuing the 'higher good'? In D. Ladkin & C. Spiller (Eds.), *Authentic leadership: Clashes, convergences and coalescences* (pp. 93–119). Cheltenham, UK: Edward Elgar.

Smith, J. A., Flowers, P., & Larkin, M. (2009). *Interpretative phenomenological analysis. Theory, method and research*. London, UK: Sage.

Sparrowe, R. (2005). Authentic leadership and the narrative self. *The Leadership Quarterly, 16*(3), 419–439. https://doi.org/10.1016/j.leaqua.2005.03.004.

Trevino, L. K., Hartman, L. P., & Brown, M. (2000). Moral person and moral manager: How executives develop a reputation for ethical leadership.

California Management Review, 42(4), 128–142. https://doi.org/10.2307/41166057.
Uleman, J. S., Adil Saribay, S., & Gonzalez, C. M. (2008). Spontaneous inferences, implicit impressions, and implicit theories. *Annual Review of Psychology, 59*(1), 329–360. https://doi.org/10.1146/annurev.psych.59.103006.093707.
Walumbwa, F. O., Avolio, B. J., Gardner, W. L., Wernsing, T. S., & Peterson, S. J. (2008). Authentic leadership: Development and validation of a theory-based measure. *Journal of Management, 34*(1), 89–126. https://doi.org/10.1177/0149206307308913.
Walumbwa, F. O., & Wernsing, T. S. (2013). From transactional and transformational leadership to authentic leadership. In M. G. Rumsey (Ed.), *The Oxford handbook of leadership* (pp. 392–400). New York: Oxford University Press.
Weick, K. E. (1995). *Sensemaking in organizations*. Thousand Oaks, CA: Sage.

8

Authentic Leadership, Embodied Leadership, and Followership from a Multi-cultural Perspective

Sharon Davis Brown

The intent of this chapter is twofold. The first is to highlight the relationship between authentic leadership, embodied leadership, and followership styles, including body–mind and nonverbal leadership and followership practices used in selected countries. The second intent is to study the relationships between the specific cultures of countries and the willingness or the ability of organisations within those countries to embrace authentic and embodied leadership and followership styles.

The conceptual framework for leadership–followership relationships borrows heavily from the seminal work of McGregor (1960). Organizations within the United States and Israel were selected for the study, based on their cultural differences in leadership and followership qualities and roles, while the culture of Israel is contrasted to that of Japan. Somatic-based leadership development assessments, such as Laban Movement Analysis, are discussed as alternatives to cognitively based assessments, such as the Myers Briggs Inventory or the 360° Assessment Instrument.

S.D. Brown (✉)
Art of Business Coaching, Beaumont, CA, USA

© The Author(s) 2018
D. Cotter-Lockard (ed.), *Authentic Leadership and Followership*, Palgrave Studies in Leadership and Followership, https://doi.org/10.1007/978-3-319-65307-5_8

This chapter adds to the scholarly conversation by furthering knowledge of effective and ineffective behaviours in leadership and followership, and by building on previous theories, assumptions, and practices within authentic leadership, embodied leadership, and followership styles.

The Problem

An authentic leadership role implies self-awareness of the leader's connection with colleagues, peers, and the organisational environment (system) at large. An absence of self-awareness may lead to ineffective leadership and may interfere with effective followership. Leaders' self-awareness is limited without knowledge of embodied leadership elements. Thus, the elements of embodied leadership are critical to effective authentic leadership.

However, there seems to be a macro-problem. Managers, who are participative and involve followers in decision-making while retaining control over implementing decisions, are open to adopting authentic or embodied leadership roles. Managers within traditional authoritarian organisations in which centralised control is retained are not. The cultures of some countries do not permit managers to deviate from traditional authoritarian styles.

Leadership Styles

Leaders and followers function within an organizational milieu that is changing. After the Industrial Revolution, leaders looked to their labour forces for their physical attributes (strength and endurance), and the followers (employees) were expected to be passive, deferential, and obedient (McGregor, 1960). However, since the onset of the technological revolution, labour is largely mechanised and leaders require followers with intellectual attributes (astuteness, creativity, persistence). Thus, the followers are expected to demonstrate extroversion, charisma, and sensitivity towards the effectiveness of the leader (McGregor, 1960).

McGregor (1960) discussed Theory X and Theory Y management styles, where Theory X is authoritarian and centralised control is retained, whereas in Theory Y, management is participative, involving the followers in decision-making but retaining control over implementing decisions. Theory X assumes that people dislike work and want to avoid it; in effect, they do not want to take responsibility. On the contrary, Theory Y assumes that people are self-motivated and thrive on responsibility ("Theory X and Theory Y," n.d.). All the authentic leadership, embodied leadership, and followership research below is an outgrowth of the Theory Y management style.

Authentic Leadership: Conceptual Framework

Researchers have not decisively agreed upon the definition of authentic leadership. Avolio and Gardner (2005) described authentic leadership as an emerging field while Luthans (2002) asserted that authentic leadership is based on positive psychology principles. Luthans applied constructs that include confidence, optimism, hope, and resilience (2002). Separately, Kernis (2003) discussed *relational orientation* that was later elaborated upon by Kernis and Goldman (2006) in which they proposed the following descriptors for authentic leadership: (1) awareness in both cognitive knowledge and in one's thoughts, feelings, motives, and values; (2) unbiased processing, such as objectivity about and acceptance of one's positive and negative attributes; (3) behaviour with respect to actions based on one's true preferences, values, and needs rather than acting merely to please others, secure rewards, or avoid punishments; and (4) relational orientation, such as achieving and valuing truthfulness and openness in one's close relationships.

Thus, authentic leadership has four core elements: (1) self-awareness, (2) unbiased processing, (3) relational authenticity, and (4) authentic behaviour and action (Avolio & Gardner, 2005; Kernis, 2003; Walumbwa, Avolio, Gardner, Wernsing, & Peterson, 2008). The term *authenticity* refers to examination of the self (Avolio & Gardner, 2005). However, a positive moral or ethical perspective is also an important element of authentic leadership (Avolio & Gardner, 2005; Luthans & Avolio, 2003).

For authentic leadership and followership to be effective, the leader and the follower must share a common purpose (Chaleff, 2009). Shamir and Eilam (2005) asserted that authentic leaders lead with an honesty derived from deep-rooted values based on the life stories that they may share with their followers, colleagues, and customers.

Self-awareness, the first core element of authentic leadership, is described as the leader's capacity to self-reflect, to be sensitive to other people's needs, to listen to other people's opinions and suggestions, and to accept responsible criticism without becoming defensive (Avolio & Gardner, 2005). Walumbwa et al. (2008) defined self-awareness as "demonstrating an understanding of how one derives and makes meaning of the world and how that meaning making process impacts the way one views himself or herself over time" (p. 95). A lack of self-awareness may create friction in the boardroom as an unwillingness to consider other people's opinions (unbiased processing), and may reduce cooperation with decision-making. As shown in the cross-cultural case studies that follow, not all leaders possess these skills and some do not wish to. In traditional hierarchical organisations, leaders often prefer an autocratic leadership style (McGregor, 1960).

From the practitioner viewpoint, George, Sims, McLean, and Mayer described authentic leadership as "(1) pursuing purpose with passion; (2) practicing solid values; (3) leading with heart; (4) establishing enduring relationships; (5) demonstrating self-discipline" (as cited in Gardner, Cogliser, Davis, & Dickens, 2011, p. 1123). From a practitioner's perspective, leaders show their authenticity through their actions while scholars may view this refined explanation as pedantic.

Embodied Leadership: Conceptual Framework

Embodied leadership is a body–mind theoretical concept that, like authentic leadership, encourages leaders to be mindful of their thoughts, actions, trustworthiness, and moral compass. However, embodied leadership stresses leaders' awareness of their body language in addition to their cognitive skills (Moore, 2005). Thus, embodied leadership is a subset of authentic leadership and these two leadership styles share similar qualities (Kernis, 2003; Ladkin & Taylor, 2010; Sheets-Johnstone, 2010).

By definition, the authentic leadership role requires self-awareness of the leader's connection with colleagues, peers, and the organisational environment (system) at large. However, an absence of self-awareness or reflexivity, a skill that "requires a process of seeking, receiving, and giving feedback, and also entails changes in behaviour" (Carmeli, Sheaffer, Binyamin, Reiter-Palmon, & Shimoni, 2014, p. 129) may lead to ineffective leadership and may interfere with effective followership. As such, without knowledge of the elements associated with embodied leadership, leaders are limited in their self-awareness. Thus, the elements of embodied leadership are critical to effective authentic leadership. The leaders who practice embodied leadership skills can more effectively connect with their followers in a synergistic relationship, although leaders' exact mannerisms may differ from culture to culture.

Most of us use our bodies to communicate nonverbally, whether consciously or not. Most of us use our voices to communicate verbally. We spend years consciously developing our abilities to communicate cognitive ideas by learning to talk and listen in turns. Most of us are only peripherally aware of our nonverbal communications. Somatic contemplative routines such as Feldenkrais'(1972) movement awareness or Gendlin's (1978) *focusing*, a method created to generate the *felt sense* that serves as a system to learn about physical body changes to make the implicit explicit, are practiced to increase a person's somatic awareness. Other body-based routines include authentic movement (Pallaro, 1999), which is a meditative practice with one person moving in a quiet space with eyes closed while a witness views the mover, yoga, and mindfulness practices (Kabat-Zinn, 1994) that increase leaders' sensitivity towards their colleagues. These practices may assist leaders and followers to use somatic awareness as an intuitive, nonverbal dimension of embodied communication.

Laban Movement Analysis, Action Profiling™, and Movement Pattern Analysis are systems that practitioners use to conceptualise and notate nonverbal movement patterns used in fields as diverse as dance choreography, assembly line factory worker movement patterns, and management decision-making (Moore, 2005). This notation is analogous to scoring a musical symphony for an orchestra. Notating nonverbal movement patterns and scoring a musical composition utilise written symbols to map the respective modality. Towards this end, knowledgeable consultants who apply the principles of Laban Movement Analysis or a similar nonverbal movement system can train the leaders to acquire and develop the skills to become authentic embodied leaders and effective followers (Bartenieff & Lewis, 1980; Moore, 2005, 2014).

Ladkin and Taylor (2010) described the concept of the *true self*, where leaders and followers display and observe somatic cues to connect with the bodily based felt sense of authenticity. Leaders can gain an understanding of the true self through an embodied education, for example, by using the Laban Movement Analysis principle of *affinities* and *disaffinities*. This principle addresses the concept of aligning people's words with their nonverbal actions. Thus, when verbal expression is aligned with the body language displayed (affinity), it is conveyed as being authentic. When words and nonverbal expression are not aligned (disaffinity), it is viewed as being inauthentic. This concept helps us understand when someone is being genuine or being insincere.

Walumbwa et al. (2008) described moral development as a requirement to achieve leadership authenticity, yet they did not prescribe a system to identify such behaviour. Laban Movement Analysis is one system that can enable a practitioner to discriminate between authentic and inauthentic behaviours. Although Laban Movement Analysis does not measure moral development, it does measure when movement actions and speech content do not mesh. When words and nonverbal expressions are not aligned, a practitioner will view this as disaffinity (Moore, 2005). In this regard, the Laban Movement Analysis principle of affinities and disaffinities dovetails with Ladkin and Taylor's (2010) concept of inner and outer expressions. When the *inner world* (somatic sensations) of leaders or followers is in sync with their *outer expression* (verbal language), they are likely to be viewed as authentic.

Ladkin (2013) advocated an embodied leadership model based on the *felt experience* (p. 321). She suggested that "bodies have a critical role in creating this felt sense through the very way in which perception works" (Ladkin, 2013, p. 322). The perception that Ladkin described is based on our bodily senses of seeing, hearing, smelling, feeling, and touching. Her model assumes that the leaders or the followers have a heightened skill set to use their physical senses in this manner. She also discussed reflexivity and suggested that "pressing the flesh" in a handshake as an interactive phenomenon strengthens the shared exchange between leaders and followers by means of an inter-subjective interaction rather than a linguistic communication.

Learning to stay in the present moment is best practiced through some form of somatic awareness, like taking a few deep breaths or taking a self-inventory of physical tension, strained muscles, or accelerated heartbeat. Slowing down breathing or releasing muscle tension are ways to return to the present moment. From a somatic perspective, authentic leadership is an act of balancing organisational objectives with the unconscious tensions within the body (Ladkin & Taylor, 2010).

Leaders and followers function in organisations that are constantly changing. Sheets-Johnstone (1981) used a phenomenological and somatic perspective to describe bodily sensations, which, when combined with cognitive awareness, mirror and act as a response to organisational changes. Thus, the study of nonverbal movement is the study of change. This includes the inner and outer dualities (somatic sensations vs. verbal language) described above: physically, how one is aware of bodily sensations; spatially, how one navigates the external environment and, dynamically, how one applies different energies to applied tasks (gentle or forceful, direct or indirect, open or closed). Brendel and Bennett (2016) examine how *somatic resonance* occurs when the leaders learn to respond to situations and relationships after having learned to observe their inner selves to access unconscious patterns of thought, emotion, and automatic reactions to others. Brendel and Bennett (2016) further suggested that as leaders learn to access their inner state, they are better positioned to be more open to new perceptions and alternative possibilities for action.

To suggest that an embodied model is successful within a leadership–followership context is complex due to the difficulty of measuring success empirically. Leaders and followers alike may describe the presence or absence of connecting to the felt experience, but as Ladkin (2013) conveyed, subjective experiences are easily ignored in a world that embraces measurements and objective studies.

Embodied leadership requires a set of skills that allows leaders to listen to their bodily senses as part of their leadership role. It takes a special kind of leader to embrace an embodied leadership practice where the goal is to maximise the connection with the leadership team, colleagues, and customers. Towards this end, an embodied leadership skill set can be transferred to followership roles with success.

Followership: Conceptual Framework

Researchers use subtle conceptual variations when explaining followership and the literature shows a developmental progression in the definitions of follower characteristics. Meindl (1995) introduced the *follower-centred approach* to describe follower traits, emotions, and attitudes. In the same year, Chaleff (1995) coined the term *courageous follower* to describe the followers who choose to question their leaders' actions and decisions rather than remaining silent. Chaleff (2009) later modified his courageous follower term to define the unbalanced relationship between leaders and followers with the core values of mutual respect and honesty; the follower supports the leader's vision and final decision. The Pearce and Manz (2005) model of *shared leadership* advocates diminishing rigid roles that can inhibit best business practices by encouraging a dynamic and interactive synergy based on mutual respect. Avolio et al. (2004) also postulate that underlying trust is the essential required feature for the leader–follower relationship to thrive and that trust is initiated when leaders encourage diverse follower viewpoints as long as these viewpoints support their working relationship and the organisation's core mission. Uhl-Bien and Pillai (2007) suggested that the followers express their own viewpoints when engaging with the leaders, while Shamir (2007) suggested that "reverse[ing] the lens" is a trait where the followers are actively engaged to create and maintain leadership outcomes. In this regard, Shamir suggested that the followers are co-producers in organisational outcomes and their role is vital to the functioning of the organisation.

de Zilwa (2014) enumerated a relational conceptual framework for *authentic followership* that relies on the (1) the follower's capacity to think and behave, (2) the nature of the dyadic relationship between the leader and follower along with the follower's secure attachment to the leader, and (3) the context with which the follower engages with the organisational structure, culture, norms, and political conditions so that these conditions provide a supportive environment for authentic followership.

The term *relational dynamics* coined by Uhl-Bien, Riggio, Lowe, and Carsten (2014) to describe mutual influence between the leader and follower is similar to the concepts that others have described as *proactive follower* (Carsten, Uhl-Bien, West, Patera, & McGregor, 2010) and courageous follower (Chaleff, 1995). Followership is the essential backbone of the constructive authentic leadership process (Uhl-Bien et al., 2014).

Effective followers are critical thinkers, and, as such, they carefully question potential leadership decisions with a thoughtful, provoking inquiry. For example, the effective follower may ask questions such as, "Is there another way we might be able to solve this business problem?" or "What is the downside of this decision compared with another intervention?" These types of questions are designed to challenge the leaders so that they have multiple perspectives from which to make sound business decisions. This type of interaction should not be viewed as being anti-leader, but rather as an attempt to work collaboratively with the leader and the leadership team.

The somatic practices discussed in the section "Authentic Leadership: Conceptual Framework" above also apply to followers. When somatic practices are used by both leaders and followers, the result can be an increase in flexible synergy and embodied communication among members of the organisational team.

Multi-Cultural Case Studies

Earlier in this chapter, the author described the conceptual framework for Theory X, Theory Y, authentic leadership, embodied leadership, and followership roles. This section highlights cultural differences and how leaders and followers from the United States and Israel perform their respective roles, particularly as it pertains to their self-awareness, unbiased processing, relational authenticity, authentic behaviours, cognitive skills, and the connections with colleagues, peers, and the organisational environment.

Since only one case study is used from each country, the author does not mean to imply that the characteristics of the chosen examples exist in every organisation within that country, only that cultural differences exist between countries.

United States

S. Jobs, a co-founder of Apple Industries, was a well-recognised, though complex, leader. Although some writers focus on his genius, others focus on his acerbic personality. He was passionate about his work and a perfectionist who was hyper-focused, artistic, compulsive, and controlling. He often set impossible deadlines and, upon receiving employee push-back, would devolve into temper tantrums. His personality traits shaped the way he approached business (Knickerbocker, 2011). Based on the inflexible way he led others, he appeared to lack self-awareness. However, he was driven by his vision of the products he developed. For example, during the development of the iPod, he insisted that the music must be quickly accessed by no more than three clicks.

Jobs' career went through several peaks and valleys. During the first 10 years of Apple, there was marked growth of the Macintosh computer. Jobs hired J. Sculley to work on the business side of the company; however, an interpersonal conflict ensued between the two, and the board of directors sided with Sculley. In effect, Jobs, then 30 years of age, was relieved of his duties at the company he co-founded.

As Jobs described in a 2005 Stanford speech, his sense of career, identify, self-efficacy, and self-worth were challenged (as cited in Richardson & Arthur, 2013). Thus, it appeared that upon being fired, Jobs conducted a self-assessment, an act of self-awareness that led to the most productive years of his professional career, his time at NeXt and Pixar. Jobs asserted that the loss of the Apple Industries leadership position allowed him to develop new opportunities for growth and redirection and to plan new career alternatives (as cited in Richardson & Arthur, 2013; Zikic & Klehe, 2006; Zikic & Richardson, 2007). Reflecting, Jobs claimed that getting fired was the best thing that could have happened to him (Richardson & Arthur, 2013).

Upon his return to Apple in 2005, he continued leading in the Theory X, autocratic style. He discontinued the production of the Macintosh computer and focused on technological products such as the iPod, iPad, iTunes, and iPhone. During this period of his life, Jobs continued developing creative products that customers did not yet know they needed. He produced a wealth of products and, at that time, Apple Industries revenue exceeded that of Mobil/Exxon (Yu, 2013).

Jobs typically lacked real-time self-awareness, dismissed or undermined other people's opinions, and was a difficult person to work for and with (Isaacson, 2012). However, during his 2005 Stanford graduation speech, Jobs shared with the graduating audience a need to "listen to their hearts and heads, do what is important to them, pursue their ambitions, and take charge of and responsibility for their careers" (Richardson & Arthur, 2013, p. 46). This statement showed a softer side of Jobs, but one that did not transfer into his leadership style. Nevertheless, Jobs remains an icon in the creation of products that combine art, technology, and functionality.

The brief somatic analyses given below are based on YouTube videos.

During a 2010 demonstration to a large audience, which was failing due to Wi-Fi overload, Jobs paced back and forth along the stage (CNET, 2010). It was not a true temper tantrum as his voice was soft, but his tone was sarcastic. His torso was *bound*; a term describing limited flexibility, which in this example signifies annoyance with the situation. He gestured in a *free flow* manner; his arms wide open within the horizontal plane, which shows receptivity to his audience. The audience complied with his request to turn off their Wi-Fi devices so that his demonstration could continue.

Separately, Jobs demonstrates his ability to connect with his audience during the introduction of the iPhone in 2007 (Stark, 2012). Throughout the presentation, Jobs paces along the length of the stage using *sustained* even *flow* and using his arms bilaterally to gesture in an open manner as if to invite his audience closer, an example of affinity. To emphasise a point, Jobs makes large sweeping flowing gestures that capture the attention of his audience. When the audience applauds, Jobs pauses before adding more dialogue. Jobs' posture is upright, but not rigid, as he displays an uncanny ability for patience.

His body language in this video shows a man who is passionate about the product he is introducing. He seemingly takes his time; he listens to the audience by waiting for the applause to stop before he resumes talking. He speaks softly but deliberately. He displays an affinity by *spreading* his arms open *indirectly* but in a *sustained* manner. According to the principles of Laban Movement Analysis, this gesture shows a propensity towards alignment (affinity) between his words and his nonverbal actions.

Israel

H. Lipskin is the CEO of Keepers Child Safety, a start-up company in Jerusalem, Israel, that has been in business for one year and has 10 employees (personal communication, October 11, 2016). Their business product is a computer application that allows parents to monitor and track their child's activity on smart phones to detect and prevent cyber-bullying. Keepers Child Safety launched their product in beta version (soft launch) testing in early November 2016. Success will be determined by "the prevention of suicide" and failure "by the loss of life" (H. Lipskin, personal communication, October 11, 2016). Their ability to continue is contingent upon success and global market factors that will affect their ability to raise money (H. Lipskin, personal communication, October 11, 2016).

The small size of the company makes the structural fluidity between the leader and followers transparent. This is evidenced by how Lipskin views himself "as a member of the team" (personal communication, October 11, 2016). He also described the company's organisational culture as "unofficial," in which employees are engaged in the process and enjoy their work. This is Lipskin's first start-up business, and he has had no prior experience as a manager. He described his greatest leadership challenges as meeting deadlines and the responsibility for success or failure (H. Lipskin, personal communication, October 11, 2016).

The followers in Israeli companies are comfortable challenging their leaders (Senor & Singer, 2009). This was supported by Lipskin's (personal communication, October 11, 2016) reflections in which he noted, "Last time I had an idea … the R&D leader told me it's a bad idea and explained why and we decided to give up on my idea." Challenging leadership is part of the culture of Israeli organisations as well as the Israeli military (Senor & Singer, 2009).

B. Brown, a University of California undergraduate and an unpaid intern hired by Keepers Child Safety during the summer of 2016, shared his experience working in the company with this author. This was his second internship in Israel, so he had some cultural familiarity. Per Brown, Lipskin told him at their first meeting that "By hiring me he would be in a no-lose scenario. Either his company would get something out of me, or he wouldn't lose anything" (B. Brown, personal communication, October 30, 2016).

Commenting on his first week at work Brown said,

> My second day of work [the day after the interview] the company had a meeting with a senior executive of Cisco and a couple other high-level people. As the questions began, no one from the actual team was speaking up, so I started talking with only a bare-bones background in the company, and no background in business. Somehow, I was articulate enough to impress the executive enough for him to continue backing the project. Hanan was quite impressed with my actions and gave me the task of reworking our business model and executive summary documents to meet our new plans (and [in] the quality English that investors expected). In spite of being an intern, I was, in effect, a member of senior staff and was treated as such. I tried hard to support Hanan as my boss, even (and especially) when our visions of the company did not align. (B. Brown, personal communication, October 30, 2016)

Brown also shared his reflections on the structural fluidity and transparency within this culturally influenced leader–follower dyad:

> As an intern in the U.S., I would have barely been on the fringes of those sorts of decisions. As an intern in an Israeli startup, I was thrust right into the middle of the mess and told 'figure it out'. It's a very horizontal organizational structure, where the leaders are really more of a 'first among equals' than an overlord. Hanan and Doron [co-founder] both expected their subordinates (myself included) to tell them when we thought they were wrong, and why. (B. Brown, personal communication, October 30, 2016)

Lipskin's leadership style is an example of Theory Y in that management is participative, assumes that people are self-motivated and thrive on responsibility, and involves subordinates in decision-making while retaining the control to implement decisions.

From the follower's perspective, Brown observed,

> When in the office the general attitude was pretty relaxed. Hanan and Doron tended to be pretty open to ideas and opinions of others. On the other hand, when Hanan really wanted something done a certain way that was just the way it had to be, even if there were [other] potential ways of going about it. The thing that I really remember is the frenetic energy

Hanan seemed to just barely control most of the time. He was always intensely pursuing some goal or project, and as soon as that goal or project was finished (or fell through) he would immediately take up another one. (B. Brown, personal communication, April 16, 2017)

As there are no videos of Lipskin, the following brief conceptual analysis is based on what might be expected from Brown's observations.

The principles of Laban Movement Analysis refer to motion factors that move along four continua; those for *weight*, *time*, *space*, and *flow*. Within the time continuum, Lipskin would likely show a sense of urgency. Within the space continuum, Lipskin would likely show movement qualities that are indirect, as he can attend to multiple tasks simultaneously. However, he also has the ability to be extremely focused. Thus, at various times he demonstrates both ends of the space continuum.

A person may be an embodied leader with or without specific outside coaching or training. If Lipskin were trained as an embodied leader, he would be able to consciously ensure that his nonverbal and verbal expressions were synchronised, and thus display authenticity. He may or may not currently do so unconsciously, but without video, any claims to his embodied leadership are uncertain.

Cultural Differences in Leadership–Followership Roles

This section explores cultural differences between the United States, Israel, and Japan in leadership–followership roles. Japan is included in this discussion due to the cultural pervasiveness of a rigid hierarchical social structure that contrasts with the more egalitarian Israeli leadership culture.

The Industrial Revolution was marked by a series of stages demarcating specific levels of progression (Greenwood, 1999). The "third wave" was marked by a technical revolution that began in the 1950s with the invention of the computer and includes the utilisation of robotics (Greenwood, 1999). Initially, computers were used in academic and industrial research, but since the 1980s computer use has evolved to include personal computers and the spread of networking (Greenwood, 1999). Companies that have emerged from this technological revolution include IBM, Microsoft, Apple Industries, Google, and Facebook. Because of this technological revolution, skilled workers are increasingly replaced by machines or technology support, for example, switching machines replacing telephone operators, robotic welders replacing skilled manual welders, and vending machines replacing food servers.

During the first two stages of the Industrial Revolution in the United States, the prevailing relationship between leaders and followers was Theory X. During the third stage of the Industrial Revolution in the United States, some organisations moved to a Theory Y form of the leader–follower relationship (McGregor, 1960). In 1976, when S. Wozniak and S. Jobs founded Apple Computer, this shift was still in its infancy.

Israel is a small, Jewish, democratic society surrounded by larger Arab, authoritarian countries predominately inhospitable to Israel. For 68 years, 18- to 23-year-old Israeli men and women have been required to serve in the Israeli defence forces where they learn combat tactics and survival skills. In the book *Start Up Nation: The Story of Israel's Economic Miracle*, Senor and Singer (2009) described a socially homogenised leadership culture where hierarchical structure is minimal. Senor and Singer noted, "Israeli soldiers are not defined by rank; they are defined by what they are good at" (p. 50). Opinion is strongly valued irrespective of one's official rank. As such, lower ranked individuals are expected to challenge higher-ranking individuals. After their initial time with the defence forces, Israelis are placed on reserve status, but have frequent "call-ups" for training, emergencies, or combat. Relationships that develop during the army years and during higher education, along with a competitive drive to succeed, make the Israeli society ripe for entrepreneurship, high technology, and scientific invention (Senor & Singer, 2009).

The Israeli culture invests in human capital. Steinberg (2011), commenting on the cost that Israel invests in human capital, stated that "tuition at Israel's renowned public universities is about $2,714 per year, thanks in large part to government subsidies. Compared with other developed countries, Israel ranks eighth out of the OECD's 26 countries for tuition rates." Israelis excel at teamwork and innovation

(Senor & Singer, 2009). In fact, Israel Venture Capital Research (as cited in Senor & Singer, 2009) indicated, "The country boasts more startups per capita than any other country and currently has 70 companies listed on the Nasdaq." In Israeli culture, business leaders are known to practice what Carsten et al. (2010) called relational authenticity. As in the military, members of an Israeli business team have no problem raising issues with their nominal leader, provided they have reliable facts. They are expected to take responsibility for assigned tasks rather than follow explicit orders. This is true of Keepers Child Safety where Lipskin encourages employees to "tak[e] as much responsibility as possible … that if the employee got a big responsibility and he is the 'owner' of the mission, he will perform better than if I tell him exactly what to do" (personal communication, October 11, 2016). Israeli author A. Oz wrote, "a culture of doubt and argument, an open-ended game of interpretations, counter-interpretations, reinterpretations, opposing interpretations" are the norm and not the exception in Israeli business and leadership culture (as cited in Senor & Singer, 2009, p. 51).

Formed as a country in 1948, Israel has experienced many waves of culturally diverse immigration and remains a heterogeneous country without full assimilation of minorities. As full Israeli egalitarianism has not been achieved, some authors, seemingly in contrast to Senor and Singer (2009), have suggested that Israel needs further policy reforms (Cohen-Almagor, 2014). However, it should be noted that the focus of Senor and Singer (2009) was on the assimilation and egalitarian aspects of the Israeli leadership culture that form the basis of an entrepreneurial culture.

Historically, Japan is a much older country than the United States or Israel. Prior to the Meiji Restoration of 1868, Japan had a feudal samurai (warrior) society (Garon, 1994) and was largely closed to outside contact (Bernhofen & Brown, 2004). After the Meiji Restoration, Japan closely followed Western models, including industrialisation, and became a world power (Huntington, 1996).

In 1908, Kobayashi Sakutaro came to the United States and noticed that American workers "followed rules, came to work on time, [and] never loafed," but he claimed to not find these attributes among Japanese workers (Gordon, 1990, p. 239). He asserted that Japanese workers needed constant instruction and that supervisors were in a difficult situation (Gordon, 1990).

The key issue for workers was the moral authority of the factory or enterprise to exact diligent labour in exchange for pay (Gordon, 1990). As stated by Gordon (1990), "During WWI and the 1920s, workers in Japan ... raised vigorous demands [regarding] the treatment [that] they required before offering a sustained commitment to their employers" (p. 241). These demands were not necessarily particular to Japan, but to the changing role of the labour force around the globe. Their demands included secure jobs and the security of severance pay where dismissals could not be prevented; secure, predictable, implicit seniority (rather than incentive) based wages; and respect as human beings, Japanese citizens and employees of the firm (Gordon, 1990).

Gordon (1990) claimed that state and government bureaucrats were responsible for setting standards of fair wages to promote "social harmony" between managers and workers. From the mid-1930s to the end of World War II, there was an effort to systemise labour management in Japan, although this war period was a time of deprivation and coercion for the typical Japanese worker (Gordon, 1990). These labour management practices were developed using a Theory X structure and continue to this day. This researcher has found no evidence in the literature of a Theory Y management style in use in Japan; however, W. Ouchi (1981) writes about the hierarchical clan (Type Z or Theory Z) in Japanese industrial organisations.

Although challenging the leader is an accepted practice within a Theory Y Israeli business culture, a Theory X leader from Japan who relocates to Israel for an employment opportunity may feel uncomfortable with the followers' seemingly aggressive nature and lack of respect. An understanding of an organisation's culture and the culture of the country where the organisation conducts business is essential for an individual to be successful.

Summary

Leaders and followers function within an organisational milieu that is changing. After the Industrial Revolution, leaders looked to their labour forces for their physical attributes (strength and endurance), and followers were expected to be passive, deferential, and obedient. Today, labour is largely mechanised. Thus, leaders often require followers with intellectual attributes (astuteness, creativity, persistence), and followers are expected to demonstrate extroversion, charisma, and sensitivity towards the leader's effectiveness. As scholars study this new dynamic between leaders and followers, new characteristics are modelled to describe new ways of engagement. Thus, the studies of authentic leadership, embodied leadership, and followership are emerging fields within Theory Y organisations.

An authentic leader exhibits self-awareness, unbiased processing, relational authenticity, and authentic behaviours. Embodied leadership is a subset of authentic leadership and stresses the leaders' awareness of their body language in addition to their cognitive skills. When the inner world (somatic sensations) of leaders or followers is in sync with their outer expression (verbal language), they are likely to be viewed as authentic. Thus, the elements of embodied leadership are critical to effective authentic leadership. Although the literature on leadership and followership suggested that somatic awareness and reflexivity could enhance leader and follower roles, insufficient information was evident within the case studies presented to support that argument.

Jobs, a co-founder of Apple Industries, was a complex leader with exceptional vision, but he needed the intellectual attributes of his followers to create the products of that vision. If Jobs was a Theory Y, authentic, and embodied leader, his followers would likely have been happier. Would he still have been able to fashion his vision into reality? We cannot know.

Lipskin, a co-founder and CEO of Israeli start-up Keepers Child Safety, viewed his role as a member of the team. His authentic leadership style is an example of Theory Y and is "relational" to the extent of allowing a summer intern to initiate and take on a leadership role more often expected from long-term senior staff. Towards this end, followers are engaged in the process and enjoy their work.

The US case study illustrates a transition stage where a Theory X leader had conflicts with a seemingly Theory Y leaning followership. The Israeli case study and the Japanese and Israeli cultural examples show that countries' cultural climates impact their organisational cultural climates and the structure of leader–follower interaction: the Japanese concepts of honour and a rigid hierarchical structure (Theory X) and the Israeli socially homogenised military and leadership cultures with minimal hierarchical structure (Theory Y).

Authentic leadership, embodied leadership, and followership add new perspectives in which to view organisational roles. Organisations are complex systems based on the personal strengths of leaders and followers. Thus, cultural and organisational norms often determine ways to lead, follow, and thrive in business.

References

Avolio, B., & Gardner, W. (2005). Authentic leadership development: Getting to the root of positive forms of leadership. *The Leadership Quarterly, 16*(3), 315–338.

Avolio, B., Gardner, W., Walumbwa, F., Luthans, F., & May, D. (2004). Unlocking the mask: A look at the process by which authentic leaders impact follower attitudes and behaviors. *The Leadership Quarterly, 15*(6), 801–823.

Bartenieff, I., & Lewis, D. (1980). *Body movement: Coping with the environment.* New York: Routledge.

Bernhofen, D., & Brown, J. (2004). A direct test of the theory of comparative advantage: The case of Japan. *Journal of Political Economy, 112*(1), 48–67.

Brendel, W., & Bennett, C. (2016). Learning to embody leadership through mindfulness and somatics practice. *Advances in Developing Human Resources, 18*(3), 409–425.

Carmeli, A., Sheaffer, Z., Binyamin, G., Reiter-Palmon, R., & Shimoni, T. (2014). Transformational leadership and creative problem-solving: The mediating role of psychological safety and reflexivity. *The Journal of Creative Behaviour, 48*(2), 115–135.

Carsten, M. K., Uhl-Bien, M., West, B. J., Patera, J. L., & McGregor, R. (2010). Exploring social constructions of followership: A qualitative study. *The Leadership Quarterly, 21*(3), 543–562.

Chaleff, I. (1995). *The courageous follower.* San Francisco: Benett.

Chaleff, I. (2009). *The courageous follower: Standing up to and for our leaders* (3rd ed.). San Francisco: Berrett-Koehler.

CNET. (2010, June 7). *Steve Jobs demo fail.* Retrieved from https://www.youtube.com/watch?v=znxQOPFg2mo

Cohen-Almagor, R. (2014). Reconciling liberalism and Judaism? Human rights in Israel. In J. Carby-Hall (Ed.), *Essays on human rights: A celebration of the life of Dr. Janusz* (pp. 136–163). Warsaw, Poland: Ius et Lex Foundation.

de Zilwa, D. (2014). A new conceptual framework for authentic followership. In L. M. Lapierre & M. K. Carsten (Eds.), *Followership: What is it and why do people follow?* (pp. 47–72). Bingley, UK: Emerald.

Feldenkrais, M. (1972). *Awareness through movement: Easy-to-do health exercises to improve your posture, vision, imagination, and personal awareness*. New York: Harper Collins.

Gardner, W., Cogliser, C., Davis, K., & Dickens, M. (2011). Authentic leadership: A review of the literature and research agenda. *The Leadership Quarterly, 22*(6), 1120–1145.

Garon, S. (1994). Rethinking modernization and modernity in Japanese history: A focus on state-society relations. *The Journal of Asian Studies, 53*(2), 346–366.

Gendlin, E. (1978). *Focusing*. New York: Bantam Books.

Gordon, A. (1990). Japanese labour relations during the twentieth century. *Journal of Labor Research, XI*(3), 239–252.

Greenwood, J. (1999). The third industrial revolution: Technology, productivity and income equality. *Economic Review, 35*(2), 2–12.

Huntington, S. (1996). *The clash of civilizations and the remaking of world order*. New York: Touchstone.

Isaacson, W. (2012). The real leadership lessons of Steve Jobs. *Harvard Business Review, 90*(4), 92–102.

Kabat-Zinn, J. (1994). *Wherever you go, there you are: Mindless meditation in everyday life*. New York: Hyperion.

Kernis, M. (2003). Toward a conceptualization of optimal self-esteem. *Psychological Inquiry, 14*(1), 1–26.

Kernis, M., & Goldman, B. (2006). From thought and experience to behavior and interpersonal relationships: A multicomponent conceptualization of authenticity. In A. Tesser, J. V. Wood, & D. A. Staple (Eds.), *On building, defending, and regulating the self: A psychological perspective* (pp. 31–52). New York: Psychology Press.

Knickerbocker, B. (2011, August 25). Steve Jobs and Apple: How his vision transformed the way we work and play. *Christian Science Monitor*. Retrieved from http://www.csmonitor.com/USA/2011/0825/Steve-Jobs-and-Apple-How-his-vision-transformed-the-way-we-work-and-play

Ladkin, D. (2013). From perception to flesh: A phenomenological account of the felt experience of leadership. *Leadership, 9*(3), 320–334.

Ladkin, D., & Taylor, S. (2010). Enacting the 'true self': Towards a theory of embodied authentic leadership. *The Leadership Quarterly, 21*(1), 64–74.

Luthans, F. (2002). The need for and meaning of positive organizational behaviour. *Journal of Organizational Behavior, 23*(6), 695–706.

Luthans, F., & Avolio, B. (2003). Authentic leadership development. In K. S. Cameron, J. E. Dutton, & R. E. Quinn (Eds.), *Positive organizational scholarship: Foundations of a new discipline* (pp. 241–258). San Francisco: Berrett-Koehler.

McGregor, D. (1960). *The human side of enterprise*. New York: McGraw Hill.

Meindl, J. (1995). The romance of leadership as a follower-centric theory: A social constructionist approach. *The Leadership Quarterly, 6*(3), 329–341.

Moore, C.-L. (2005). *Movement and making decisions: The body-mind connection in the workplace*. New York: Dance & Movement Press.

Moore, C.-L. (2014). *Meaning in motion: Introducing Laban movement analysis*. Denver, CO: MoveScapeCenter.

Ouchi, W. (1981). Theory Z: How American business can meet with the Japanese challenge. *Business Horizons, 24*(6), 82–83.

Pallaro, P. (Ed.). (1999). *Authentic movement: A collection of essays by Mary Starks Whitehouse, Janet Adler and Joan Chodorow*. Philadelphia: Jessica Kingsley.

Pearce, C., & Manz, C. (2005). The new silver bullets of leadership: The importance of self- and shared leadership in knowledge work. *Organizational Dynamics, 34*(2), 130–140.

Richardson, J., & Arthur, M. (2013). Just three stories: The career lessons behind Steve Jobs. *Journal of Business and Management, 19*(1), 45–57.

Senor, D., & Singer, S. (2009). *Start-up nation: The story of Israel's economic miracle*. New York: Twelve.

Shamir, B. (2007). From passive recipients to active co-producers: Followers' roles in the leadership process. In B. Shamir, R. Pillai, M. C. Bligh, & M. Uhl-Bien (Eds.), *Follower-centered perspectives on leadership: A tribute to the memory of James R. Meindl* (pp. ix–xxxvi). Greenwich, CT: Information Age.

Shamir, B., & Eilam, G. (2005). 'What's your story?' A life stories approach to authentic leadership development. *The Leadership Quarterly, 16*(3), 395–417.

Sheets-Johnstone, M. (1981). Thinking in movement. *Journal of Aesthetics and Art Criticism, 39*(4), 399–407.

Sheets-Johnstone, M. (2010). Kinesthetic experience: Understanding movement inside and out. *Body, Movement and Dance in Psychotherapy, 5*(2), 111–127.

Stark, J. (2012, September 26). *Highlights of Steve Jobs 2007 iPhone Announcement*. Retrieved from https://www.youtube.com/watch?v=GE1pd3HktwA

Steinberg, J. (2011, August 16). Just how expensive is it to live in Israel? *Jewish Telegraph Agency*. Retrieved from http://www.jta.org/2011/08/16/news-opinion/israel-middle-east/just-how-expensive-is-it-to-live-in-israel

Theory X and Theory Y. (n.d.). *Understanding team member motivation*. Retrieved from https://www.mindtools.com/pages/article/newLDR_74.htm

Uhl-Bien, M., & Pillai, R. (2007). The romance of leadership and the social construction of followership. In B. Shamir, R. Pillai, M. C. Bligh, & M. Uhl-Bien (Eds.), *Follower-centered perspectives on leadership: A tribute to the memory of James R. Meindl* (pp. 187–210). Greenwich, CT: Information Age.

Uhl-Bien, M., Riggio, R. E., Lowe, K. B., & Carsten, M. K. (2014). Followership theory: A review and research agenda. *The Leadership Quarterly, 25*(1), 83–104.

Walumbwa, F., Avolio, B., Gardner, W., Wernsing, T., & Peterson, S. (2008). Authentic leadership: Development and validation of a theory-based measure. *Journal of Management, 34*(1), 89–126.

Yu, H. (2013). Decoding leadership: How Steve Jobs transformed Apple to spearhead a technological informed economy. *Journal of Business and Management, 19*(1), 33–44.

Zikic, J., & Klehe, U.-C. (2006). Job loss as a blessing in disguise: The role of career exploration and career planning in predicting reemployment quality. *Journal of Vocational Behavior, 69*(3), 391–409.

Zikic, J., & Richardson, J. (2007). Unlocking the careers of business professionals following job loss: Sensemaking and career exploration of older workers. *Canadian Journal of Administration Sciences, 24*(1), 58–73.

9

Authentic Leadership and Followers' Cheating Behaviour: A Laboratory Experiment from a Self-Concept Maintenance Perspective

Susanne Braun and Lars Hornuf

Unethical conduct is a prevailing phenomenon in organizations. The Association of Certified Fraud Examiners (2014) projects a potential global fraud loss of more than $3.7 trillion per year. Losses are estimated to comprise 5% of organizational revenues and to last for an average of 18 months before detection. Among the most tangible costs are losses related to theft. Retail businesses in the United States have inventory losses of approximately $42 billion per year, with employee theft accounting for 43% of lost revenue (Deyle, 2014). Means to reduce unethical conduct in

S. Braun (✉)
Durham University Business School, Durham University, Durham, UK

Center for Leadership and People Management, Ludwig Maximilian University Munich, Munich, Germany

L. Hornuf
Faculty of Business Studies & Economics, University of Bremen, Bremen, Germany

Max Planck Institute for Innovation and Competition, Munich, Germany

© The Author(s) 2018
D. Cotter-Lockard (ed.), *Authentic Leadership and Followership*, Palgrave Studies in Leadership and Followership, https://doi.org/10.1007/978-3-319-65307-5_9

organizations are needed. We studied whether authentic leadership buffers followers' unethical behaviour in the form of cheating in professional contexts (i.e., work-related settings; Djawadi & Fahr, 2015).

The behavioural ethics literature is concerned with factors that influence how individuals make ethical decisions (Bazerman & Gino, 2012), individuals' compliance with generally accepted moral norms in organizations (Treviño, Weaver, & Reynolds, 2006), moral identity (Shao, Aquino, & Freeman, 2008), and the normalization of unethical behaviour (Ashforth & Anand, 2003) in organizations. According to this literature, unethical conduct encompasses specific unethical behaviours (e.g., lying, cheating, stealing) or behaviours that do not reach some minimal moral standard (e.g., dishonesty, disobedience of the law; Treviño et al., 2006). In behavioural economics, scholars have systematically analysed individuals' cheating behaviour in laboratory studies (Conrads, Irlenbusch, Rilke, & Walkowitz, 2013; Fischbacher & Föllmi-Heusi, 2013; Houser, Vetter, & Winter, 2012), in online experiments (Gill, Prowse, & Vlassopoulos, 2013), and in the field (Abeler, Becker, & Falk, 2014; Ariely, Garcia-Rada, Hornuf, & Mann, 2014; Djawadi & Fahr, 2015; Ichino & Maggi, 2000). Most of this work addressed the question whether individuals cheat and how pervasive cheating is across contexts. With some notable exceptions (Abeler et al., 2014; Erat & Gneezy, 2012; Lundquist, Ellingsen, Gribbe, & Johannesson, 2009), extensive evidence shows that individuals cheat (Alberti & Güth, 2013; Bucciol, Landini, & Piovesan, 2013; Djwadi & Fahr, 2015; Gino, Ayal, & Ariely, 2009; Mann, Garcia-Rada, Houser, & Ariely, 2014), especially when the risk of detection is low (Effron, Bryan, & Murnighan, 2015).

Rather than questioning whether individuals cheat, we analysed whether cheating persists under the influence of intervening factors. We specifically focused on the influence of authentic leadership as described in the following paragraph. Previous research showed that the extent to which followers perceive their leaders as being authentic related positively to followers' satisfaction in their job and with their leader, trusting and effective relations between leaders and followers as well as within teams, and followers' job-related engagement (Banks, McCauley, Gardner, & Guler, 2016; Gardner, Cogliser, Davis, & Dickens, 2011; Peus, Wesche, Streicher, Braun, & Frey, 2012). Authentic leadership "extends well beyond bottom-line success" and thereby contributes to advancements "in the greater society by tackling public policy issues and addressing organizational and societal problems" (Avolio, Gardner, Walumbwa, Luthans, & May, 2004, p. 802). Regarding followers' unethical conduct (e.g., cheating), however, very little is known about variations in response to perceptions of authentic leadership (Cianci, Hannah, Roberts, & Tsakumis, 2014).

Our study served to contribute to a better theoretical and practical understanding of authentic leadership in four ways. First, we addressed the question, which factors reduce the probability that individuals will engage in unethical conduct in the face of spontaneous opportunities to cheat for their own benefit, but at the expense of their organization. Second, the study integrated authentic leadership literature with behavioural economics. Third, we analysed cheating in a carefully designed laboratory experiment. Study designs that allow causal conclusions have provided relevant insights into the effects of followers' perceptions of authentic leadership (Braun & Peus, 2016). Fourth, we tested a range of variables that may affect cheating in interaction with authentic leadership (i.e., gender, cheating norm, victimization). Overall, based on the results of this research, we cannot conclude that authentic leadership attenuates followers' cheating.

Theory and Hypotheses

Based on self-concept maintenance theory (Ariely, 2012; Mazar, Amir, & Ariely, 2008), this research aimed to contribute to a better understanding of the phenomenon of cheating as well as the influencing factors in professional contexts, including perceptions of authentic leadership, cheating norms, and victimization. The economic standard model of crime and punishment predicts cheating as the result of cost–benefit calculations (Becker, 1968, 1993). It includes three main predictors: (a) the expected benefits, (b) the probability of detection, and (c) the magnitude of punishment expected in case of detection. Results from behavioural law and economics underscore the relevance of these three variables, which differ in their impact on cheating (Nagin & Pogarsky, 2003).

A growing body of research has been devoted to studying influence factors on unethical conduct in organizational contexts. Cohn, Fehr, and Maréchal (2014) demonstrated that the professional background of the banking industry increases dishonesty, although not necessarily through competition or competitive incentives but through the prevalence of materialistic values. Treviño (1986) proposed a person-situation interactionist model suggesting that individual as well as contextual factors influence whether unethical behaviour occurs in organizations. The immediate job context (e.g., reward structures, time pressure) and organizational culture form part of the contextual factors. Brass, Butterfield, and Skaggs (1998) reviewed factors that influence unethical conduct at multiple organizational levels. Their model of unethical decision-making included the types of relationships (e.g., strength, status, asymmetry) in organizations. Strong ties between leaders and followers are likely to increase the buffering effects of leadership on cheating behaviour. A recent review confirmed the relevance of factors at multiple levels, including individual-level cognitive moral development, moral identity, or emotional states (e.g., guilt, shame), and ethical group climates, organizational climates, and leadership (Treviño et al., 2006). Accordingly, we considered authentic leadership as one of the contextual factors with the potential to reduce cheating.

Self-Concept Maintenance

The theory of self-concept maintenance (Ariely, 2012; Mazar et al., 2008) suggests that individuals' self-concept predicts cheating. According to this theory, individuals engage in dishonest behaviours if they can maintain a positive self-concept. The self-concept consists of all inferences that individuals make about themselves and is inherently relational. Individuals' "sense of self, including thoughts, feelings, motives, and self-regulatory strategies may thus vary as a function of relations with significant others" (Anderson & Chen, 2002, p. 619). We reasoned that authentic leaders are significant others, who influence followers' self-concepts and affect their cheating behaviour.

Individuals internalize norms and standards (e.g., honesty, diligence, community) of the society that surrounds them. Compliance with such norms is rewarding, while non-compliance is likely to result in social punishment. Mazar et al. (2008) proposed that (dis)honesty is part of an internal reward and punishment system, which influences an individual's self-concept. If individuals transgress against honesty norms, their self-concept is negatively affected. Accordingly, self-concept maintenance theory suggests "a magnitude range of dishonesty within which people can cheat, but their behaviours, which they would usually consider dishonest, do not bear negatively on their self-concept" (Mazar et al., 2008, p. 634). That is, if they can still consider themselves honest below a certain perceptual threshold, individuals are likely to cheat. This theory has received initial empirical support (Mazar et al., 2008), but also opens controversy around the question of which factors promote or prevent cheating.

Authentic Leadership

Previous research indicated that specific forms of leadership in organizations promote desirable outcomes and prevent undesirable ones (Hiller, DeChurch, Murase, & Doty, 2011). Authentic leaders "know who they are, what they believe and value, and they act upon those values and beliefs while transparently interacting with others" (Avolio et al., 2004, p. 802). Kernis (2003, p. 13) describes the modern understanding of authenticity as "reflecting the unobscured operation of one's true, or core, self in one's daily enterprise." Authentic leadership goes beyond the idea of 'being true to oneself'. Four dimensions characterize authentic leadership (Walumbwa, Avolio, Gardner, Wernsing, & Peterson, 2008) as implemented in this research: (a) self-awareness (i.e., leaders who are aware of their own strengths and weaknesses), (b) relational transparency (i.e., leaders who emphasize open and transparent communication), (c) internalized moral perspective (i.e., leaders who act in accordance with strong moral convictions and values), and (d) balanced processing (i.e., leaders who consider multiple perspectives before decision-making).

Authentic leaders take on a positive role modelling function for their followers (Gini, 1997). Followers' perceptions of authentic leadership relate to a variety of positive behaviours, such as followers' work engagement (Wang & Hsieh, 2013), extra-effort (Peus et al., 2012), creativity (Rego, Sousa, Marques, & Pina e Cunha, 2012), and job performance (Leroy, Palanski, & Simons, 2011). Furthermore, authentic leadership facilitates positive attitudes, such as followers' own authenticity (Leroy, Anseel, Gardner, & Sels, 2015) and feelings of empowerment and satisfaction (Wong & Laschinger, 2013). Studies of the mechanisms through which followers' perceptions of authentic leadership support these positive outcomes revealed trust in the leader (Clapp-Smith, Vogelgesang, & Avey, 2009) and predictability of the leader (Peus et al., 2012) as relevant variables.

Authenticity is directly linked to morality (Gino, Kouchaki, & Galinsky, 2015). The inherent value system of authentic leaders comprises universal and self-transcendent values, which emphasize collective functioning (e.g., justice, responsibility, honesty) rather than egocentric concerns (Howell & Avolio, 1992). Followers' perceptions of authentic leadership in turn drive perceptions of leaders' behavioural integrity (Leroy et al., 2011). Initial empirical evidence suggests that authentic leadership reduces followers' unethical decision-making in the face of temptation (Cianci et al., 2014) and relates positively to followers' fairness perceptions (Kiersch & Byrne, 2015). Moreover, authentic leadership appears to be negatively related to organizational deviance (Erkutlu & Chafra, 2013).

Drawing on the four dimensions of authentic leadership introduced above, authentic leaders fulfil positive ethical role modelling functions (internalized moral perspective). They influence followers' ethical views through close trusting relationships (relational transparency). Authentic leaders are also ethical in that they realize what their own limitations are (self-awareness), and that they explicitly consider different views that underlie difficult ethical decisions (balanced processing).

In summary, in line with self-concept maintenance theory, we expected that authentic leaders lower the threshold under which followers can still consider themselves honest, and hence followers are less likely to cheat when given opportunities to do so. We assumed that followers who perceive their leaders as authentic should be less likely to cheat.

Hypothesis 1 Followers' perceptions of authentic leadership negatively predict cheating. Participants in the authentic leadership condition are less likely to cheat than participants in the non-authentic leadership condition.

Cheating Norm

Our second hypothesis concerns interactions between followers' perceptions of authentic leadership and a cheating norm as predictors of unethical conduct in organizations. The theory of self-concept maintenance implies that cheating depends on internalized norms and standards. These are established through socialization (interaction with meaningful others, such as parents, siblings, friends, and colleagues). Therefore, it is likely that social interaction also increases or decreases internally held thresholds of acceptable conduct in professional contexts (e.g., Cohn et al., 2014). This assumption is in line with social learning theory (Bandura, 1965) and social norms theory (Cialdini, Reno, & Kallgren, 1990). It also concurs with Gino et al.'s (2009) findings that cheating is contagious. In their studies, cheating increased when participants witnessed in-group members cheating successfully. However, when the possibility of cheating was made salient, but not enacted by an in-group member, cheating decreased (Gino et al., 2009).

We concurred with the view that social contagion positively influences unethical conduct. We expected that participants who become aware of a cheating norm are more likely to cheat. However, we also proposed that the values set by authentic leadership counteract this influence. The buffering influence of authentic leadership on followers' unethical behaviour will be stronger than a perceived cheating norm. Followers who perceive their leaders as authentic should be less likely to cheat when they observe successful cheating behaviour.

Hypothesis 2 Cheating norm and followers' perceptions of authentic leadership interact to predict cheating. Authentic leadership moderates the impact of a cheating norm on cheating. When participants observe cheating, they are less likely to cheat in the authentic leadership condition than in the non-authentic leadership condition.

Victimization

Our third hypothesis concerns interactions between followers' perceptions of authentic leadership and victimization as predictors of unethical conduct in organizations. We analysed the influence of victimization and subsequent retaliation through cheating. This view builds on the concept of social reciprocity. Evolutionary game theory suggests that the tit-for-tat strategy, in which a party will first cooperate and then subsequently replicate an opponent's previous move, is the most successful strategy in many cases of direct competition (Axelrod, 1984). Research in organizational psychology suggests that retaliation occurs in response to perceived fairness violations (Skarlicki & Folger, 1997). Thus, we expected that participants are more likely to retaliate through cheating when they experience being cheated by others (i.e., victimization).

However, we again proposed that perceptions of authentic leadership counteract this influence. Even if others cheat them, followers of authentic leaders will be unlikely to retaliate through cheating. The buffering influence of authentic leadership on followers' unethical behaviour should be stronger than the perceived victimization. Followers who see their leaders as authentic should be less likely to cheat when they are victimized than followers under the influence of non-authentic leadership.

Hypothesis 3 Victimization and followers' perceptions of authentic leadership interact to predict cheating. Authentic leadership moderates the impact of victimization on cheating. When participants are victimized, they are less likely to cheat in the authentic leadership condition than in the non-authentic leadership condition.

Methods

We tested the above stated hypotheses in a laboratory experiment with students at a German university. We analysed data with t-tests, Mann–Whitney U-tests, and conducted robustness checks.

Sample and Procedure

We recruited participants over the course of two weeks in April 2015 at a German university. Our initial sample was 424 participants. To ensure that participants were not excessively familiar with experimental research methods, we *ex ante* decided to limit our study to individuals who reported being students of fields different from psychology (57 psychology students or non-students were excluded). Twenty-four participants who were interrupted during the study due to technical problems or personal issues were also excluded. Four students repeatedly took part in our study. We counted only their first appearance. With these constraints, our final sample included 343 individuals.

Table 9.1 provides demographic data of the participants. Participants differed in age (25% were under 21 years of age, 50% were between 21 and 25 years, and 25% were above 25 years of age), gender (117 men vs. 218 women), previous work experience (191 experience vs. 147 no experience), marital status (155 single vs. 168 in a relationship), and current standard of living (278 very well-off or living comfortably vs. 53 just getting along or poor). A male leader was randomly assigned to instruct 50% of the participants through a video message, while a female leader instructed the other 50%. Finally, 25% of participants believed that less than 31% of participants had earned more than they themselves did, 50% believed that 31–60% had earned more, and 25% believed that 61% or more had earned more. On average, participants believed that only 45% had earned more than they themselves did, providing a first indication that they must have been aware of their cheating behaviour.

Design and Manipulations

Study Setup

A fictitious supervisor supposedly from a personnel economics institute at the university instructed the participants in our study. The instruction was delivered through a video message, which we recorded with two professional actors (male and female). Participants were randomly assigned

Table 9.1 Descriptive statistics

		N	Mean	Median	SD	Min	Max
Age		333	23.35	22	5.06	17	57
Under 21	[1]	92	[1] vs. [3]: $p = 0.0619$, $P > \|z\| = 0.0802$				
Between 21 and 25	[2]	177					
Over 25	[3]	74					
Expectations		337	44.56	45	19.49	0	91
Less than 31%	[4]	96	[4] vs. [6]: $p = 0.6890$, $P > \|z\| = 0.6198$				
Between 31% and 60%	[5]	163					
Over 61%	[6]	82					
Semester		327	5.82	5	3.73	1	22
Work experience		338	0.57	1	0.50	0	1
Yes	[7]	191	[7] vs. [8]: $p = 0.7939$, $P > \|z\| = 0.8496$				
No	[8]	147					
Gender		335	0.35	0	0.48	0	1
Male	[9]	117	[9] vs. [10]: $p = 0.1809$, $P > \|z\| = 0.0733$				
Female	[10]	218					
Marital status							
Single	[11]	155	[11] vs. [12]: $p = 0.1314$,				
In a relationship	[12]	168	$P > \|z\| = 0.0687$				
Married	[13]	6					
Divorced	[14]	2					
Other	[15]	2					
Prefer not to answer	[16]	10					
Living standard							
Very well-off	[17]	6	[17–19] vs. [20–22]: $p = 0.9273$,				
Living very comfortably	[18]	149	$P > \|z\| = 0.9960$				
Living comfortably	[19]	123					
Just getting along	[20]	43					
Nearly poor	[21]	4					
Poor	[22]	6					
Prefer not to answer	[23]	12					

Differences report p-values on a two-sided t-test between means as well as Prob > z for Mann–Whitney U-tests

to receive the video message from a male or female supervisor. In a first step, the supervisors introduced themselves and made clear that instructions would be delivered through a video message owing to time constrains. While the content of the message explaining the task was the same in all study conditions, the supervisors' self-introduction varied in authentic leadership.

Authentic Leadership

Participants were randomly assigned to a supervisor who made a self-introduction with either high or low levels of authentic leadership or no further information about the leadership style was provided. In a second step, the supervisor explained the task, which participants would subsequently undertake. Through the video message format, we ensured that the instruction was uniformly delivered to all participants and only varied in authentic leadership expressed.

We developed variations of high and low levels of authentic leadership based on existing, validated study materials (Braun & Peus, 2016; Cianci et al., 2014). The ways in which supervisors described themselves in the video referred to the four dimensions of authentic leadership: (a) self-awareness (e.g., wanting to know about one's strengths and weaknesses vs. avoiding others' feedback), (b) relational transparency (e.g., asking for others' opinions, even if they run counter to one's own views vs. asking to consent with one's views), (c) internalized moral perspective (i.e., aligning actions with personal values vs. compliance with external pressures), and (d) balanced processing (e.g., integrating all perspectives vs. following one's own opinion). In the third video, where participants received no further information about the authentic leadership style, the supervisor described their general role (e.g., professional background, expertise, research and teaching goals).

Cheating Target

As part of the video message, participants were informed that their earnings would be paid from the supervisor's project budget. We also made clear that any profits on the participants' side would result in equal levels of losses on the supervisors' side. Thus, in contrast with previous studies, this setup made explicit who would be the beneficiary (participants) and who would be the target (supervisors and organizations) of possible cheating. After the task was explained, 97% of participants indicated having understood the video message and the task. The remaining 3% asked for a written explanation and read the instructions again until they fully understood the task.

Cheating Norm and Victimization

Recent research has shown that cheating behaviour can be contagious (Gino et al., 2009; Weisel & Shalvi, 2015). To determine whether authentic leadership can mitigate such tendencies, we introduced two additional influencing factors: cheating norm and victimization, both of which make the possibility of cheating behaviour more salient. For this purpose, we distributed participants randomly across two rooms in the experimental laboratory with six (room 1) and four (room 2) individual workstations. Each room had one experimenter supervising the study. Participants worked on mobile tablets equipped with keyboards and headsets.

At a standardized point in time during the study, participants received an online message that the chat function of their tablet had been activated. Participants in the *cheating norm* condition then received a fake message supposedly from another participant in the second room. The message read that the other participant had discovered how to cheat on the task and would cheat from now on. Participants in the *victimization* condition received a fake message supposedly from an experimenter in the second room. The message read that the experimenter had discovered that another participant had taken the participant's €2 show-up fee for arriving on time at the experimental laboratory. Seven study conditions resulted from the variations of authentic leadership, cheating norm, victimization, and a neutral baseline condition. Table 9.2 summarizes the conditions.

Table 9.2 Study conditions

Condition	No.						
		Factor 1: Authentic		Factor 2: Cheating norm		Factor 3: Victimization	
		High	Low	Yes	No	Yes	No
Baseline	[1]				X		X
Authentic	[2]	X					
Non-authentic	[3]		X				
Authentic and cheating norm	[4]	X		X			X
Non-authentic and cheating norm	[5]		X	X			X
Authentic and victimization	[6]	X			X	X	
Non-authentic and victimization	[7]		X		X	X	

Dependent Measure

To examine cheating, we adapted a task developed by Jiang (2013), which we refer to as the die task. The die task involves rolling a physical die over 40 repeated trials. On each trial, participants were instructed to mentally choose a side of the die (top or bottom) before rolling it. They were asked to remember their choice, roll the die, and, when the outcome was visible, report the outcome on the chosen side in a box on their screen. Participants knew that they would be paid 5 cents per dot on the chosen side. If a participant selected the "top" side of the die before rolling it and consequently rolled only one dot on that side of the die, they faced a trade-off to honestly report having rolled one dot or to dishonestly report having chosen "bottom" and report six dots. Thus, on any roll for which the unfavourable side is initially chosen, participants can cheat by claiming to have chosen the higher-earning side. While it is impossible to identify whether a participant cheated on any given trial, in a large sample choosing the favourable earnings side should statistically not occur on more than 50% of the trials (see Mann, Garcia-Rada, Hornuf, Tafurt, & Ariely, 2016; Mann, Garcia-Rada, Hornuf, & Tafurt, 2016 for a virtual version of the test).

Results

Descriptive Statistics

Differences in reported high rolls for the first 10 trials (before additional information was given in Conditions 4–7, cheating norm and victimization) revealed that individual characteristics had no significant effect on cheating. Women reported the favourable side with the larger number of dots 2.7% more frequently than men. This difference was, however, only marginally significant for the non-parametric test and not significant for the t-test (t-test, $p = 0.1809$, Mann–Whitney U-test, $P > |z| = 0.0733$). Singles cheated 2.9% less than those in a relationship (t-test, $p = 0.1314$, Mann–Whitney U-test, $P > |z| = 0.0687$), and participants who were (self-reported) poorer cheated as much as those who lived comfortably or were very well-off (t-test, $p = 0.9273$, Mann–Whitney U-test, $P > |z| = 0.9960$). Likewise, we found no difference for participants with and without previous work experience (t-test, $p = 0.7939$, Mann–Whitney U-test, $P > |z| = 0.8496$).

Self-Concept Maintenance

In line with previous field and laboratory experiments (Ariely et al., 2014; Jiang, 2013), we found that participants cheated, but not to the fullest extent possible. In the baseline Condition 1, the distribution of reported outcomes shifted to the right of the binomial distribution (Fig. 9.1, Panel A), with participants declaring 61.8% high rolls on average, which is statistically different from the fair outcome of 50.0% (Table 9.3, Column [1]). Moreover, we found no significant change in cheating behaviour when splitting the sample at the mean of 20 rolls ($p = 0.1178$). Thus, there is no indication that participants adapted to the die task the longer they took part in it. These findings are in line with self-concept maintenance theory, and previous findings by Mazar et al. (2008).

Authentic Leadership

To determine whether authentic leadership negatively predicted cheating, in Condition 2 and Condition 3 an authentic and non-authentic leader, respectively, presented the die task through a video message. As a manipulation check, we asked participants 16 questions from a validated version (Hörner, Weisweiler, & Braun, 2015) of the Authentic Leadership Inventory (Neider & Schriesheim, 2011). For each of the questions, participants evaluated how authentic the leader appeared to them on a scale from 0% to 100%. When averaging the results of these 16 questions, we found that participants in the authentic leader condition rated the authenticity of the actors twice as high (67%) as those in the non-authentic leader condition (33%). The baseline condition, which did not include a specific introductory statement by the leader, was perceived statistically different and in-between (60%) the non-authentic

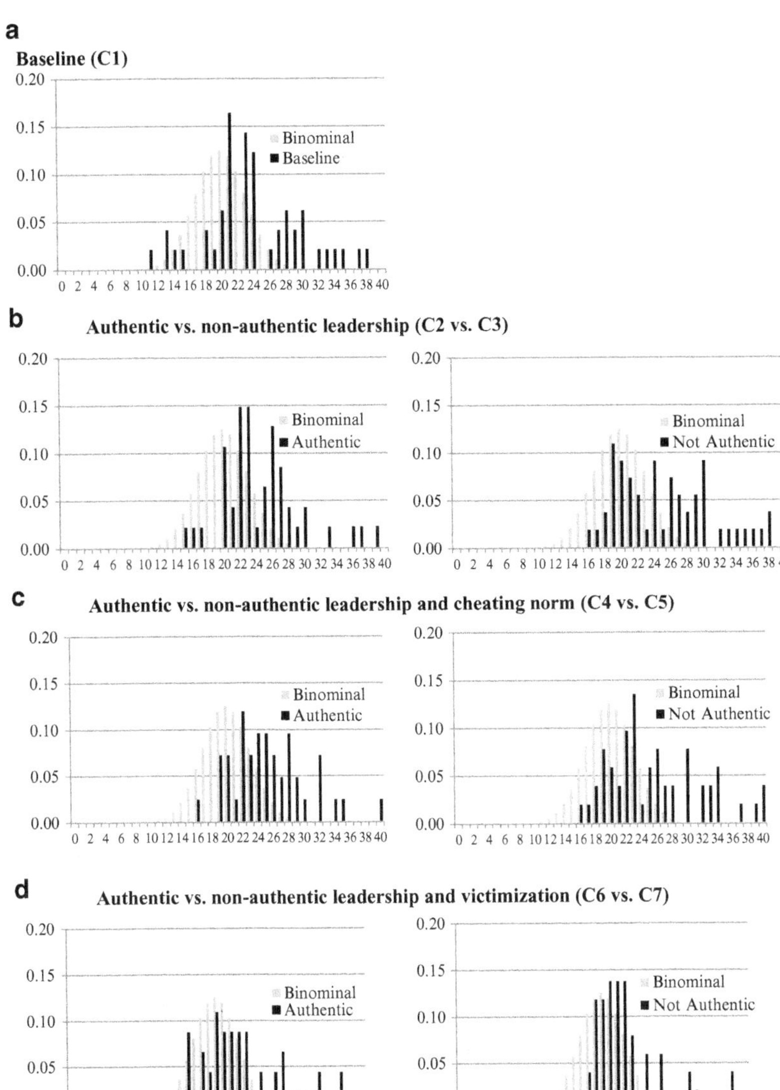

Fig. 9.1 Distribution of average reported outcomes in the cheating-of-mind task

Table 9.3 Differences in cheating

		High rolls in %					(1)	(2)	(3)	(4)
		N	Mean	SD	Min	Max	Diff. 50%	Diff. [1]	Diff. Cond.	Diff. 10 vs. 30
Condition 1 (baseline)	**[1]**	49	61.8	13.8	32.5	95.0	$p = 0.0000$***			$p = 0.9109$
Condition 2 (authentic)	**[2]**	47	61.8	12.1	40.0	97.5	$p = 0.0000$***	$p = 0.9755$ $P > \|z\| = 0.8802$	**[2] vs. [3]** $p = 0.4752$	$p = 0.1909$
Condition 3 (non-authentic)	**[3]**	42	63.5	12.3	40.0	100.0	$p = 0.0000$***	$p = 0.5101$ $P > \|z\| = 0.8066$	$P > \|z\| = 0.7315$	$p = 0.4670$
Condition 4 (authentic and cheating norm)	**[4]**	46	61.5	13.1	42.5	92.5	$p = 0.0000$***	$p = 0.5596$ $P > \|z\| = 0.6035$	**[4] vs. [5]** $p = 0.7529$	$p = 0.7062$
Condition 5 (non-authentic and cheating norm)	**[5]**	55	63.7	15.2	40.0	100.0	$p = 0.0000$***	$p = 0.3854$ $P > \|z\| = 0.6287$	$P > \|z\| = 0.9362$	$p = 0.1972$
Condition 6 (authentic and victimization)	**[6]**	52	64.4	15.4	40.0	100.0	$p = 0.0000$***	$p = 0.9096$ $P > \|z\| = 0.6353$	**[6] vs. [7]** $p = 0.4606$	$p = 0.1222$
Condition 7 (non-authentic and victimization)	**[7]**	51	59.7	11.0	40.0	95.0	$p = 0.0000$***	$p = 0.3936$ $P > \|z\| = 0.2001$	$P > \|z\| = 0.6400$	$p = 0.3429$

Differences report p-values on a two-sided t-tests as well as Prob > z for a Mann–Whitney U-tests. (1) is the between-subjects variation for rolls 1–40 from the fair outcome of 50% high rolls, (2) is the between-subjects variation for rolls 1–40 from the baseline condition, (3) is the between-subjects variation for rolls 1–40 between the authentic and non-authentic leadership conditions, and (4) reports the difference for the within-subject variation for rolls 1–10 and rolls 11–40 for the respective condition (t-test, $p = 0.0000$) and authentic leader conditions (t-test, $p = 0.0031$). Participants indeed perceived the actors in the video more or less authentic in line with the condition under which they were instructed.

However, for Conditions 2 and 3 we found that participants cheated just as much as participants in the baseline Condition 1 (see Fig. 9.1, Panel B, and Table 9.3, Column [2]). Authentic leadership did not affect individual cheating behaviour, as participants in Condition 2 reported, on average, just as many high rolls as those in the baseline condition. Participants in Condition 3 reported 63.7% high rolls, which represented no significant statistical difference from Condition 2 (Table 9.3, Column [3]). Instruction by an authentic leader did not per se change individual cheating. Therefore, our results did not support Hypothesis 1.

Cheating Norm

In the next step, we tested the interaction between a cheating norm and authentic leadership. For this purpose, we showed individuals a chat message in which another participant informed them that it was possible to cheat during the die task. The other participant indicated having decided to report only the high side as an outcome (cheating norm). Under an authentic leader, participants in Condition 4 cheated with 63.5% high rolls in a similar magnitude to those in the baseline condition (see Fig. 9.1, Panel C). When a non-authentic leader delivered the instructions and participants were informed about the possibility of cheating, participants reported 63.3% high rolls, which was no different from those in either the baseline condition or Condition 5 (Table 9.3, Columns [2] and [3]). We also tested whether cheating behaviour varied within subjects rather than between conditions. We therefore compared the first 10 rolls with the next 30 rolls (i.e., after participants had received the cheating norm information). Participants did not change their cheating behaviour after being informed about cheating by others (Table 9.3, Column [4]). Therefore, our results did not support Hypothesis 2.

Victimization

Finally, we tested the interaction between being cheated by a fellow participant (victimization) and authentic leadership. We found that participants reported 61.3% high rolls in the authentic leadership condition and 59.2% in the non-authentic condition (see Fig. 9.1, Panel D), which was not statistically different from either those in the baseline condition or each other (Table 9.3, Columns [2] and [3]). Finally, we again compared the first 10 rolls with the next 30 rolls when participants received the information about being the victim of others' cheating. Again, participants did not change their cheating behaviour when being cheated by others (Table 9.3, Column [4]). Therefore, our results did not support Hypothesis 3.

Robustness

As a robustness check, we investigated whether the gender of the participants or the leader or a combination of the two had a significant impact on cheating. The results showed that participants perceived the male actor on average no more or less authentic than the female actor (p = 0.7484). We again found no differences in outcomes. Cheating occurred at the same magnitude regardless of whether the participants or leaders were male or female (Fig. 9.2, Panel B and C).

Finally, we tested whether the expectations of others' cheating influenced the individual propensity to cheat. We found that individuals, who believed that less than 31% of the other participants had earned more than they themselves did, cheated about the same as those who believed that more than 61% of the other participants had earned more than they themselves did (Table 9.1, columns [4] and [6]).

Discussion and Conclusion

We investigated authentic leadership as a potential remedy for followers' cheating as well as moderating factors of the environment (i.e., a cheating norm and victimization). In doing so, we integrated leadership research and behavioural economics, used a carefully designed laboratory experiment

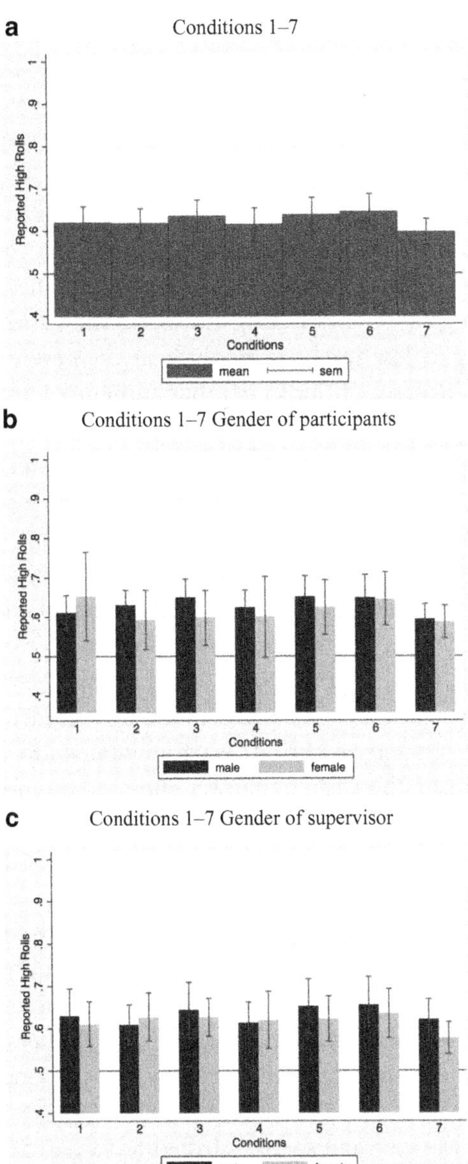

Fig. 9.2 Differences in cheating behaviour by conditions and gender

with video variations of authentic leadership and a cheating-of-mind task, and tested a range of variables that may affect cheating. In line with self-concept maintenance theory (Ariely, 2012; Mazar et al., 2008), we found participants to engage in minor acts of cheating, but not to the fullest extent possible. This finding reflects organizational practice, where people may not "necessarily do something that is totally dishonest, but in small ways let things slide that they really should not let slide" (Mathys, 2002, p. 90 f.).

Cheating did not change significantly under the influence of authentic leadership, contingent on a cheating norm or the experience of being cheated. Cheating at low levels seems difficult to prevent at least in the short term. Previous research indicated that authentic leadership prevents employees from unethical decision-making (Cianci et al., 2014). While this might hold true in general, restrictions to this assumption must be made considering our findings. First, cheating at low levels (e.g., taking smaller items from one's organization) may not induce cheating costs; rather, followers may perceive minor theft or dishonesty as acts of trivial offense, and those who engage in such acts will likely maintain their positive self-concept. Consequently, cheating at low levels continues and, in sum, negatively affects organizational functioning. Second, while we assumed that authentic leadership affects unethical conduct, this might not be the case in the short term. In our experimental study that included a short-term relationship between a follower and a newly introduced supervisor, authentic leadership did not impede followers' cheating behaviour.

Perceptions of leadership vary between countries and are influenced by implicit assumptions about what good leadership is (Javidan & Dastmalchian, 2009). While we conducted this research in Germany, the concept of authentic leadership was first introduced in the United States (Avolio et al., 2004) and the majority of studies originated in this context (Gardner et al., 2011). Schneider and Schröder (2012) compared cultural representations of managers in Germany and the United States over time. While in the United States, perceptions of managers as charismatic figures increased, the German sample shifted toward a view of managers as coercive figures. Similarly, Peus, Braun, and Knipfer (2015) showed in an interview study, that women managers in the United States placed more emphasis on authentic leadership than women in other countries (especially China and India). Future studies need to analyse whether cultural contexts attenuate positive effects of authentic leadership.

Taken together, the above interpretations are useful to think about further developments in the field of authentic leadership. Firstly, we consistently found that participants cheated despite a short-term authentic leadership intervention. However, other forms of interventions may counteract unethical behaviour in professional contexts. Secondly, while experimental variations of authentic leadership are generally effective, future research needs to test more specific theoretical predictions as to which types of outcomes authentic leadership affects, and which ones it does not. A recent network analysis of leadership by Meuser et al. (2016) suggested that this specific leadership style may be impactful in promoting positive emotions (e.g., enjoyment at work) and preventing negative ones (e.g., fear of failure), but less directly related to specific unethical behaviours such as cheating.

Advanced theoretical models should also consider the conditions under which authentic leadership is more or less effective in response to cheating. Vidyarthi, Anand, and Liden (2014) suggested that "individuals' conformity to social influence is positively related to the strength and immediacy of influencers" (p. 233). Previous research found that the impact of leadership on group performance increased with task interdependence (e.g., leader-member exchange differentiation; Liden, Erdogan, Wayne, & Sparrowe, 2006). Ibarra (2015) criticized that current views describe authentic leadership as a gold standard, which may hinder its impact. The paradox of authenticity is that if leaders apply a too rigid strategy, they may actually appear as less rather than more authentic. Since leaders need to accommodate a range of different roles, they also have different selves in the present as well as in the future. Being authentic means not sticking to one of these selves rigidly, but rather developing a sense of a complex, multifaceted self that provides room for adaptation.

Limitations and Future Research

We conducted an experimental laboratory study with a student sample and one specific measure of cheating. Most students were 25 years of age or younger (81%) and many did not have work experience to date (44%). Hence, their experience with leaders was likely limited and a more experienced working adult sample may have responded differently to authentic leadership. Moreover, we tested the impact of one specific authentic leadership variation. While this variation built on existing, validated study materials (Braun & Peus, 2016; Cianci et al., 2014), it represented only a small part of organizational reality. Leaders and followers typically interact on a daily basis over longer periods of time. The video recording with actors did not enable two-way interactions between leaders and followers over time. Also, participants did not have any opportunities to validate the leaders' self-descriptions (e.g., to compare them to colleagues' opinions). We cannot answer the question whether specific dimensions of authentic leadership (e.g., internalized moral perspective) buffer cheating more than others. Future research can advance the current variation of authentic leadership to test this. Finally, we cannot rule out the possibility that long-term exposure to authentic leadership in organizations does indeed reduce unethical conduct (Shamir, 2011).

Practical Implications

Based on our findings we cannot conclude that followers' perceptions of authentic leadership are an immediate remedy in the face of tendencies toward unethical conduct, such as followers' cheating. Nevertheless, many previous studies demonstrated the positive impact of authentic leadership (Banks et al., 2016; Gardner et al., 2011). In general, management training often covers approaches to increase self-knowledge and self-consistency, factors that precede authentic leadership (Peus et al., 2012). Opportunities for self-reflection support self-concept clarity, including clarity about one's values and moral convictions (e.g., constructing one's life story; Shamir & Eilam, 2005).

Given the findings of this research, we caution against the conclusion that simply training managers in authentic leadership will prevent followers from cheating for their own gain. Instead, organizations need to consider the impact of the interaction between authentic leaders and their followers in the long run (Shamir, 2011). Moreover, previous literature suggested that successful prevention of unethical conduct in organizations requires addressing factors such as opportunity, incentives or pressures, and rationalization of inappropriate actions (Murphy & Dacin, 2011).

To avoid organizational members' lacking awareness of or rationalizing their cheating behaviour, organizations' ethical values, code of conduct, and sanctions must be aligned (McCabe, Treviño, & Butterfield, 1996; Nitsch, Baetz, & Hughes, 2005).

Acknowledgements We gratefully acknowledge the support of David Schindler and the team of the Munich Experimental Laboratory for Economic and Social Sciences. We also thank Ximena Garcia-Rada and the participants in the Workshop on Experimental Labour and Personnel Economics (Institute for Labour Law and Industrial Relations in the European Union) as well as the Workshop on the Autonomy at Work and Employee Involvement: Causes and Consequences (Institute for Employment Research) for their helpful comments and suggestions. We are highly indebted to Anna Fuhrmann and Xueqian Chen for their excellent research assistance. We also thank Matthias Schmitt, Karolina Nieberle, David Goretzko, and Mark Bärthel for their help in running the experiment. Finally, we gratefully acknowledge the financial support of the Fritz Thyssen Foundation.

Appendix 1

List and Definition of Variables

Dependent Variable:

High roll: 0 = Participants reported that they had rolled a 1, 2, or 3. 1 = Participants reported that they had rolled a 4, 5, or 6.

Explanatory Variables:

Age: Participants' age as of April 2015.

Education: Reply to the question "What is the highest level of education you have completed?" 0 = none, 1 = "Hauptschule" (lower-level high school), 2 = "Realschule" (high school), 3 = "Abitur / Fachabitur" (college), 4 = "Bachelor / Fachhochschulabschluss" (3–4 years of university), 5 = "Master / Diplom" (4–5 years of university) and 6 = "Promotion / Aufbaustudium" (doctoral degree, post-graduate degree).

Expectations: Reply to the question "What is the percentage of participants who have earned more than you in the die task?"
Gender: Gender, 0 = female, 1 = male.
Living standard: Reply to the question "What describes your standard of living?" on a scale from 1 = very well-off to 6 = poor.
Material standard: Reply to the question "What is your marital status". 1 = single, 2 = In a relationship, 3 = married, 4 = divorced, 5 = other, 6 = prefer not to answer.
Semester: Number of semester participants had studied as of April 2015.
Work experience: Reply to the question whether the participant had previous work experience in an organization, 0 = no, 1 = yes.

References

Abeler, J., Becker, A., & Falk, A. (2014). Representative evidence on lying costs. *Journal of Public Economics, 113*, 96–104. https://doi.org/10.1016/j.jpubeco.2014.01.005.

Alberti, F., & Güth, W. (2013). Studying deception without deceiving participants: An experiment of deception experiments. *Journal of Economic Behavior & Organization, 93*, 196–204. https://doi.org/10.1016/j.jebo.2013.04.001.

Andersen, S. M., & Chen, S. (2002). The relational self: An interpersonal social-cognitive theory. *Psychological Review, 109*, 619–645. https://doi.org/10.1037/0033-295X.109.4.619.

Ariely, D. (2012). *The (honest) truth about dishonesty*. New York: HarperCollins Publishers.

Ariely, D., Garcia-Rada, X., Hornuf, L., & Mann, H. (2014). The (true) legacy of two really existing economic systems. *Munich Discussion Papers in Economics 2014–26*. Retrieved from SSRN: http://ssrn.com/abstract=2457000

Ashforth, B. E., & Anand, V. (2003). The normalization of corruption in organizations. *Research in Organizational Behavior, 25*, 1–52. https://doi.org/10.1016/S0191-3085(03)25001-2.

Association of Certified Fraud Examiners. (2014). *Report to the nations on occupational fraud and abuse*. Austin, TX: Association of Certified Fraud Examiners. Retrieved from https://www.acfe.com/rttn/docs/2014-report-to-nations.pdf.

Avolio, B. J., Gardner, W. L., Walumbwa, F. O., Luthans, F., & May, D. R. (2004). Unlocking the mask: A look at the process by which authentic leaders impact follower attitudes and behaviors. *The Leadership Quarterly, 15*, 801–823. https://doi.org/10.1016/j.leaqua.2004.09.003.

Axelrod, R. (1984). *The evolution of cooperation*. Cambridge, MA: Basic Books.

Bandura, A. (1965). Influence of models' reinforcement contingencies on the acquisition of imitative responses. *Journal of Personality and Social Psychology, 1*, 589–595. https://doi.org/10.1037/h0022070.

Banks, G. C., McCauley, K. D., Gardner, W. L., & Guler, C. E. (2016). A meta-analytic review of authentic and transformational leadership: A test for redundancy. *The Leadership Quarterly, 27*, 634–652. https://doi.org/10.1016/j.leaqua.2016.02.006.

Bazerman, M. H., & Gino, F. (2012). Behavioral ethics: Toward a deeper understanding of moral judgment and dishonesty. *Annual Review of Law and Social Science, 8*, 85–104. https://doi.org/10.1146/annurev-lawsocsci-102811-173815.

Becker, G. S. (1968). Crime and punishment: An economic approach. *Journal of Political Economy, 76*, 169–217.

Becker, G. S. (1993). Nobel lecture: The economic way of looking at behavior. *Journal of Political Economy, 101*, 385–409. https://doi.org/10.1086/259394.

Brass, D. J., Butterfield, K. D., & Skaggs, B. C. (1998). Relationships and unethical behavior: A social network perspective. *Academy of Management Review, 23*, 14–31. Retrieved from http://amr.aom.org/content/23/1.toc.

Braun, S., & Peus, C. (2016). Crossover of work–life balance perceptions: Does authentic leadership matter? *Journal of Business Ethics*, 1–19. https://doi.org/10.1007/s10551-016-3078-x.

Bucciol, A., Landini, F., & Piovesan, M. (2013). Unethical behavior in the field: Demographic characteristics and beliefs of the cheater. *Journal of Economic Behavior & Organization, 93*, 248–257. https://doi.org/10.1016/j.jebo.2013.03.018.

Cialdini, R. B., Reno, R. R., & Kallgren, C. A. (1990). A focus theory of normative conduct: Recycling the concept of norms to reduce littering in public places. *Journal of Personality and Social Psychology, 58*, 1015–1026. https://doi.org/10.1037/0022-3514.58.6.1015.

Cianci, A. M., Hannah, S. T., Roberts, R. P., & Tsakumis, G. T. (2014). The effects of authentic leadership on followers' ethical decision-making in the face of temptation: An experimental study. *The Leadership Quarterly, 25*, 581–594. https://doi.org/10.1016/j.leaqua.2013.12.001.

Clapp-Smith, R., Vogelgesang, G. R., & Avey, J. B. (2009). Authentic leadership and positive psychological capital: The mediating role of trust at the group level of analysis. *Journal of Leadership & Organizational Studies, 15*, 227–240. https://doi.org/10.1177/1548051808326596.

Cohn, A., Fehr, E., & Maréchal, M. A. (2014). Business culture and dishonesty in the banking industry. *Nature, 516*, 86–89. https://doi.org/10.1038/nature13977.

Conrads, J., Irlenbusch, B., Rilke, R. M., & Walkowitz, G. (2013). Lying and team incentives. *Journal of Economic Psychology, 34*, 1–7. https://doi.org/10.1016/j.joep.2012.10.011.

Deyle, E. (2014). *The new barometer: The global retail theft barometer*. Retrieved from http://www.odesus.gr/images/nea/eidhseis/2015/3.Global-Retail-Theft-Barometer-2015/GRTB%202015_web.pdf

Djawadi, B. M., & Fahr, R. (2015). "… and they are really lying": Clean evidence on the pervasiveness of cheating in professional contexts from a field experiment. *Journal of Economic Psychology, 48*, 48–59. https://doi.org/10.1016/j.joep.2015.03.002.

Effron, D. A., Bryan, C. J., & Murnighan, J. K. (2015). Cheating at the end to avoid regret. *Journal of Personality and Social Psychology, 109*, 395–414. https://doi.org/10.1037/pspa0000026.

Erat, S., & Gneezy, U. (2012). White lies. *Management Science, 58*, 723–733. https://doi.org/10.1287/mnsc.1110.1449.

Erkutlu, H., & Chafra, J. (2013). Effects of trust and psychological contract violation on authentic leadership and organizational deviance. *Management Research Review, 36*, 828–848. https://doi.org/10.1108/MRR-06-2012-0136.

Fischbacher, U., & Föllmi-Heusi, F. (2013). Lies in disguise – An experimental study on cheating. *Journal of the European Economic Association, 11*, 525–547. https://doi.org/10.1111/jeea.12014.

Gardner, W. L., Cogliser, C. C., Davis, K. M., & Dickens, M. P. (2011). Authentic leadership: A review of the literature and research agenda. *The Leadership Quarterly, 22*, 1120–1145. https://doi.org/10.1016/j.leaqua.2011.09.007.

Gill, D., Prowse, V., & Vlassopoulos, M. (2013). Cheating in the workplace: An experimental study of the impact of bonuses and productivity. *Journal of Economic Behavior & Organization, 96*, 120–134. https://doi.org/10.1016/j.jebo.2013.09.011.

Gini, A. (1997). Moral leadership and business ethics. *Journal of Leadership & Organizational Studies, 4*, 64–81. https://doi.org/10.1177/107179199700400406.

Gino, F., Ayal, S., & Ariely, D. (2009). Contagion and differentiation in unethical behavior: The effect of one bad apple on the barrel. *Psychological Science, 20*, 393–398. https://doi.org/10.1111/j.1467-9280.2009.02306.x.

Gino, F., Kouchaki, M., & Galinsky, A. D. (2015). The moral virtue of authenticity. How inauthenticity produces feelings of immorality and impurity. *Psychological Science, 26*, 1–14. https://doi.org/10.1177/0956797615575277.

Hiller, N. J., DeChurch, L. A., Murase, T., & Doty, D. (2011). Searching for outcomes of leadership: A 25-year review. *Journal of Management, 37*, 1137–1177. https://doi.org/10.1177/0149206310393520.

Hörner, K., Weisweiler, S., & Braun, S. (2015). *Authentic leadership and follower stress perception and coping – Model testing and validation of the Authentic Leadership Inventory*. 75th Annual Meeting of the Academy of Management, Vancouver, BC. Retrieved from http://proceedings.aom.org/content/2015/1/10922.short

Houser, D., Vetter, S., & Winter, J. (2012). Fairness and cheating. *European Economic Review, 56*, 1645–1655. https://doi.org/10.1016/j.euroecorev.2012.08.001.

Howell, J. M., & Avolio, B. J. (1992). The ethics of charismatic leadership: Submission or liberation? *Academy of Management Review, 6*, 43–54. https://doi.org/10.5465/ame.1992.4274395.

Ibarra, H. (2015). The authenticity paradox. *Harvard Business Review, 93*, 52–59. Retrieved from https://hbr.org/2015/01/the-authenticity-paradox.

Ichino, A., & Maggi, G. (2000). Work environment and individual background: Explaining regional shirking differentials in a large Italian firm. *Quarterly Journal of Economics, 115*, 1057–1090. https://doi.org/10.1162/003355300554890.

Javidan, M., & Dastmalchian, A. (2009). Managerial implications of the GLOBE project: A study of 62 societies. *Asia Pacific Journal of Human Resources, 47*, 41–58. https://doi.org/10.1177/1038411108099289.

Jiang, T. (2013). Cheating in mind games: The subtlety of rules matters. *Journal of Economic Behavior & Organization, 93*, 328–336. https://doi.org/10.1016/j.jebo.2013.04.003.

Kernis, M. H. (2003). Toward a conceptualization of optimal self-esteem. *Psychological Inquiry, 14*, 1–26. https://doi.org/10.1207/S15327965PLI1401_01.

Kiersch, C. E., & Byrne, Z. S. (2015). Is being authentic being fair? Multilevel examination of authentic leadership, justice, and employee outcomes. *Journal of Leadership & Organizational Studies, 22*, 292–303. https://doi.org/10.1177/1548051815570035.

Leroy, H., Anseel, F., Gardner, W. L., & Sels, L. (2015). Authentic leadership, authentic followership, basic need satisfaction, and work role performance: A cross-level study. *Journal of Management, 41*, 1677–1697. https://doi.org/10.1177/0149206312457822.

Leroy, H., Palanski, M. E., & Simons, T. (2011). Authentic leadership and behavioral integrity as drivers of follower commitment and performance. *Journal of Business Ethics, 107*, 255–264. https://doi.org/10.1007/s10551-011-1036-1.

Liden, R. C., Erdogan, B., Wayne, S. J., & Sparrowe, R. T. (2006). Leader-member exchange, differentiation, and task interdependence: Implications for individual and group performance. *Journal of Organizational Behavior, 27*, 723–746. https://doi.org/10.1002/job.409.

Lundquist, T., Ellingsen, T., Gribbe, E., & Johannesson, M. (2009). The aversion to lying. *Journal of Economic Behavior & Organization, 70*, 81–92. https://doi.org/10.1016/j.jebo.2009.02.010.

Mann, H., Garcia-Rada, X., Hornuf, L., & Tafurt, J. (2016). What deters crime? Comparing the effectiveness of legal, social, and internal sanctions across countries. *Frontiers in Psychology, 7*, 1–13. https://doi.org/10.3389/fpsyg.2016.00085.

Mann, H., Garcia-Rada, X., Hornuf, L., Tafurt, J., & Ariely, D. (2016). Cut from the same cloth: Similarly dishonest individuals across countries. *Journal of Cross-Cultural Psychology, 47*, 858–874. https://doi.org/10.1177/0022022116648211.

Mann, H., Garcia-Rada, X., Houser, D., & Ariely, D. (2014). Everybody else is doing it: Exploring social transmission of lying behavior. *PloS One, 9*(10), e109591. https://doi.org/10.1371/journal.pone.0109591.

Mathys, N. J. (2002). A conversation with C. Richard Panico: Leading an ethically-based organization. *Journal of Leadership & Organizational Studies, 9*, 89–101. https://doi.org/10.1177/107179190200900208.

Mazar, N., Amir, O., & Ariely, D. (2008). The dishonesty of honest people: A theory of self-concept maintenance. *Journal of Marketing Research, 45*, 633–644. https://doi.org/10.1509/jmkr.45.6.633.

McCabe, D. L., Treviño, L. K., & Butterfield, K. D. (1996). The influence of collegiate and corporate codes of conduct on ethics-related behavior in the workplace. *Business Ethics Quarterly, 6*, 461–476. https://doi.org/10.2307/3857499.

Meuser, J. D., Gardner, W. L., Dinh, J. E., Hu, J., Liden, R. C., & Lord, R. G. (2016). A network analysis of leadership theory: The infancy of integration. *Journal of Management, 42*, 1374–1403. https://doi.org/10.1177/0149206316647099.

Murphy, P. R., & Dacin, M. T. (2011). Psychological pathways to fraud: Understanding and preventing fraud in organizations. *Journal of Business Ethics, 101*, 601–618. https://doi.org/10.1007/s10551-011-0741-0.

Nagin, D. S., & Pogarsky, G. (2003). An experimental investigation of deterrence: Cheating, self-serving bias, and impulsivity. *Criminology, 41*, 167–194. https://doi.org/10.1111/j.1745-9125.2003.tb00985.x.

Neider, L. L., & Schriesheim, C. A. (2011). The authentic leadership inventory (ALI): Development and empirical tests. *The Leadership Quarterly, 22*, 1146–1164. https://doi.org/10.1016/j.leaqua.2011.09.008.

Nitsch, D., Baetz, M., & Hughes, J. C. (2005). Why code of conduct violations go unreported: A conceptual framework to guide intervention and future research. *Journal of Business Ethics, 57*, 327–341. https://doi.org/10.1007/s10551-004-8203-6.

Peus, C., Braun, S., & Knipfer, K. (2015). On becoming a leader in Asia and America: Empirical evidence from women managers. *The Leadership Quarterly, 26*, 55–67. https://doi.org/10.1016/j.leaqua.2014.08.004.

Peus, C., Wesche, J. S., Streicher, B., Braun, S., & Frey, D. (2012). Authentic leadership: An empirical test of its antecedents, consequences, and mediating mechanisms. *Journal of Business Ethics, 107*, 331–348. https://doi.org/10.1007/s10551-011-1042-3.

Rego, A., Sousa, F., Marques, C., & Pina e Cunha, M. (2012). Authentic leadership promoting employees' psychological capital and creativity. *Journal of Business Research, 65*, 429–437. https://doi.org/10.1016/j.jbusres.2011.10.003.

Schneider, A., & Schröder, T. (2012). Ideal types of leadership as patterns of affective meaning: A cross-cultural and over-time perspective. *Social Psychology Quarterly, 75*, 268–287. https://doi.org/10.1177/0190272512446755.

Shamir, B. (2011). Leadership takes time: Some implications of (not) taking time seriously in leadership research. *The Leadership Quarterly, 22*, 307–315. https://doi.org/10.1016/j.leaqua.2011.02.006.

Shamir, B., & Eilam, G. (2005). "What's your story?" A life-stories approach to authentic leadership development. *The Leadership Quarterly, 16*, 395–417. https://doi.org/10.1016/j.leaqua.2005.03.005.

Shao, R., Aquino, K., & Freeman, D. (2008). Beyond moral reasoning: A review of moral identity research and its implications for business ethics. *Business Ethics Quarterly, 18*, 513–540. https://doi.org/10.5840/beq200818436.

Skarlicki, D. P., & Folger, R. (1997). Retaliation in the workplace: The roles of distributive, procedural, and interactional justice. *Journal of Applied Psychology, 82*, 434–443. https://doi.org/10.1037/0021-9010.82.3.434.

Treviño, L. K. (1986). Ethical decision making in organizations: A person-situation interactionist model. *Academy of Management Review, 11*, 601–617. Retrieved from http://wweb.uta.edu/management/lavelle/New%20Folder/Trevino%201986.pdf.

Treviño, L. K., Weaver, G. R., & Reynolds, S. J. (2006). Behavioral ethics in organizations: A review. *Journal of Management, 32*, 951–990. https://doi.org/10.1177/0149206306294258.

Vidyarthi, P. R., Anand, S., & Liden, R. C. (2014). Do emotionally perceptive leaders motivate higher employee performance? The moderating role of task interdependence and power distance. *The Leadership Quarterly, 25*, 232–244. https://doi.org/10.1016/j.leaqua.2013.08.003.

Walumbwa, F. O., Avolio, B. J., Gardner, W. L., Wernsing, T. S., & Peterson, S. J. (2008). Authentic leadership: Development and validation of a theory-based measure. *Journal of Management, 34*, 89–126. https://doi.org/10.1177/0149206307308913.

Wang, D. S., & Hsieh, C. C. (2013). The effect of authentic leadership on employee trust and employee engagement. *Social Behavior and Personality: An International Journal, 41*, 613–624. https://doi.org/10.2224/sbp.2013.41.4.613.

Weisel, O., & Shalvi, S. (2015). The collaborative roots of corruption. *Proceedings of the National Academy of Sciences, 112*, 10651–10656. https://doi.org/10.1073/pnas.1423035112.

Wong, C. A., & Laschinger, H. K. (2013). Authentic leadership, performance, and job satisfaction: The mediating role of empowerment. *Journal of Nursing Management, 69*, 947–959. https://doi.org/10.1111/j.1365-2648.2012.06089.x.

10

Authentic Leadership and Authenticity: An Existential Perspective

Cloé Fortin, Louis Baron, and Cécile Renucci

Organisations today are facing unprecedented turmoil. The current economic and humanitarian crises have increased the fragility of organisations that were already confronted with an accelerating pace of change, the arrival of new actors in a sharing economy (e.g., Uber and Airbnb), strong competition from emerging economies, and an ongoing accumulation of financial scandals. Recent economic, geopolitical, and technological developments and the ethical abuses of corporations such as WorldCom and Enron have further undermined the internal stability of

C. Fortin (✉)
Industrial and Organizational Psychology, Université du Québec à Montréal, Montréal, Québec, Canada

L. Baron
Department of Organisation and Human Resources, Université du Québec à Montréal School of Management, Montréal, Quebec, Canada

C. Renucci
Industrial and Organizational Psychology, Université du Québec à Montréal, Montréal, Quebec, Canada

© The Author(s) 2018
D. Cotter-Lockard (ed.), *Authentic Leadership and Followership*, Palgrave Studies in Leadership and Followership, https://doi.org/10.1007/978-3-319-65307-5_10

businesses (Northouse, 2010). It is in these challenging times of instability that the need for leadership is most acutely felt (Dinh et al., 2014), especially positive forms of leadership that can help restore the confidence of stakeholders—investors, employees, and customers—who have become increasingly intolerant of inconsistencies between the principles espoused by leaders and their actual conduct (Walumbwa, Avolio, Gardner, Wernsing, & Peterson, 2008). In this context, some businesses are adapting by implementing new forms of work organisations in which employees at all levels are called upon to exercise leadership (McCrimmon, 2010). These developments require the use of life skills which encourage leaders to become more aware of their values, to behave ethically, and thus become capable of coherently guiding their organisations (Clapp-Smith, Vogelgesang, & Avey, 2008). Leadership behaviours and the development of positive and effective leaders are thus among the foremost concerns for many organisations (Day, Fleenor, Atwater, Sturm, & McKee, 2014). A growing number of authors have argued that the adoption of authentic leadership (AL) – characterised by transparent intentions and coherence between actions and espoused values – is needed to achieve sustainable business performance (Avolio & Gardner, 2005).

In recent years, the scientific community has worked to define and refine the concept of AL (Luthans & Avolio, 2003) to analyse its positive implications for individuals and organisations (Walumbwa, Luthans, Avey, & Oke, 2011) and to suggest ways to develop such leadership within organisations (Baron & Parent, 2015; Berkovich, 2014; Gardner, Avolio, Luthans, May, & Walumbwa, 2005). Recently, the conceptualisation of AL has attracted various criticisms from the scientific community (Algera & Lips-Wiersma, 2012; Berkovich, 2014; Lawler & Ashman, 2012). These authors point out inconsistencies in the literature as to the place of authenticity in the concept of AL and the failure to take into consideration dynamic variables, such as relational and interpersonal processes, that influence the development of AL.

To examine these criticisms, the purpose of this chapter is to apply two different perspectives historically used to defined authenticity: the existential perspective and the psychological perspective. Second, using a correlational design, this chapter explores the relationship between authenticity and AL in a French-Canadian population using a quantitative approach. Finally, the discussion focuses on the influence of these concepts on all members of an organisation, both the leaders and the followers, as well as their relationships.

Theoretical Background

Authenticity

Historically, the concept of authenticity has been explored and defined from two perspectives: the existentialist philosophical (or interpersonal) perspective and the psychological (or individual) perspective. The existentialist meanings given to authenticity have been set out in terms of individual virtues and ethical choices, whereas the psychological meanings have been structured in terms of individual traits and identities (Novicevic, Harvey, Ronald, & Brown-Radford, 2006).

Originally, the existentialist perspective of authenticity was developed by Sartre and Heidegger. They defined authenticity as a dynamic state that can be achieved through one's relationships with others (Berkovich, 2014; Heidegger, 1962; Sartre, 1943, 1946). Similarly, Barrett-Lennard (1998) suggested that authenticity is possible when individuals are able to consistently integrate their feelings, perceptions and actions in their relationships with themselves and others. Thus, the concept of authenticity as defined from an existentialist perspective refers to the context: individuals are authentic in the moment, depending on their choices and through their interpersonal relationships.

The concept of authenticity was later examined from a psychological perspective. The definition proposed by Harter (2002) is the most widely used in the literature on AL. It defines authenticity as

> owning one's personal experiences, be they thoughts, emotions, needs, wants, preferences or beliefs, processes captured by the injunction to 'know oneself'. The exhortation 'To thine own self be true' further implies that one acts in accord with the true self, expressing oneself in ways that are consistent with inner thoughts and feelings. (Harter, 2002, p. 382)

According to this definition, authenticity is a question of identity: authentic individuals act in accordance with their beliefs and values (Novicevic et al., 2006).

The definition of authenticity put forward by Wood, Linley, Maltby, Baliousis, and Joseph (2008) was used in this study. Inspired by Rogers' (1961) person-centred psychology and the work of Barrett-Lennard (1998), they proposed a model (see Fig. 10.1) that conceptualises authenticity as consistency between three domains of experience: (a) *the person's primary experience*, that is, their true self, including actual physiological states, emotions, and schematic beliefs); (b) *their symbolised awareness*, that is, their experience as consciously perceived; and (c) *their externalised*

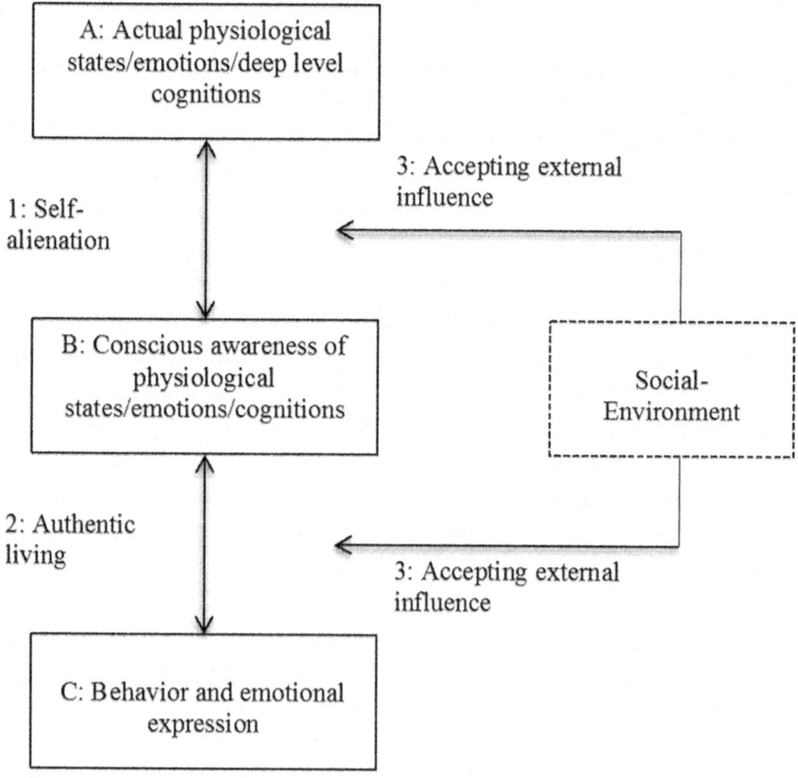

Fig. 10.1 The person-centred conception of authenticity from Wood et al. (2008)

behaviours and communication. The first component of authenticity, *self-alienation*, is experienced in reaction to the contradictions between their 'real' experience (physiological states, emotions, schematic beliefs) and their symbolised awareness (aspects of experience represented in cognitive awareness). This dimension of authenticity can be experienced as a "subjective experience of not knowing oneself, or feeling out of touch with the true self" (Wood et al., 2008, p. 386).

The second component, *authentic living*, represents the congruence between symbolised awareness and behaviour. This dimension of authenticity is manifested by the individual behaving and expressing themselves in a way that is consistent with their conscious awareness (Wood et al., 2008). In other words, authentic living refers to one's ability to be true to oneself and live, as much as possible, in accordance with one's values and beliefs. Finally, *acceptance of external influence* is manifested as the extent to which one acknowledges and agrees to conform to the expectations of others and introject their opinions. By being aware of the influence of others, one can develop a deeper understanding of oneself, making it possible to avoid or limit unwanted influences and thus to be more authentic.

Authentic Leadership

In recent years, numerous researchers have focused on defining AL (Avolio, Gardner, Walumbwa, Luthans, & May, 2004; Luthans & Avolio, 2003; Shamir & Eilam, 2005; Walumbwa et al., 2008). AL was initially defined as

> [...] a process that draws from both positive psychological capacities and a highly developed organizational context, which results in both greater self-awareness and self-regulated positive behaviors on the part of leaders and associates, fostering positive self-development. (Luthans & Avolio, 2003, p. 243)

Later, researchers associated with the Gallup Leadership Institute proposed a more operational conceptualisation of AL which helped consolidate its theoretical underpinnings. According to this group, authentic leaders have positive psychological capacities, are self-aware, have self-regulated positive behaviours, and work in a highly developed organisational context they help create. Drawing on Kernis' (2003) conception of authenticity, the self-based model of AL developed by Gardner et al. (2005), which includes propositions from Ilies, Morgeson, and Nahrgang (2005), identified several distinguishing features associated with authentic self-regulation processes, including four dimensions.

First, *self-awareness* refers to the meaning that individuals bring to their lives and how that meaning influences the way they see themselves over time. In other words, this aspect of AL refers to the leader's knowledge and understanding in terms of values, identity, emotions, motivations, and goals. Second, *relational transparency* refers to presenting one's 'authentic self' to others. Third, *balanced processing* of information refers to the ability of the leader to objectively analyse all relevant data before making a decision, including seeking views that differ from their own. Finally, *authentic behaviour* refers to a process of self-regulation guided by personal values and standards forming the basis for decision-making and undertaking action. This last dimension was renamed to 'internalised moral perspective' by Walumbwa et al. (2008) in their study on the development of a theory-based measure of AL. As they summarised in their validation study of the four-factor conceptualisation:

> Kernis (2003) advanced a developmental model that posits attainment of authenticity produces 'optimal' levels of self-esteem. That is, when individuals come to know and accept themselves, including their strengths and weaknesses, they display high levels of stable, as opposed to fragile, self-esteem. Such individuals are also relatively free of the defensive biases displayed by less mature persons and consequently more comfortable forming transparent, open, and close relationships with others. Furthermore, they display authentic behavior that reflects consistency between their values, beliefs, and actions. (Walumbwa et al., 2008, p. 93)

Recently, this conceptualisation of AL, based on the psychological view of authenticity, has sparked criticism from various authors who approach these concepts from an existentialist perspective. First, Lawler and Ashman (2012) point out an inconsistency in the literature regarding the place of authenticity in the concept of AL, stating that "[whilst] the number of articles discussing authenticity in relation to leadership may be increasing, few overtly relate the concept to philosophical foundations or identify ways in which the interpretations of the concept might have altered over time" (Lawler & Ashman, 2012, p. 327). In addition, Algera and Lips-Wiersma (2012) have suggested that the concept of authenticity as currently embedded in the concept of AL is limited because, as yet, insufficient effort has been devoted to developing a full understanding of the ontological roots of authenticity. According to these authors, authenticity is primarily a concept pertaining to humans, and it must be understood in that regard before being applied to the leadership context. Algera and Lips-Wiersma (2012) consider that the developers of AL have not examined authenticity thoroughly enough to justify incorporating it into the AL concept. This gap worries some researchers (Algera & Lips-Wiersma, 2012; Berkovich, 2014; Lawler, 2005; Lawler & Ashman, 2012) who see significant inconsistencies related to it, particularly with regard to the understanding of AL and AL development programmes.

First, they point out that the dominant conception of AL encourages holding on to unrealistic expectations of oneself and others. These inconsistencies directly affect the authenticity of leaders, the authenticity of the relationship between the leaders and their followers, and the authenticity of the followers. Indeed, these authors suggest that if an organisation attempts to portray an image that is inconsistent with the interpersonal or organisational reality as experienced by its members, they may develop a sense of incoherence and meaninglessness. In contrast, at the individual level, acknowledging, accepting, and addressing such inauthenticity could foster positive self-development for members of the organisation (Algera & Lips-Wiersma, 2012).

The same authors propose that our understanding of authenticity, and thus of AL, necessarily has an influence on the development of leader training programmes. In this regard, Cooper, Scandura, and Schriesheim (2005) suggest that traditional training programmes would not produce the desired changes in terms of the life skills and personal skills needed to exercise AL. These authors explain that AL, largely because of its contextual aspect, should not be considered the same as other aspects of leadership for which a set of skills can be acquired through training programmes. To that end, they stress the importance of an independent assessment of authenticity "[regardless] of how authenticity is measured, however, it will be essential to conduct an assessment of it to ensure that any training intervention to develop authentic leaders is genuine" (Cooper et al., 2005, p. 477).

To address these limitations and deepen our understanding of AL, some researchers have proposed the adoption of a conceptualisation of AL developed from an existentialist perspective (Algera & Lips-Wiersma, 2012; Berkovich, 2014; Ford & Lawler, 2007; Lawler & Ashman, 2012). They suggest that it is critical to adopt a different approach—one based on an understanding of relational and interpersonal processes that presuppose individual authenticity. These authors further argue that such an approach would be an interesting avenue to pursue, as it would support ontological research on the concept of authenticity, focus on the place of authenticity in the concept of AL and recognise the inter-subjective relational dynamics in the development of authenticity and AL.

This chapter puts forward a critical analysis of the psychological and dominant conception of AL with a view to assessing its similarities and differences with an existentialist conception of AL and discusses the potential impacts on followership. To accomplish this, two specific research objectives were formulated. The first objective was to assess the extent to which authenticity is related to AL as conceptualised from the psychological perspective. The second objective was to determine the extent to which authenticity is related to AL as conceptualised from the existentialist perspective. The AL development model put forward by Berkovich (2014), which uses an existentialist point of view, was used to address the second objective of this study (see Fig. 10.2 for an adapted version of the model).

In the theoretical model of AL development proposed by Berkovich (2014), the interaction of eight components (self-exposure, open-mindedness, respect, critical thinking, empathy, care, contact, and mutuality) is posited to foster the personal development of both leaders and followers as well as the development of AL. Specifically, these eight components, in the context of an authentic relationship between the leader and another individual, contribute to the development of AL. Supported by the relationship with the other person, these eight components may stimulate authentic attitudes and behaviours in the developing individuals and foster the development of AL in the leader.

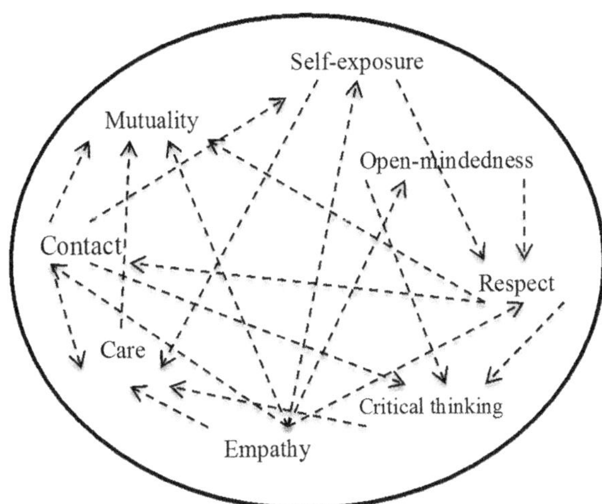

Fig. 10.2 Adapted model of authentic leadership development from Berkovich (2014)

Considering the interest in AL and its development, on the one hand, and the lack of consensus regarding the link between authenticity and AL, on the other, this study is part of a process of comparative analysis of the postulated relationships between these variables. To assess the similarities and differences between the psychological and existential perspectives regarding the relationship between authenticity and AL, we formulated four hypotheses.

The first hypothesis concerns the link between authenticity and AL. As discussed above, AL as conceptualised by Walumbwa et al. (2008) and authenticity as defined by Wood et al. (2008) develop in similar ways, through awareness of one's thoughts and emotions, through behaviours and emotional expression, as well as through acceptance of external influence. In the same vein, it is possible that authenticity is associated with AL. However, self-alienation is not a dimension found in AL theory. Accordingly, it is possible that the four-component model of AL is not related to the self-alienation dimension, but may be related to authenticity and its two sub-dimensions, authentic living and acceptance of external influence. To evaluate the possible links between authenticity and AL as conceptualised from a psychological perspective, the first hypothesis focuses on the three dimensions of authenticity in relation to AL.

H_1: Authenticity and its three sub-dimensions (self-alienation, acceptance of the influence of others, and authentic living) are positively correlated with AL.

The next three hypotheses focus on the link between authenticity and the AL development model proposed by Berkovich (2014). According to Berkovich (2014), various components, including self-exposure (defined as a form of openness to others), empathy (defined as the ability to recognise the emotional experience of others), and critical thinking (defined as a process of awareness of one's own thoughts and perceptions and those of others), foster the development of AL. Whereas authenticity, as defined by Wood et al. (2008), develops through awareness of one's emotions and cognitions, through one's behaviour and emotional expressiveness, and through contact with one's social environment. It is possible that the three dimensions mentioned above may also influence the development of authenticity.

H_2: Self-exposure is positively correlated with authenticity.
H_3: Critical thinking is positively correlated with authenticity.
H_4: Empathy is positively correlated with authenticity.

Methods

Participants and Data Collection

Given the objectives of this study, the target population included persons who hold or have held leadership positions. However, since the inclusion criteria needed to describe this population cannot be precisely operationalised, a convenience sample was assembled to obtain a representation of the target population. More specifically, the study sample was made up of postgraduate students at a French-Canadian university, enrolled either in a specialised MBA for management consultants or in a Master's programme in Human Resources. The participants were contacted by email.

Because of the importance of relationships with others in the AL development model proposed by Berkovich (2014), all the selected participants had to have attended a course focusing on the development of personal management skills within the previous two years. To be admissible, the courses needed to meet two criteria: the objectives of the course had to be mainly oriented towards personal development, and the teaching methods used needed to include some form of ongoing interaction among students.

Measurements

Authentic Leadership

The Authentic Leadership Questionnaire developed by Walumbwa et al. (2008) was used to measure AL. The questionnaire consists of 16 items measuring the construct's four dimensions (self-awareness, relational transparency, balanced processing of information, and internalised moral perspective). The respondents indicated how often they used different behaviours on a scale from 0 (*never*) to 4 (*frequently*). Since previous studies found that first-order factors failed to add any meaningful incremental validity beyond that of the shared core higher factor (Baron, 2016; Walumbwa et al., 2008), the authors chose to use the general factor in the analysis. The four dimensions contribute to the internal consistency of the overall AL scale (Cronbach's alpha = 0.77).

Authenticity

Authenticity was assessed using the authenticity scale (Grégoire, Baron, Ménard & Lachance, 2014; Wood et al., 2008; for the French version). This measure is based on the person-centred conception of authenticity proposed by Wood et al. (2008) and includes three subscales: self-alienation, authentic living, and acceptance of external influence. A 7-point Likert scale from 1 (*Does not describe me at all*) to 7 (*Describes me very well*) was used. The alpha coefficients for our data were similar to those obtained in the validation study (overall score, α = 0.85; self-alienation, α = 0.82; authentic living, α = 0.74 and acceptance of external influence, α = 0.83). Regarding the psychometric properties of the scale, the validation study by Wood et al. (2008) indicates good validity and good internal consistency.

Components of the AL Development Model

Empathy, critical thinking, and self-exposure were also measured in this study. Based on their interactions with other variables, these variables were selected to be most representative of the chosen model. Together, these three variables are related to all the other variables in the model proposed by Berkovich (2014).

Empathy

Empathy was measured using the 17-item Empathy Assessment Index, developed and validated by Lietz et al. (2011). The items were measured using a 5-point Likert scale. The validation analysis indicated that the Index has good internal consistency (α = 0.82).

Critical Thinking.

Critical thinking was measured using the Critical Thinking Disposition Scale (Sosu, 2013). The questionnaire consists of 11 items evaluated using a 5-point Likert scale from 1 (*totally disagree*) to 5 (*totally agree*). The results of exploratory factor analyses and confirmatory factor analyses indicate that the scale's 11 items show good content validity.

Self-Exposure

Self-exposure was measured using the *quantity* dimension of the Revised Self-disclosure Scale (Wheeless & Grotz, 1976). This dimension assesses both the frequency and duration of self-disclosure messages in which the respondents choose to expose themselves in their communication with others. This dimension of the self-disclosure scale was chosen because it represents the definition of self-exposure used in this study and suffices for measurement of this variable. The definition put forward by Cozby (1973, cited in Wheeless & Grotz, 1976) explains that the nature of the message does not necessarily have to be considered for it to be classified as a form of self-disclosure. This dimension is measured using four questions on a 7-point Likert scale from 1 (*totally disagree*) to 7 (*completely agree*). The internal consistency analysis of the instrument demonstrated its validity and accuracy ($\alpha = 0.78$).

Results

Descriptive Analyses

Descriptive analyses were conducted to determine the distribution of our sample. The results show that in general, the data are reliable and normally distributed. Regarding the control variables, the average age of the participants was 33 years, the majority (95%) held a university diploma, 64% were women, and they had 5 years of managerial experience on average.

Statistical Analysis

To verify our first hypothesis, that authenticity and its three subdimensions are positively correlated with AL, we carried out correlation analyses. Table 10.1 shows the Pearson's correlation coefficients (r) between each of the variables and AL.

The results show that there is a statistically significant positive correlation between the extent of AL and the measures for authentic living, acceptance of external influence, and authenticity. The self-alienation subscale is the only variable that was not correlated with AL ($r(100) = 0.167$, n.s.). These results thus partially confirm H_1.

Hypotheses H_2, H_3 and H_4 posited positive correlations between authenticity and the three dimensions of the AL development model: self-exposure, critical thinking, and empathy. To validate these hypotheses,

Table 10.1 Correlations between authenticity and authentic leadership

Variable	N	AL (r)
Self-alienation	100	0.167
Authentic living	100	0.508[a]
Acceptance of external influence	100	0.270[a]
Authenticity	100	0.366[a]

AL authentic leadership
[a]Correlations with a 0.01 significant level (two-tailed)

Table 10.2 Correlations between the components of the AL model and authenticity

Variable	N	Authenticity (r)
Self-exposure	99	00.175
Empathy	98	00.386[a]
Critical thinking	97	00.385[a]

Note that the number of participants varies according to missing data in certain sections of the questionnaire
[a]Correlations with a 0.01 significant level (two-tailed)

further correlation analyses were conducted, the results of which are presented in Table 10.2.

The results indicate that there are statistically significant positive correlations between the measures of critical thinking and authenticity and between the measures of empathy and authenticity. H_3 and H_4 are thus confirmed. However, no significant association was found between self-exposure and authenticity. H_2 is thus rejected.

Discussion

Hypotheses Test Conclusions

The confirmed or partially confirmed hypotheses are consistent with the theoretical models and empirical studies that form the conceptual framework for this study. Our first hypothesis posited that authenticity and its three dimensions are positively correlated with AL. The results show that indeed, authenticity and two of its dimensions – acceptance of the influence of others and authentic living – are positively correlated with AL, but that there was no significant correlation between AL and the self-alienation dimension of authenticity.

The positive correlations between authenticity and two of its dimensions with AL partially corroborate the postulate of Walumbwa et al. (2008) that authenticity is linked to AL. The correlation between AL and the acceptance of external influence supports the position of Gardner et al. (2005) regarding the notion of the influence of others as an antecedent to AL. According to these authors, the development of AL is particularly influenced by the organisational climate, which is itself modulated by employee development. Development of AL would thus be influenced by the interactions of leaders with their followers. Furthermore, the results support the link between AL and authentic living (i.e., living in accordance with one's values and beliefs), supporting the theoretical model of Shamir and Eilam (2005) and the study results of Peus, Wesche, Streicher, Braun, and Frey (2012). According to these authors, self-awareness is an antecedent of AL, and AL develops in tandem with the leader's identity as a central element of their self-concept. Leaders can develop AL and authenticity by maintaining consistency between their cognitions (seeing oneself as a leader) and behaviour (consistently adopting the role of a leader).

However, considering that according to Wood et al. (2008) authenticity has three dimensions and one of the three dimensions, self-alienation, is not correlated with AL, it is not possible to say that authenticity, in its complete form, is linked to AL as conceptualised in the model developed by Walumbwa et al. (2008). Recognition of this aspect of the self is necessary to the development of authenticity, as it allows the individual to acknowledge previously unknown aspects of their identity and thus to gain control over them (Barrett-Lennard, 1998). Hypothesis 1 was partially supported, because of the lack of a significant correlation between self-alienation and AL, indicating that authentic leaders, as defined in the four-component model, may be unaware of this part of themselves. This finding is consistent with the work of Algera and Lips-Wiersma (2012), Berkovich (2014), and Lawler and Ashman (2012) who suggest that authenticity, as conceptualised in the model of AL proposed by Walumbwa et al. (2008), is not fully representative of authenticity as defined by Wood et al. (2008). Moreover, this finding leads to interesting reflections regarding the mechanisms that might impede access to awareness of this aspect of oneself.

First, the lack of correlation between AL and self-alienation is consistent with the work by Tate (2008) showing that authentic leaders are more likely to have a low level of self-monitoring. According to Ilies et al. (2005), self-monitoring is a form of active surveillance that helps leaders control their behaviour to act in accordance with perceived expectations from the social environment. Given that our data reveal no correlation between self-alienation and AL, it is possible that the leaders with low levels of self-monitoring may pay little attention to themselves and others, which would explain their difficulty in gaining awareness of the alienated parts of themselves.

An important nuance regarding measurement issues should be pointed out when interpreting this finding. Because the assessment of self-alienation is based on awareness of this part of oneself, although the instrument developed by Wood et al. (2008) only measures the *presence* of this variable, it is difficult to objectively interpret this result. The presence of self-alienation, as measured using the authenticity scale of Wood et al. (2008), does not necessarily mean that the person is less authentic. Indeed, individuals who develop self-awareness—as may be the case for the participants in the professional development courses that were required for enrolment in this study—may realise that they do not know themselves very well, even though this insight helps them know themselves better than most people do. Conversely, individuals may believe that they know themselves well and are not alienated, when in fact they are unaware of the parts of themselves which they do not suspect exist. According to this logic, it appears difficult to know whether a person is alienated because of an awareness that seeks to limit the alienated parts of himself or herself or simply because they do not know themselves very well. These reflections corroborate the work of Algera and Lips-Wiersma (2012) and Guignon and Pereboom (2001) regarding the need for awareness of self-alienation in the development of the authenticity, and put the interpretation of the first hypothesis into perspective. This exposition raises the age-old questions posed by Socrates in 400 B.C. regarding wisdom and self-awareness. Who is the more alienated individual? The person who knows that he does not know or the one who thinks he knows when he does not?

Self-Awareness, Authenticity, and Mindfulness

These analyses underline the importance of self-awareness in the concept of authenticity. A study by Hodgin and Knee (2002) provides some thoughts for further reflection. They suggest multiple parallels between authenticity, mindfulness, and self-determined motivation. Specifically, they propose that individuals who are motivated in a self-determined manner would tend to possess a "readiness to perceive ongoing experience accurately, without distorting or attempting to avoid the experience and a willingness to assimilate novel experiences into self-structures" (Hodgin & Knee, 2002, p. 88). In the same vein, the lack of correlation between self-alienation and AL can be examined using the concept of mindfulness. Mindfulness is defined as "the awareness that emerges through paying attention on purpose, in the present moment, and non-judgmentally to the unfolding of experience moment by moment" (Kabat-Zinn, 2006, p. 145). Mindfulness makes it possible for individuals to set aside their personal filters to establish direct contact with their experience. By integrating awareness of internal and external experiences, the present and dynamic context, and a non-judging attitude, the practice of mindfulness could make it possible for individuals to become aware of self-alienation and to develop greater authenticity. In addition, from the follower's perspective, Gardner et al. (2005) suggest that self-awareness may help authentic leaders encourage followers to engage in a process of self-discovery whereby they nurture their strengths. In short, the integration of authenticity in the concept of AL, as used by the authors who adopt the psychological perspective of AL, is supported by this finding.

An Existentialist Perspective of Authentic Leadership

We also examined the factors associated with the existentialist perspective of AL, as set out in Hypotheses 2, 3, and 4. The confirmation of Hypotheses 3 and 4 provides support for the postulate that the components of the model proposed by Berkovich (2014) are indeed associated with authenticity. According to that model, critical thinking and empathy stimulate authentic behaviour in leaders. Through their capacity to recognise the emotional experience of others and to exercise critical thinking regarding new ideas, leaders should be able to become more authentic (Berkovich, 2014).

Finally, Hypothesis 2, which postulated that self-exposure was correlated with authenticity, was rejected. One possible explanation is that this variable may not have been well represented. We chose to evaluate self-exposure using the 'quantity' dimension of the self-disclosure scale that measures the frequency and duration of self-exposure behaviour. In light of the rejection of this hypothesis, it is possible that a measure of the nature of the self-disclosure messages may have been needed to evaluate this variable in a more representative way.

Impact of Authentic Leadership and Authenticity on Followers

These results have many implications for authentic followership. First, the results associated with our first hypothesis supports the work of Algera and Lips-Wiersma (2012) and Petriglieri and Stein (2012), according to whom leaders may tend to unconsciously shape their self-conceptions to develop or maintain a socially valued and desirable role. This mechanism may impede the development of self-awareness in leaders and followers, and explain the lack of a correlation between self-alienation and AL. Considering that in the psychological perspective leaders are autonomous with respect to their development, it is conceivable that inauthenticity would be normatively maintained in organisations where the leaders develop in accordance with this perspective. As mentioned above, this notion has considerable consequences for the authenticity of leaders and followers. If an organisation, evoking collective awareness, attempts to portray a perfect image of itself and if that image is inconsistent with the interpersonal or organisational reality as experienced by its members, they may experience a sense of incoherence and meaninglessness.

Second, from a follower's point of view, the results also corroborate the postulate put forward by researchers regarding the importance of recognising the role of inter-subjective relationship dynamics in the development of authenticity and AL. These researchers propose that both leaders and followers can develop authenticity when the relating individuals engage in genuine dialogue. Such dialogue may foster openness regarding different interpretations and experiences of others as well as providing an opportunity to receive feedback from others (DeRue & Wellman, 2009). This openness and exchange of information may help individuals who work with others to recognise the importance of inter-subjectivity. Indeed, certain authors explain that dialogue may help individuals recognise inter-subjectivity when they take another person's thoughts into consideration in constructing their own judgements (Lawler & Ashman, 2012) and develop shared meaning (norms, values, and symbols shared between two people; Berkovich, 2014). In the same vein, Ashman and Lawler (2008) explain that the development of authenticity requires interpersonal interactions. Dialogue may offer an opportunity for individuals to coherently integrate the meanings they give to others, the world, and themselves.

This notion has substantial implications. To recognise others as having their own subjective and objective freedom implies that leaders should rely less on traditional modes of control and more on developing communications which are co-created by those involved in the leadership process (Lawler & Ashman, 2012). In the same vein, DeRue and Wellman's (2009) study of the role of experience in the leadership development process showed that feedback contributes to the learning process. These authors explain that in organisations, individuals receive feedback through informal sources such as interpersonal interactions, which offer clues on how others perceive and evaluate their behaviour, enabling everyone to learn from others (DeRue & Wellman, 2009). Thus, if leaders and followers recognise the importance of dialogue in the creation of identity and authenticity, they could endorse modes of communication in which everyone in the organisation has an opportunity to express themselves and learn by sharing their ideas. In summary, access to feedback through dialogue may help individuals become more self-aware and develop a more accurate understanding of their skills, which may, in turn, foster the development of authenticity. The results regarding our first hypothesis are consistent with the suggestions of Gardner et al. (2005), Peus et al. (2012) and those of Shamir and Eilam (2005), and they support the proposed relationship between relational dynamics and the development of authenticity.

Study Limitations

The limitations of this study may impact the quality of the data and the validity of the resulting analysis and conclusions. First, the small sample size reduced the statistical power of the study (Fortin, 2010) and may have hampered our ability to detect statistically significant relationships between variables. Second, the self-evaluative nature of the questionnaires represents an important limitation. Steffens, Mols, Haslam, and Okimoto (2016) demonstrated that the perception of AL depends on the collective. On the contrary, it is possible that common methods bias could explain the correlation between our different self-rated measures, particularly common rated effects. In a future study, it would be helpful to collect data not only from the managers but also from subordinates to obtain more objective measures.

Third, our non-probabilistic sampling method represents a limit to the generalisation of the results. Although the choice of convenience sampling is based on practical considerations, random errors cannot be calculated and it is impossible to know to what extent the volunteers behaved in the same way as those who decided not to answer the questionnaire (Vallerand & Hess, 2000). Fourth, although participants were students enrolled in an MBA in Management Consulting or in a Master's in HR, they were not necessarily all in a leadership position at the moment of their participation, which limits the representativeness of the results.

The final limit is the incomplete theoretical analysis, particularly regarding the model proposed by Berkovich (2014). One goal of this study was to explore authenticity and AL as viewed from the existentialist perspective. To do this, the model proposed by Berkovich (2014) was chosen and some components of this model were selected to assess their pertinence. Of the model's eight components, we measured three selected components thought to represent all components of the model. This procedure limited the applicability of this model. Moreover, Berkovich (2014) also suggests that the interaction between the model's components influences their development and thus the development of AL. This possibility was not explored in our study; it was not possible to test for associations between the components because only three of them were evaluated. The model proposed by Berkovich (2014) was thus only partially measured, limiting the validity of any inferred associations based on that model.

Avenues for Further Research

The above-mentioned limitations can lead to various avenues for future research. This study could be replicated using a different methodology: the use of a probability sampling technique, a longitudinal design, a control group, and multivariate analyses would generate less biased data and facilitate nuanced interpretation of the results. In addition, research to replicate this study could test the entire Berkovich (2014) model, including all eight components. This would make it possible to test Berkovich's (2014) hypothesis that the interactions among these components fosters their development and the development of AL. Finally, a promising avenue for further research would be to include the followers as participants in a quantitative data collection, to test the relationships between AL, authenticity and the dimensions of the Berkovich's relational model of AL development.

More broadly speaking, this study also opens several other lines of enquiry concerning authenticity and AL. To understand how authenticity can be developed at the organisational level, future research could explore the organisational factors that play a role in hindering or facilitating opportunities for personal and collective growth.

Conclusion

With regard to the self-alienation dimension (awareness of a part of oneself that is alienated or inauthentic), the findings of this study improve our understanding of AL by integrating this concept as being necessary to positive self-development. Self-alienation or inauthenticity can be considered and integrated in a positive light, both for the individual in the organisational context and for the organisation itself. Confronting one's own inauthenticity can enable individuals to develop as differentiated and integrated persons among the other members of the organisation (Algera & Lips-Wiersma, 2012). This lucid awareness of themselves may help leaders and followers to find meaning in their life and their work, especially since by becoming aware of their limitations they are then able to confront them.

For the organisation, the recognition that inauthenticity is inevitable, both individually and organisationally, could lead to thoughtful discussions and the development of a working environment guided by ethics. By recognising organisational limits of authenticity, the organisation's leaders and followers may be able to establish greater coherence between the organisation's needs, values, and principles and thus serve as an example. In this regard, Algera and Lips-Wiersma (2012) suggest that this awareness may lead organisations to recognise the importance of considering the aspirations of the individuals who work there, "…since an organization requires collective meanings and commonly agreed upon principles, it is important to understand how such meanings and principles can be identified in a way that recognizes that individuals already have meanings" (p. 127).

The findings of this study help advance our knowledge by highlighting the influence of others on individual self-development. Recognising that all members of the organisation can act as agents of change, organisations may choose to orient their training programmes to include a wider group of employees, not just the leaders. For example, training programmes could be implemented in which individuals from different groups in the organisation's hierarchy can interact, discuss, and learn together. In the same vein, these considerations suggest that organisations would benefit by designating facilitators to, for example, help members of the organisation to discuss, debate and reflect together. These facilitators could, first, foster the collective engagement of the leaders, the employees and the organisation (Bakker & Demerouti, 2008) and, second, provide the leaders more opportunities to grow through their relationships with others, based on feedback from different shared value systems (Morgeson, DeRue, & Karam, 2009). In summary, this chapter highlights various aspects of authenticity and AL, such as self-alienation and inter-subjectivity that had been little explored before.

References

Algera, P. M., & Lips-Wiersma, M. (2012). Radical authentic leadership: Co-creating the conditions under which all members of the organization can be authentic. *The Leadership Quarterly, 23*(1), 118–131. https://doi.org/10.1016/j.leaqua.2011.11.010.

Ashman, I., & Lawler, J. (2008). Existential communication and leadership. *Leadership, 4*(3), 253–269. https://doi.org/10.1177/1742715008092361.

Avolio, B. J., & Gardner, W. L. (2005). Authentic leadership development: Getting to the root of positive forms of leadership. *The Leadership Quarterly, 16*(3), 315–338. https://doi.org/10.1016/j.leaqua.2005.03.001.

Avolio, B. J., Gardner, W. L., Walumbwa, F. O., Luthans, F., & May, D. R. (2004). Unlocking the mask: A look at the process by which authentic leaders impact follower attitudes and behaviors. *The Leadership Quarterly, 15*(6), 801–823. https://doi.org/10.1016/j.leaqua.2004.09.003.

Bakker, A. B., & Demerouti, E. (2008). Towards a model of work engagement. *Career Development International, 13*(3), 209–223. https://doi.org/10.1108/13620430810870476.

Baron, L. (2016). Authentic leadership and mindfulness development through action learning. *Journal of Managerial Psychology, 31*(1), 296–311. https://doi.org/10.1108/JMP-04-2014-0135.

Baron, L., & Parent, E. (2015). Developing authentic leadership within a training context: Three phenomena supporting the individual development process. *Journal of Leadership & Organizational Studies*, 1–17. https://doi.org/10.1177/1548051813519501.

Barrett-Lennard, G. (1998). *Carl Rogers' helping system: Journey & substance.* London: Sage.

Berkovich, I. (2014). Between person and person: Dialogical pedagogy in authentic leadership development. *Academy of Management Learning & Education, 13*(2), 245–264.

Clapp-Smith, R., Vogelgesang, G. R., & Avey, J. B. (2008). Authentic leadership and positive psychological capital: The mediating role of trust at the group level of analysis. *Journal of Leadership & Organizational Studies, 15*(3), 227–240. https://doi.org/10.1177/1548051808326596.

Cooper, C. D., Scandura, T. A., & Schriesheim, C. A. (2005). Looking forward but learning from our past: Potential challenges to developing authentic leadership theory and authentic leaders. *The Leadership Quarterly, 16*(3), 475–493. https://doi.org/10.1016/j.leaqua.2005.03.008.

Cozby, P. C. (1973). Self-disclosure: A literature review. *Psychological Bulletin, 79*(2), 73.

Day, D. V., Fleenor, J. W., Atwater, L. E., Sturm, R. E., & McKee, R. A. (2014). Advances in leader and leadership development: A review of 25years of research and theory. *The Leadership Quarterly, 25*(1), 63–82. https://doi.org/10.1016/j.leaqua.2013.11.004.

DeRue, D. S., & Wellman, N. (2009). Developing leaders via experience: The role of developmental challenge, learning orientation, and feedback availability. *Journal of Applied Psychology, 94*(4), 859–875. https://doi.org/10.1037/a0015317.

Dinh, J. E., Lord, R. G., Gardner, W. L., Meuser, J. D., Liden, R. C., & Hu, J. (2014). Leadership theory and research in the new millennium: Current theoretical trends and changing perspectives. *The Leadership Quarterly, 25*(1), 36–62. https://doi.org/10.1016/j.leaqua.2013.11.005.

Ford, J., & Lawler, J. (2007). Blending existentialist and constructionist approaches in leadership studies. *Leadership & Organization Development Journal, 28*(5), 409–425. https://doi.org/10.1108/01437730710761724.

Fortin, M. F. (2010). *Fondements et étape du processus de recherche: Méthodes quantitatives et qualitatives. Fondements et étapes du processus de recherche* (2e éd., p. 632). Montréal, QC: Chenelière Éducation.

Gardner, W. L., Avolio, B. J., Luthans, F., May, D. R., & Walumbwa, F. (2005). 'Can you see the real me?' A self-based model of authentic leader and follower development. *The Leadership Quarterly, 16*(3), 343–372. https://doi.org/10.1016/j.leaqua.2005.03.003.

Grégoire, S., Baron, L., Ménard, J., & Lachance, L. (2014). The authenticity scale: Psychometric properties of a French translation and exploration of its relationships with personality and well-being. *Canadian Journal of Behavioural Science*, 1–10. https://doi.org/10.1037/a0030962.

Guignon, C., & Pereboom, D. (2001). *Existentialism: Basic writings*. Indianapolis, IN: Hackett Publishing.

Harter, S. (2002). Authenticity. In C. R. Snyder & S. Lopez (Eds.), *Handbook of positive psychology* (pp. 382–394). Oxford, UK: Oxford University Press.

Heidegger, M. (1962). *Being and time* (translated, p. 589). London: SCM Press.

Hodgin, H., & Knee, C. (2002). The integrating self and conscious experience. In E. L. Deci & R. M. Ryan (Eds.), *Handbook of self-determination research* (pp. 87–100). Rochester, NY: The University of Rochester Press.

Ilies, R., Morgeson, F. P., & Nahrgang, J. D. (2005). Authentic leadership and eudaemonic well-being: Understanding leader–follower outcomes. *The Leadership Quarterly, 16*(3), 373–394. https://doi.org/10.1016/j.leaqua.2005.03.002.

Kabat-Zinn, J. (2006). Mindfulness-based interventions in context: Past, present, and future. *Clinical Psychology: Science and Practice, 10*(2), 144–156. https://doi.org/10.1093/clipsy.bpg016.

Kernis, M. H. (2003). Toward a conceptualization of optimal self-esteem. *Psychological Inquiry, 14*, 1–26.

Lawler, J. (2005). The essence of leadership? Existentialism and leadership. *Leadership, 1*(2), 215–231. https://doi.org/10.1177/1742715005051860.

Lawler, J., & Ashman, I. (2012). Theorizing leadership authenticity: A Sartrean perspective. *Leadership, 8*(4), 327–344. https://doi.org/10.1177/1742715012444685.

Lietz, C., Gerdes, K., Sun, F., Mullins Geiger, J., Wagaman, M. A., & Segal, E. (2011). The empathy assessment index (EAI): A confirmatory factor analysis of a multidimensional model of empathy. *Journal of the Society for Social Work and Research, 2*(2), 104–124. https://doi.org/10.5243/jsswr.2011.6.

Luthans, F., & Avolio, B. (2003). Authentic leadership development. In K. S. Cameron, J. E. Dutton, & R. E. Quinn (Eds.), *Positive organizational scholarship* (pp. 241–258). San Francisco: Berrett-Koehler.

McCrimmon, M. (2010). A new role for management in today's post-industrial organization. *Ivey Business Journal Online*. Retrieved from http://iveybusinessjournal.com/publication/a-new-role-For-management-in-todays-post-industrial-organization/

Morgeson, F. P., DeRue, D. S., & Karam, E. P. (2009). Leadership in teams: A functional approach to understanding leadership structures and processes. *Journal of Management, 36*(1), 5–39. https://doi.org/10.1177/0149206309347376.

Northouse, P. G. (2010). *Leadership: Theory and practice* (5th ed.p. 435). London: Sage.

Novicevic, M. M., Harvey, M. G., Ronald, M., & Brown-Radford, J. A. (2006). Authentic leadership: A historical perspective. *Journal of Leadership & Organizational Studies, 13*(1), 64–76. https://doi.org/10.1177/10717919070130010901.

Petriglieri, G., & Stein, M. (2012). The unwanted self: Projective identification in leaders' identity work. *Organization Studies, 33*(9), 1217–1235. https://doi.org/10.1177/0170840612448158.

Peus, C., Wesche, J. S., Streicher, B., Braun, S., & Frey, D. (2012). Authentic leadership: An empirical test of its antecedents, consequences, and mediating mechanisms. *Journal of Business Ethics, 107*(3), 331–348. https://doi.org/10.1007/s10551-011-1042-3.

Rogers, C. R. (1961). *On becoming a person: A therapist's view of psychotherapy.* London: Constable.

Sartre, J.-P. (1943). *L'Être et le Néant* (Éditions G., p. 722). Paris, France: Librairie Gallimard.

Sartre, J.-P. (1946). *L'Existentialisme est un humanisme* (Éditions N., p. 144). Paris, France: Librairie Gallimard.

Shamir, B., & Eilam, G. (2005). 'What's your story?' A life-stories approach to authentic leadership development. *The Leadership Quarterly, 16*(3), 395–417. https://doi.org/10.1016/j.leaqua.2005.03.005.

Sosu, E. M. (2013). The development and psychometric validation of a critical thinking disposition scale. *Thinking Skills and Creativity, 9*, 107–119. https://doi.org/10.1016/j.tsc.2012.09.002.

Steffens, N. K., Mols, F., Haslam, S. A., & Okimoto, T. G. (2016). True to what we stand for: Championing collective interests as a path to authentic leadership. *The Leadership Quarterly, 27*(5), 726–744.

Tate, B. (2008). A longitudinal study of the relationships among self-monitoring, authentic leadership, and perceptions of leadership. *Journal of Leadership & Organizational Studies, 15*, 16–29.

Vallerand, R. J., & Hess, U. (2000). *Méthodes de recherche en psychologie.* Montréal, QC: G. Morin, Ed.

Walumbwa, F. O., Avolio, B. J., Gardner, W. L., Wernsing, T. S., & Peterson, S. J. (2008). Authentic leadership: Development and validation of a theory-based measure. *Journal of Management, 34*(1), 89–126. https://doi.org/10.1177/0149206307308913.

Walumbwa, F. O., Luthans, F., Avey, J. B., & Oke, A. (2011). Authentically leading groups: The mediating role of collective psychological capital and trust. *Journal of Organizational Behavior, 32*, 4–24. https://doi.org/10.1002/job.

Wheeless, L. R., & Grotz, J. (1976). Conceptualization and measurement of reported self-disclosure. *Human Communication Research, 2*(4), 338–346. https://doi.org/10.1111/j.1468-2958.1976.tb00494.x.

Wood, A. M., Linley, P. A., Maltby, J., Baliousis, M., & Joseph, S. (2008). The authentic personality: A theoretical and empirical conceptualization and the development of the authenticity scale. *Journal of Counseling Psychology, 55*(3), 385–399. https://doi.org/10.1037/0022-0167.55.3.385.

11

Conceptualising Authentic Followers and Developing a Future Research Agenda

Joseph Crawford, Sarah Dawkins, Angela Martin, and Gemma Lewis

The twenty-first century has brought with it many challenges that potentially undermine organisational effectiveness. One such challenge is increased awareness of the unethical and/or ineffective decisions of the leaders (Gardner, Cogliser, Davis, & Dickens, 2011). Recent examples of unethical/ineffective leadership decisions include the oil spill in Mexico, greed-driven leaders who contributed to the global financial crisis and Japan's nuclear disaster. Yet, when a crisis emerges, the focus is often solely on the leader(s), with little consideration of the followers who elect, appoint, and support the leaders.

J. Crawford (✉) • G. Lewis
Tasmanian School of Business and Economics, University of Tasmania, Newnham, TAS, Australia

S. Dawkins • A. Martin
Tasmanian School of Business and Economics, University of Tasmania, Hobart, TAS, Australia

© The Author(s) 2018
D. Cotter-Lockard (ed.), *Authentic Leadership and Followership*, Palgrave Studies in Leadership and Followership, https://doi.org/10.1007/978-3-319-65307-5_11

In addressing these leadership complexities, researchers often turn to approaches that foster and sustain ethical, effective, and enduring positive leadership behaviours. However, contemporary leadership theory extends beyond the leader, to include the followers, peers, culture, and context (Avolio, 2007). The collective context is important, as some 'collectives' will be harder to lead than others depending on environmental and political factors (de Zilwa, 2014). Although a leader may be defined as an individual who is able to influence a collective towards common goals (Northouse, 2016), the *process* of leadership is more complex, encompassing not only the influence of an individual leader on the followers but also the influence of the followers on their leader(s).

Crawford, Lewis, Martin, and Dawkins (2017) argue that the leader represents only one of the four domains of leadership: (1) the leader, (2) the follower, (3) the leadership process, and (4) the followership process. Although the *follower* has been identified as a domain of leadership, it is often overlooked. This individual, or a group of individuals, can make a leader's role relatively simple, or substantially difficult (Jung & Avolio, 1999).

In this chapter, our focus will centre on the follower. In doing so, our primary aim is to support previous calls to enhance the conceptual clarity of the authentic leader and related constructs, including the authentic followers (Crawford et al., 2017). As such, we will not focus on authentic followership (AF: the process), but rather on the authentic followers (the individual/group) and provide a case for its necessary independence as a construct. Subsequent to our review of the authentic follower, we believe it is important that we first briefly define the authentic leader, to provide context to the reader. We then explore the two-way relationship between the authentic leaders and the followers. Subsequently, we will address how an authentic follower interacts with the leaders, can be a leader, and interact in teams. Finally, several directions for future research that progresses understanding of the follower in the authentic leadership (AL) process will be discussed.

Authentic Followers

The followers have often been considered as extraneous to leadership theory, particularly in situational and contingency leadership theories (Fiedler, 1967; House & Mitchell, 1975). In these theories, leaders adapt their behaviour based, in part, on the follower attributes such as loyalty, skill, maturity, cooperation, experience, and confidence. Although the followers have an interrelated role with the leaders, researchers have generally neglected the study of followership (Agho, 2009), even though the followers are worth understanding in their own right (Shamir, 2007). At the turn of the century this changed, with the emergence of charismatic followership (Howell & Shamir, 2005) and AF (de Zilwa, 2014). However, a primary challenge of AF models is the lack of distinction between AF (the process) and the authentic followers (the individuals).

Undertaking a conceptual analysis of the authentic followers is important for several reasons. First, there is an inherent and practical need for the leaders and the followers to adopt ethical and effective behaviours to prevent and/or address issues related to ineffective and/or unethical leadership. Unethical leadership practices have increased over the past three decades, and the role of leadership scholars should be to understand the problem and propose solutions. Second, a loss of authenticity in organisations (a by-product of the industrial era) has resulted in organisational members being treated as mere cogs in a system, as opposed to individual humans (Erickson, 1995). We argue that the followers not be perceived as cogs in an expanding global economy, but rather actors with independent self-concepts. As such, we suggest that the followers be positioned as an important part of the leadership process. Third, although leadership is widely considered a collective construct (Avolio, Walumbwa, & Weber, 2009), most leadership theories focus dominantly on the individual leader. Recent conceptualisations of the authentic leaders include the notion of 'the collective' in its definition (Crawford et al., 2017), but greater consideration of the follower is still required. To this end, the theory surrounding the authentic followers and their independence requires alignment with best practice.

Finally, there remains a need to conceptualise the authentic followers as related to, but distinct from, the authentic leaders. To date, research that considers the authentic follower as an independent construct has not been extensively explored. For example, Avolio and Gardner (2005) briefly discuss the followers, but only after first proposing how a leader influences the followers' self-awareness, self-regulation, and clarity of self-concept. Furthermore, Gardner et al. (2011, p. 1141) argue that practitioners and scholars have emphasised the importance of AF as a 'central component of the authentic leadership (AL) process'. The complexity of the authentic leader–follower dyad is underlined by a number of key assumptions. The first of these is that for a person to be an authentic follower, they must have an existing relationship with the authentic leader. This is evident in discussion of the emergence of the authentic followers as typically taking place *after* the follower has interactions with an authentic leader. To reiterate, a follower is different from followership, with the former being an individual capable of engaging in followership, and the latter being the process of following in some way.

Authenticity of the follower is likely to be as important in AL development as the authenticity of the leader, yet no known empirical studies have focused on this. As such, notions of what a follower *is*, from the AL literature, should not foreshadow the definition of an authentic follower, as a related, but independent construct. That is, the two elements of the AL process related to the followers (follower self-awareness and follower self-regulation) should not predetermine the dimensionality of an authentic follower, but rather *inform* it. Furthermore, the absence of an authentic leader should not eliminate the potential for the authentic followers. The authentic followers, as is demonstrated throughout this chapter, are crucially important to the AL process.

Thus, we provide the following conceptualisation of the authentic follower, comprising two dimensions: psychological capacity for authenticity and positive organisational engagement:

> An authentic follower is an individual who, through their capacity for authenticity and positive organisational engagement, is self-managing and follows leaders with whom they share values.

Understanding Authentic Leadership

AL was originally conceptualised as the synergy between predecessor theories: transformational leadership, psychological capital (PsyCap), and the capacity and development of ethical and moral perspectives (Luthans & Avolio, 2003). The concept of AL was later considered a higher order construct, with four first-order dimensions: self-awareness, relational transparency, balanced processing, and an internalised moral perspective (Kernis & Goldman, 2006; Walumbwa, Avolio, Gardner, Wernsing, & Peterson, 2008). From this perspective, AL can be defined as given below:

> A pattern of leader behavior that draws upon and promotes both positive psychological capacities and a positive ethical climate, to foster greater self-awareness, an internalized moral perspective, balanced processing of information, and relational transparency on the part of leaders working with followers, fostering positive self-development. (Walumbwa et al., 2008, p. 94)

As outlined previously, more recent conceptualisations of leadership emphasise a process between the leader and the surrounding collective such as the followers, peers, and superiors (Avolio et al., 2009). As such, when an authentic leader is conceptualised as comprising characteristics that are predominantly inward-focused (e.g. an internalised moral perspective), there appears to be little consideration of the collective. Although Walumbwa et al. defined AL (the process), there is pertinence in first understanding each individual participant in this process. In a more recent conceptualisation (Crawford et al., 2017), authentic leaders are defined as follows:

> **An authentic leader** influences and motivates followers to achieve collective goals through their sincerity and positive moral perspective, enabled through heightened awareness and balanced processing.

Thus, an authentic leader exhibits five behavioural dimensions:

Awareness (A) is having insight into the behaviours of groups and individuals, including ones' self.

Sincerity (S) is presenting one's true self to others honestly and openly in all relationships, with consideration to context.

Balanced processing (B) is the tendency to consider all relevant information available and using this to make decisions that benefit the collective (e.g. followers).

Positive moral perspective (M) is commitment to one's intrinsic ethical framework and a willingness to subdue personal interests and ego to facilitate collective interests.

Informal influence (I) is the ability to inspire and motivate individuals to accomplish collective goals of their own volition.

The Effects of Authentic Leadership on Followers

A growing body of empirical research has demonstrated the positive effect the authentic leaders can have on the followers. High leader authenticity is associated with lower follower burnout (Wong & Cummings, 2009a), follower identification with the leader (Wong, Spence Laschinger & Cummings, 2010) and higher levels of job performance; consideration of group needs; trust in leadership (Wong & Cummings, 2009b); organisational citizenship behaviours; organisational commitment; work happiness (Jensen & Luthans, 2006); satisfaction with supervisors (Walumbwa et al., 2008) and well-being (Rahimnia & Sharifirad, 2015) among the followers.

In contrast, research investigating the influence of the authentic followers on their leaders is sparse. The 'authentic leadership process' described by Avolio and Mhatre (2012) has nine facets including the following: positive PsyCap, positive moral perspective, leader self-awareness, leader self-regulation, leadership processes and behaviours, follower self-awareness and regulation, follower development, organisational context, and veritable and sustainable performance which exceeds expectations. Thus, only two of the facets of the AL process are specific to the followers and followership (follower self-awareness and regulation and follower development), with follower development an expected outcome related to the leader, as opposed to being a follower characteristic in its own right.

As a result, the current understanding of followership is limited to the assumption that the influence between a leader and follower(s) is one-way. Farrukh and Ahsan (2015) propose that individuals with low self-concept clarity will demonstrate leader dependence and shift their values to align with the values of their leader; a one-way relationship, to a degree. However, the follower with high self-concept clarity will only follow a leader with whom they share values, reflective of the two-way relationship between individuals' high self-awareness and their deep understanding of themselves (Kernis & Goldman, 2006).

A central premise of authentic leadership development (ALD) is that both the leader and the follower become more authentic over time (Avolio & Gardner, 2005). According to this premise, the followers internalise the values and beliefs of their leader through modelling processes. However, this premise can still reduce the follower to become an organisational cog, where the leader simply acts authentically and the follower copies the leader's behaviour.

Farrukh and Ahsan (2015) report that the followers who have high self-concept clarity and shared values with an authentic leader are more likely to follow an authentic leader and emulate that leader. Through the AL process, the authentic leaders are posited to increase follower self-awareness and self-regulation (Avolio & Gardner, 2005). In doing so, the followers develop greater self-concept clarity which develops the behaviours of the authentic leaders (Gardner, Avolio, Luthans, May, & Walumbwa, 2005). Although this proposition better aligns with our positioning of a follower as an independent thinker, it continues to assume that the followers only model the behaviours of the leaders and negates the possibility that the leaders may also model the behaviour of their followers.

Conceptualising Authentic Followers

Existing Conceptualisations of Authentic Followers and AF

Although authentic follower research is sparse, there have been some attempts to define the construct. Gardner et al. (2005) identify AF as an outcome of AL, treating the construct as only understandable in the context of AL. AF, from their perspective, largely models the developmental processes of AL, with a one-way relationship from AL to AF. However, given that the authentic follower is an active participant in the leader–follower exchange (Shamir, 2007), it would be remiss to assume that the direction of influence is only from the leader to the follower (de Zilwa, 2014).

Avolio and Reichard (2008) define AF as a sense of psychological ownership, trusting through vulnerability and self-disclosure, and transparency and psychological safety to offer opinions. However, authentic follower development is argued to be a worthy pursuit on its own and should not be considered as secondary to AL (de Zilwa, 2014). According to de Zilwa (2014), Avolio and Reichard's (2008) AF is far closer to treating a follower as an equal. In the same regard, Goffee and Jones (2006) focus on the needs of a follower including authenticity, an underpinning reason to be led, excitement, and feeling included. However, we suggest that here again the follower is considered to be secondary to the leader, and such conceptualisations are not conducive to empowering the followers into becoming leaders themselves.

In one of only two studies to conceptualise the authentic followers and AF other than simply for the purpose of ALD, de Zilwa (2014) defined AF as a non-linear feedback loop including the follower's psychological capacity for authenticity, a positive organisational culture, and a secure attachment between the follower and the leader. This definition describes the characteristics that need to be present for an authentic follower to emerge. However, it fails to distinguish the follower as an independent person.

By extension, where an authentic follower exists, but their leader is not an authentic leader (follower-driven dyad; Fig. 11.1), the follower's behaviours are likely to have a positive impact on the leader's behaviours and increase the leaders' authenticity (through role modelling). This would, in part, be mediated by the level of influence a follower has on the leader, whereby active followers would have greater influence than passive followers. To this end, these processes of influence could be different between leadership and followership, with different behaviours associated with each. In addition, we suggest that sources of power and influence could act as moderators in determining how much the authentic follower influences their leader. For example, similar to Fredrickson's (2003) positive spiral, an authentic follower who communicates and acts authentically to an inauthentic leader will have a positive impact on their authenticity. We do not, however, suggest that this dyad (follower-driven) would be as effective in influencing the leader's AL behaviours as the leader-driven dyad, because of differences in influence.

Kelley's (1988) matrix of follower effectiveness adopts two axes: dependent and uncritical thinkers to independent and critical thinkers (*y*-axis) and passive to active behaviour (*x*-axis). According to de Zilwa's (2014) definition, an authentic follower would be active but dependent and

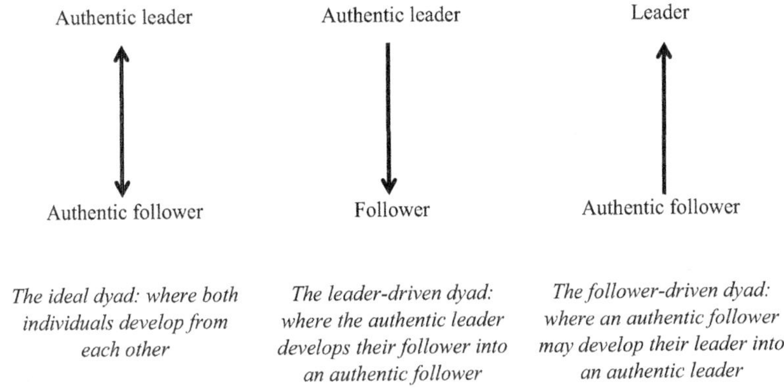

Fig. 11.1 The three dyad environments of an authentic leader and authentic follower

would fall into a 'yes-person' category, instead of being an effective 'star' follower. Kelley (1988) considers a star follower as high in independence and the ability to think critically (*y*-axis) and highly active (*x*-axis). We suggest this encapsulates part of what an authentic follower is. The separation of an authentic follower into passive and active is important. de Zilwa's (2014) definition positions an authentic follower as passive, and as such, unlikely to engage in the process of influencing. These individuals will find the leaders who share similar values and then follow, almost blindly, providing their values remain aligned. The active followers also follow the leaders who share similar values. However, a key difference is that if the leader makes a poor decision, the active follower will confront the leader and provide possible solutions with the aim to help the leader to correct the decision. The preference for many authentic leaders would be to have an active authentic follower, but authentic individuals with low influence (passive authentic followers) are also beneficial to the authentic leader, as these followers can likely be mentored by authentic leaders into active authentic followers. In summary, when conceptualising the authentic followers, it is important to consider (1) the three different possible leader–follower dyads as shown in Fig. 11.1 and (2) the effective follower category independence, critical thinking, and active involvement.

The Dimensions and Behaviours of an Authentic Follower

Psychological Capacity for Authenticity

First and foremost, we argue that an authentic follower must exhibit high degrees of the four elements of authenticity in multi-level leader–follower environments (i.e. awareness, sincerity, positive moral perspective, and balanced processing). This dimension of authenticity in the authentic followers is similar to de Zilwa's (2014) conceptualisation of AF, except that we include Crawford et al.'s (2017) revised four dimensions of authenticity as applied to the leaders. Furthermore, we suggest that these four dimensions, which may be developed in both the followers and the leaders, enable an individual to transition between being a leader and follower, depending on the context.

Although increasing authenticity in the leaders and the followers is likely to yield higher AL scores, the follower appears to have several important points of distinction from the leaders. The followers are typically argued to be the more passive member of the follower–leader relationship (Crossman & Crossman, 2011). However, the *authentic* followers tend to adopt a more active role in the dyad (de Zilwa, 2014). Similar to the leaders, the authentic followers can visualise the big and small picture, work well with others and are able to balance pursuit of their personal goals with the goals set by their leader and organisation (Kelley, 1988). However, these followers do not need a leadership title, or status, to have the strength to flourish. Furthermore, although the authentic followers are positioned as effective, they are also differentiated from effective leaders who tend to play a more active role in setting goals, achieving consensus among their followers, communicating enthusiasm and coordinating the followers (Kelley, 1988).

Positive Organisational Engagement

According to Kelley (2008), there are five main types of followers, divided by two dimensions: (1) the degree to which they are independent and think for themselves and (2) the degree of engagement they demonstrate in creating positive energy in the organisation. These five types of followers include the sheep (low in dimension 1 and dimension 2), the yes-people (low in dimension 1, high in dimension 2), the alienated (high in dimension 1, low in dimension 2), the pragmatics (do not properly align to either dimension 1 or 2) and the star followers (high in dimension 1 and dimension 2).

A star follower is the preferred type of follower and is often seen as a leader's 'right-hand person' or 'go-to person'. These followers are self-motivating, with a willingness to let their leader tap into that motivation (Bjugstad, Thach, Thompson, & Morris, 2006). According to these categories of followers, an authentic follower is most reflective of the star follower category. The authentic followers think for themselves and engage in positive organisational activities and can be separated from other followers on this basis. They can be distinguished on the basis of their capacity to be authentic and their recognition as a star follower, as seen in Fig. 11.2.

In Crawford et al.'s (2017) recent reconceptualisation of the authentic leader, a fifth dimension was added: *informal influence*. The primary reason for its inclusion was to enable clearer theoretical distinction between an authentic leader and follower(s). We extend upon this framework in Fig. 11.2 and argue that the informal influence of an authentic follower can provide benefit to distinguishing different kinds of followers: particularly passive and active followers, as discussed in Kelley (2008).

The authentic followers are likely to be 'star' followers, and thus be active. However, it may also be possible for individuals to be authentic without having informal influence. Conversely, the 'sheep' follower is likely to be a passive low-authenticity follower, as they neither think for themselves nor engage without instruction. The introvert–extrovert continuum may apply in distinguishing between the active and passive authentic followers; extroverts may tend to be more active authentic followers, whereas introverts may tend to be more passive authentic followers. The passive authentic followers may evolve towards becoming more active authentic followers as they think on their own, but may take a little longer to engage with their leader and organisation. Thus, we suggest extending Crawford et al.'s (2017) distinction between the authentic leader, authentic follower, inauthentic leader and inauthentic follower by further categorising the authentic followers into active and passive, based on their positive engagement in the organisation (which we term *positive organisational engagement*, POE) and informal influence, as seen in Fig. 11.2.

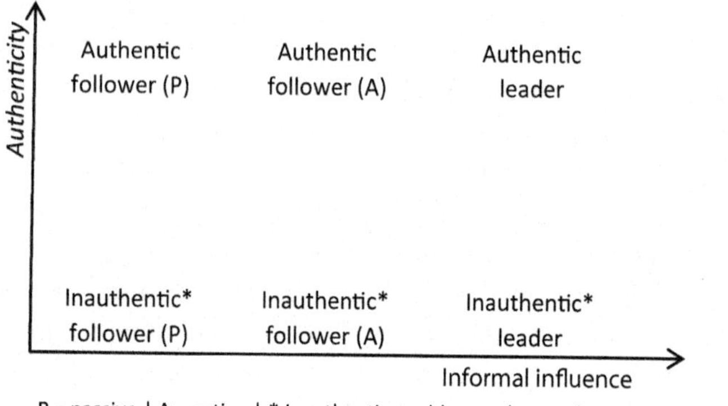

Fig. 11.2 Identifying authentic followers from other followers

Conversely, a person low in POE can be characterised by their passive involvement in the organisation and/or their negative energy. This dimension is distinct from de Zilwa's (2014) AF dimension of 'positive organisational culture and political conditions', as the requirement of a pre-existing culture is not required. A possible outcome of the ideal dyad (Fig. 11.1) is that a positive organisational culture will emerge, which can further develop other members of the organisation. However, this does not presuppose the inherent requirement for an authentic follower; but rather is an outcome of effective AL and AF. An existing positive organisational culture may be a positive mediator for the development of the authentic leaders and authentic followers. AL and AF are likely to be negatively related to high rivalry and intensity of conflict, pivotal elements of a firm's political conditions/climate (Mintzberg, 1985).

Typical Behaviour of Authentic Followers

Kelley (1988) argued that the effective followers are self-managing (and the leaders tend to delegate responsibility to them); they are committed to the organisation and its goals, are competent, focus on maximum impact, are courageous, honest, and credible. As such, we suggest that the authentic followers, using their psychological capacity for authenticity, are self-managing and likely to have high emotional intelligence. Their active involvement in developing a positive organisational climate means they may also demonstrate organisational commitment. This, we believe, is likely to result in the authentic followers seeing their leaders as co-adventurers in a worthy pursuit, especially when that leader is an authentic leader. Furthermore, when they identify operational improvements, they will have the courage to speak up, because they are emotionally invested in the organisation. Finally, their sincerity suggests that their words and actions are consistent, and they see their fellow followers as 'associates' and their leaders as equal.

In conceptualising the authentic followers, it is essential that the construct be positioned as theoretically independent of AL. We suggest that it may be possible for an authentic follower to exist without the presence of an authentic leader (Fig. 11.1), thereby negating the requirement of leader attachment for the emergence of the authentic followers (de Zilwa, 2014). To elaborate, an authentic follower with their authentic leader in one environment does not lose their authentic follower behaviours when the authentic leader leaves. When another leader (e.g. a charismatic leader) is present, the authentic follower can still exist despite having a different leader. Although this incongruence may not be the ideal, it is a likely reality. Thus, conceptualising and evaluating how both authentic leaders and authentic followers interact and behave is important in beginning to understand how these affect the innate self of those followers and leaders who are low in authenticity. However, similar to de Zilwa (2014), we suggest that leader attachment (e.g. the ideal dyad; Fig. 11.1) is likely to be more conducive to authentic leader and follower development, but the other two dyads should not be inherently sidelined from understanding the authentic leader–follower relationship because it does not reflect the 'ideal context'.

Authentic Followers and Their Relationships

The Leader

We have suggested that an ideal relationship to cultivate in organisations is an authentic leader coupled with authentic follower(s), as this relationship may enable the follower and the leader to work together as equal participants pursuing organisational goals. The effective followers keep the leaders in check (Kelley, 1988), and we argue that this is also true for the authentic followers. However, our focus now turns from the ideal dyad to the follower-driven and leader-driven dyads (Fig. 11.1).

Ideally, the authentic followers keep their leader in check and work side-by-side with their leader to achieve organisational goals. However, some followers may be inherently authentic followers, without the presence of an authentic leader. Figure 11.3 depicts an example of a middle manager who is an authentic leader in their core work context. In this context, the authentic leader develops the capabilities of their followers through role modelling (Gardner et al., 2005). However, the middle manager's leader is a senior manager, who leads a number of department middle managers. If this senior manager is not an authentic leader, it does not necessarily diminish the authentic characteristics of the middle manager. Thus, the middle manager would be an authentic follower with a leader who is not an authentic leader (follower-driven dyad). An authentic leader in one situation could be an authentic follower in another. We use formal hierarchy as an example, but there are other circumstances that can separate the individual into a leader or a follower

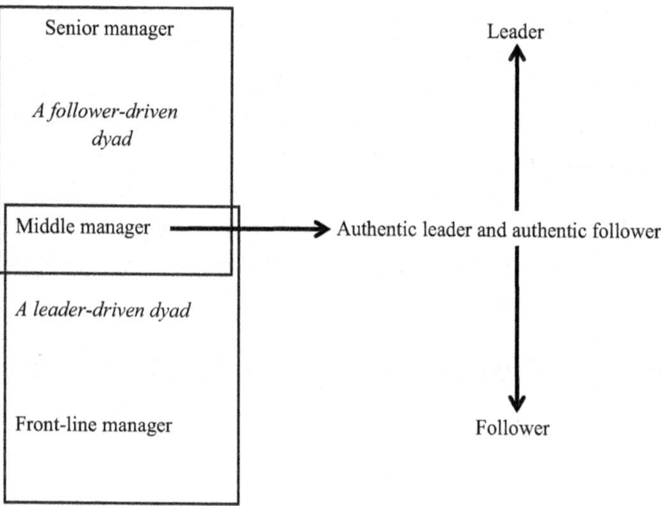

Fig. 11.3 The authentic leader/follower

(e.g. home environment, school, work, friendship groups). For example, a leader at work could be a follower in their social circle because a friend has more influence in *that* group. They would use their authentic capabilities combined with their desire for a positive organisational climate to be a positive role model to the inauthentic leader, something we posit will increase the leader's authenticity, but perhaps at a slower rate than the reverse.

Modelling is a pivotal aspect of social cognitive theory (e.g. Bandura, 1997) and is frequently cited by AL researchers (e.g. Avolio & Gardner, 2005; Avolio, Gardner, Walumbwa, Luthans, & May, 2004) as the mechanism through which the authentic leaders develop their follower(s). We have argued that the authentic leaders and authentic followers share the same psychological capacity for authenticity, and thereby propose that an authentic follower could model authentic behaviours to a non-authentic leader, improving their leadership behaviours. However, the power difference between the leaders and the followers cannot be ignored, particularly because a distinguishing feature of the leaders is their influence (Kirkman, Chen, Farh, Chen, & Lowe, 2009). Therefore, the informal power of the follower, developed through their POE and their authenticity, facilitates their modelling to the inauthentic leader. However, this process is likely to be stronger when an authentic leader models authentic behaviours to an inauthentic follower because of the difference in informal influence.

As discussed, the common features used to distinguish the leaders and the followers are the level of influence and positional power. For example, Wortman (1982, p. 373) states that 'followership is the process of attaining one's individual goals by being influenced by a leader'. Such commentary refutes former arguments that the authentic follower is not influenced by an AL (de Zilwa, 2014). It is evident that the authentic followers can maintain influence without inherently leading; equally, not all leaders require positional power to be a leader or indeed influential (e.g. Malala Yousafzai). Thus, there is a clear need to rethink the mechanisms used to measure leadership, so as to understand the differences between the authentic leaders and the followers more holistically.

The Fluidity of Authentic Leaders and Followers

In considering the authentic followers, it is important to consider how the authentic leaders and the followers coalesce. Kelley (1988, p. 2) stated that 'the reality is that most of us are more often followers than leaders'. For example, individuals may lead a committee with subordinates and also be involved in another committee where they assume a follower role. Hackman and Wageman (2007, p. 45) stated that it is 'not how do leaders and followers differ, but how can leadership models be reframed so they treat all system members as both leaders and followers?' Thus, we suggest that an authentic leader in one context can also be an authentic follower in another, different context and this should be reflected in the synergies between both constructs and their definitions. However, many conceptualisations of authentic leaders and AL are dichotomous in nature (Shamir & Eilam, 2005), ranging between an inauthentic leader and an authentic leader. This dichotomy does not allow consideration for the follower, or the coalescence between the follower and the leader (and vice versa). Crawford et al. (2017) addressed this limitation by proposing a continuum of authenticity ranging from low to high (Fig. 11.4), enabling the followers and the leaders to both be placed on the same continuum. An individual closer to the low-authenticity end of the continuum is likely to be inauthentic, pseudo-authentic or unintentionally low in authenticity. It is suggested that these individuals have potential to move along the continuum through trigger moments, authenticity development, interventions, and training (Luthans & Avolio, 2003). Conversely, an individual with high authenticity is likely to be an authentic leader or follower, depending on their level of informal influence.

Fig. 11.4 The continuum of a psychological capacity of authenticity

The Team

The nature of contemporary leadership in team contexts can shed some light on where an authentic follower ends and an authentic leader begins. As organisational structures flatten, diversify and informal structures of influence can become more complex, there is a necessity for new approaches to leadership which deal with such changes in complexity. Positional power still exists today, but the importance of informal power and emotional connections within teams is becoming evident. The role of informal social ties in team environments is of significance (Oh, Chung, & Labianca, 2004), and those informal social ties are likely to be developed by more than just the leader. Therefore, considering the role of both the authentic leader and the follower in shaping team dynamics is important when conceptualising a holistic model.

The leaders often have a visionary role, whereby they identify and motivate the achievement of organisational goals (Yukl, 2013). Thus, they still remain an important connector and potential boundary-spanner. To add, a boundary-spanner are individuals who operate between their primary organisation and its environment (Stamper & Johlke, 2003), for example, an employee with a strong connection with a supplier or customer group. We argue that each individual in the team has potential as a boundary-spanner and should not be discounted on the basis of their hierarchical status as a leader or a follower. A leader–follower dyad with an asymmetrical relationship, however, does have an effect on the abilities of those followers. This is of concern in conceptualising the authentic followers, as the follower construct must be theoretically distinct from the authentic leader construct, but organisational climate may mediate the emergence of the authentic follower.

Future Research Agenda

This chapter has provided new considerations for the definition of an authentic follower, and the relationship between the authentic followers and the authentic leaders, and leaders more generally. From the building of our conceptual foundation for the authentic followers, we believe there are many directions that future researchers in the field can pursue. In this section, we focus primarily on the critical next steps.

Empirical Validation and Measurement

In this chapter, we have proposed a two-dimensional model of the authentic follower comprising (1) psychological capacity for authenticity and (2) POE. However, empirical research is needed to assess and validate this model. We suggest that this could be conducted using a variety of research methods. Qualitative interviews with individuals who work alongside an authentic follower (and authentic followers themselves) may provide exploratory insights into how others see the authentic follower. In addition, developing quantitative measures for the authentic leaders and the follower will be important to enhancing understanding of the authentic followers, including investigation of potential antecedents and the outcomes of the authentic followers and AF. The development of quantitative measures that distinguish the authentic leader and the authentic follower from other leaders and followers would also help establish the validity of the authentic follower construct.

Authentic Leader/Follower Fluidity

One of the challenges, identified in this chapter, is the need to be able to establish where the authentic leaders end, and the authentic followers begin. Although the development of quantitative measures may be beneficial in addressing this, more research is required to understand what situations result in an authentic individual acting as either an authentic leader or authentic follower. Further to this, our proposed model of the authentic followers may require revision of AL in the future to consider potentially missing elements of the model. Understanding this fluidity would enable new work teams and individuals to comprehend their own natural group dynamics during their early formation stages. It would also enable future researchers to study how the four dimensions of authenticity are manifested differently in the authentic leaders and authentic followers.

In addition, previous research has demonstrated that the authentic followers are empowered into the authentic leaders through modelling (Gardner et al., 2005), but the point at which an authentic follower becomes an authentic leader requires further research. Such studies could consider power relationships and the level of influence of both the leader and the follower and how this affects their ability to lead and/or follow. Power may also have an effect on how the authentic followers are able to join environments which reduce their authenticity, or likewise how they may affect their leader (as hypothesised in Fig. 11.1).

Authentic Leader/Follower Emergence

Our third area for future research relates to authentic leader/follower emergence. To date, research has focused on understanding identifying the authentic leaders and their importance to organisations, yet we believe the authentic followers are valuable too. Although Gardner et al. (2011) identified four antecedents of AL compared to 30 outcomes, research on antecedents of the authentic followers is absent. Understanding the antecedents of the authentic followers may support an understanding of authentic follower emergence and enable researchers and practitioners to better understand the inherent similarities of an authentic follower and leader. Investigation of the climates in which authentic leaders/followers emerge would also be illuminating.

Team Processes

Although this chapter has largely focused on leader–follower dyads, we do not assume that this relationship exists within a vacuum. Rather, these relationships are more likely to exist with a collection of similar dyads in the form of a team (e.g. one leader and several followers). Consequently, research focused on the outcomes of AL and AF should place a particular emphasis on team processes, particularly interpersonal team processes such as conflict management, motivation/confidence building and affect management. In addition to team processes, we acknowledge that this chapter has not included in-depth discussion relating to authentic followers and their peers, and future research should attempt to address this gap. Added, our emphasis was on the authentic follower, and we did not provide depth relating to the process of AF, or better understanding the authentic relationship. We recommend future research take this mantle and continue to develop clear and parsimonious definitions for these constructs. Once a clear understanding of followership and the relationship is undertaken, it will be useful to consider how the followers transcend to become the leaders that are more effective. This understanding will enable future researchers to consider the relational and process element of AL and AF further. Finally, the authentic follower model presented in this chapter may include a third dimension surrounding team processes. Once more of the nomological network outcomes of the authentic followers and AF are understood, it may be worth considering whether a third dimension is missing, surrounding team cohesion, or interpersonal team behaviours.

Conclusion

This chapter has introduced a revised conceptualisation of the authentic follower, which draws on the existing conceptualisations and research relating to AF and AL. Specifically, we have provided a rationale for the need for greater research to be focused on the study of authentic followers, by explicating how AL relates to authentic followers. In doing so, we reviewed the existing definitions of authentic followers and followership before proposing a revised conceptualisation of the construct. Finally, we have outlined four primary areas of focus for future research including empirical measurement and validation of authentic followers primarily, authentic leader/follower fluidity, authentic leader/follower emergence and authentic followers and team processes. Thus, although this chapter has begun addressing some of the conceptual issues identified in relation extant authentic follower research, we also acknowledge that there is still much more to be done to progress understanding of the authentic followers and their importance to other followers, leaders, and organisations.

References

Agho, A. (2009). Perspectives of senior-level executives on effective followership and leadership. *Journal of Leadership & Organizational Studies, 16*(2), 159–166.

Avolio, B. (2007). Promoting more integrative strategies for leadership theory-building. *American Psychologist, 62*(1), 25–33.

Avolio, B., & Gardner, W. (2005). Authentic leadership development: Getting to the root of positive forms of leadership. *Leadership Quarterly, 16*(3), 315–338.

Avolio, B., Gardner, W., Walumbwa, F., Luthans, F., & May, D. (2004). Unlocking the mask: A look at the process by which authentic leaders impact follower attitudes and behaviors. *Leadership Quarterly, 15*(6), 801–823.

Avolio, B., & Mhatre, K. (2012). Advances in theory and research on authentic leadership. In K. Cameron & G. Spreitzer (Eds.), *The Oxford handbook of positive organizational scholarship*. Oxford, UK: Oxford University Press.

Avolio, B., & Reichard, R. (2008). The rise of authentic followership. In R. Riggio, I. Chaleff, & J. Lipman-Blumen (Eds.), *The art of followership: How great followers create great leaders and organizations*. San Francisco: Wiley.

Avolio, B., Walumbwa, F., & Weber, T. (2009). Leadership: Current theories, research and future directions. *Annual Review of Psychology, 60*(1), 421–449.

Bandura, A. (1997). *Self-efficacy: The exercise of control*. New York: Freeman.

Bjugstad, K., Thach, E., Thompson, K., & Morris, A. (2006). A fresh look at followership: A model for matching followership and leadership styles. *Journal of Behavioral and Applied Management, 7*(3), 304–319.

Crawford, J., Lewis, G., Martin, A., & Dawkins, S. (2017). *Rethinking the authentic leader: A theory-driven reconceptualization*. Manuscript submitted for publication.

Crossman, B., & Crossman, J. (2011). Conceptualising followership – A review of the literature. *Leadership, 7*(4), 481–497.

de Zilwa, D. (2014). A new conceptual framework for authentic followership. In M. C. Laurent Lapierre (Ed.), *Followership: What is it, and why do people follow?* Bingley, UK: Emerald.

Erickson, R. (1995). The importance of authenticity for self and society. *Symbolic Interaction, 18*(2), 121–144.

Farrukh, S., & Ahsan, J. (2015). Authentic leadership – A multi-component model. *Sukkur IBA Journal of Management and Business, 2*(2), 41–68.

Fiedler, F. (1967). *A theory of leadership effectiveness*. New York: McGraw-Hill.

Fredrickson, B. (2003). Positive emotions and upward spirals in organizations. In K. Cameron, J. Dutton, & R. Quinn (Eds.), *Positive organizational scholarship* (pp. 163–175). San Francisco: Berrett-Koehler Publishers.

Gardner, W., Avolio, B., Luthans, F., May, D., & Walumbwa, F. (2005). 'Can you see the real me?' A self-based model of authentic leader and follower development. *Leadership Quarterly, 16*(3), 343–372.

Gardner, W., Cogliser, C., Davis, K., & Dickens, M. (2011). Authentic leadership: A review of the literature and research agenda. *Leadership Quarterly, 22*(1), 1120–1145.

Goffee, R., & Jones, G. (2006). *Why should anyone be led by you? What it takes to be an authentic leader*. Boston: Harvard.

Hackman, J., & Wageman, R. (2007). Asking the right questions about leadership: Discussion and conclusions. *American Psychologist, 62*(1), 43–47.

House, R., & Mitchell, T. (1975). Path-goal theory of leadership. *Journal of Contemporary Business, 3*(4), 81–98.

Howell, J., & Shamir, B. (2005). The role of followers in the charismatic leadership process: Relationships and their consequences. *Academy of Management Review, 30*(1), 96–112.

Jensen, S., & Luthans, F. (2006). Entrepreneurs as authentic leaders: Impact on employees' attitudes. *Leadership & Organization Development Journal, 27*(8), 646–666.

Jung, D., & Avolio, B. (1999). Effects of leadership style and followers' cultural orientation on performance in group and individual task conditions. *Academy of Management Journal, 42*(2), 208–218.

Kelley, R. (1988). In praise of followers. *Harvard Business Review Case Services, 66*(6), 142–148.

Kelley, R. (2008). Rethinking followership. In R. Riggio, I. Chaleff, & J. Lipman-Blumen (Eds.), *The art of followership: How great followers create great leaders and organizations*. San Francisco: Wiley.

Kernis, M., & Goldman, B. (2006). A multicomponent conceptualization of authenticity: Theory and research. *Advances in Experimental Social Psychology, 38*(1), 283–357.

Kirkman, B., Chen, G., Farh, J., Chen, Z., & Lowe, K. (2009). Individual power distance orientation and follower reactions to transformational leaders: A cross-level, cross-cultural examination. *Academy of Management Journal, 52*(4), 744–764.

Luthans, F., & Avolio, B. (2003). Authentic leadership development. In K. Cameron, J. Dutton, & R. Quinn (Eds.), *Positive organizational scholarship: Foundations of a new discipline*. San Francisco: Berrett Koehler.

Mintzberg, H. (1985). The organization as political arena. *Journal of Management Studies, 22*(2), 133–154.
Northouse, P. (2016). *Leadership: Theory and practice* (7th ed.). Thousand Oaks, CA: Sage.
Oh, H., Chung, M., & Labianca, G. (2004). Group social capital and group effectiveness: The role of informal socializing ties. *Academy of Management Journal, 47*(6), 860–875.
Rahimnia, F., & Sharifirad, M. (2015). Authentic leadership and employee well-being: The mediating role of attachment insecurity. *Journal of Business Ethics, 132*(2), 363–377.
Shamir, B. (2007). From passive recipients to active co-producers: The roles of followers in the leadership process. In B. Shamir, R. Pillai, M. Bligh, & M. Uhl-Bien (Eds.), *Follower-centered perspectives on leadership: A tribute to the memory of James R. Meindl*. Stanford, CT: Information Age.
Shamir, B., & Eilam, G. (2005). 'What's your story?' A life-stories approach to authentic leadership development. *Leadership Quarterly, 16*(3), 395–417.
Stamper, C., & Johlke, M. (2003). The impact of perceived organizational support on the relationship between boundary spanner role stress and work outcomes. *Journal of Management, 29*(4), 569–588.
Walumbwa, F., Avolio, B., Gardner, W., Wernsing, T., & Peterson, S. (2008). Authentic leadership: Development and validation of a theory-based measure. *Journal of Management, 34*(1), 89–126.
Wong, C., & Cummings, G. (2009a). Authentic leadership: A new theory for nursing or back to basics? *Journal of Health Organization and Management, 23*(5), 522–538.
Wong, C., & Cummings, G. (2009b). The influence of authentic leadership behaviors on trust and work outcomes of health care staff. *Journal of Leadership Studies, 3*(2), 6–23.
Wong, C., Spence Laschinger, H., & Cummings, G. (2010). Authentic leadership and nurses' voice behaviour and perceptions of care quality. *Journal of Nursing Management, 18*(8), 889–900.
Wortman, M. (1982). Strategic management and changing leader-follower roles. *The Journal of Applied Behavioral Science, 18*(3), 371–383.
Yukl, G. (2013). *Leadership in organizations* (8th ed.). Boston: Pearson.

Index

© The Author(s) 2018
D. Cotter-Lockard (ed.), *Authentic Leadership and Followership*, Palgrave Studies in Leadership and Followership, https://doi.org/10.1007/978-3-319-65307-5

L

P

R

CPSIA information can be obtained
at www.ICGtesting.com
Printed in the USA
LVOW05*0050241217
560659LV00013B/229/P

9 783319 653068